Borderlands

Borderlands

Towards an Anthropology of the Cosmopolitan Condition

Michel Agier

Translated by David Fernbach

polity

First published in French as *La condition cosmopolite: L'anthropologie à l'épreuve du piège identitaire*, (c) Éditions La Découverte, Paris, 2013
This English edition (c) Polity Press, 2016

Polity Press
65 Bridge Street
Cambridge CB2 1UR, UK

Polity Press
350 Main Street
Malden, MA 02148, USA

ISBN-13: 978-0-7456-9679-9
ISBN-13: 978-0-7456-9680-5 (pb)

A catalogue record for this book is available from the British Library.

Library of Congress Cataloging-in-Publication Data

Names: Agier, Michel, 1953–
Title: Borderlands : towards an anthropology of the cosmopolitan condition / Michel Agier.
Other titles: Condition cosmopolite. English
Description: Malden, MA : Polity Press, 2016. | Includes bibliographical references and index.
Identifiers: LCCN 2015048690 (print) | LCCN 2016010176 (ebook) | ISBN 9780745696799 (hardcover : alk. paper) | ISBN 0745696791 (hardcover : alk. paper) | ISBN 9780745696805 (pbk. : alk. paper) | ISBN 0745696805 (pbk. : alk. paper) | ISBN 9780745696829 (mobi) | ISBN 9780745696836 (epub)
Subjects: LCSH: Cosmopolitanism. | Multiculturalism. | Globalization. | Group identity.
Classification: LCC JZ1308 .A3813 2016 (print) | LCC JZ1308 (ebook) | DDC 303.48/2--dc23
LC record available at http://lccn.loc.gov/2015048690

Typeset in 10.5 on 12pt Sabon by Servis Filmsetting Ltd, Stockport, Cheshire
Printed and bound in the UK by CPI Group (UK) Ltd, Croydon, CR0 4YY

For further information on Polity, visit our website: politybooks.com

CONTENTS

He walks on the wind. And, in the wind,
he knows himself. No four walls hem in the wind. And the wind is a
    compass
for the north in a foreign land.
He says: I come from that place. I come from here,
and I am neither here nor there.
I have two names that come together but pull apart.
I have two languages, but I have forgotten which is
the language of my dreams.
    Mahmoud Darwish, 'Counterpoint (Homage to Edward Said)', 2007

It was night.
The ninth night.
We came to a mountain pass.
The trafficker shouted: 'Stop a moment! Look back.'
We all stopped. We all looked back.
'This is your last look at your land.'
The land, beneath the whiteness of the snow, had become invisible in
    the darkness.
Only the traces of our steps.
Everyone cried. Then we ran to the border.
On the other side was an expanse covered with snow, white as a sheet
    of paper.
Not a footprint.
Not a word.
And its margins lost in the dark night.
    Atiq Rahimi, 'The Ninth Night', *Le Retour imaginaire*, 2005

PREFACE TO THE
ENGLISH EDITION

Frontières was the working title for the first French edition of this book, written between 2010 and 2012 and published in 2013. Only at the last moment was it changed to *La Condition cosmopolite*, from a desire to spell out the perspective of my reflections here. Yet *frontières* do occupy the greater part of the book, and it is this that I wanted to restore by putting 'border' back in the title for the second edition (and the present English edition), which is a much revised and modified version of the original essay. At the same time, the discussion aroused by the original publication has led me to clarify what cosmopolitan 'condition' we have in mind in speaking of the movement of migrants, of life in border spaces, and of the relationships that are formed there. The condition I discuss here is that of *ordinary* or 'banal' cosmopolitism, in a sense quite close to that of the 'banal nationalism' that Michael Billig has written about in relation to the everyday practices and little signs that exhibit the belonging of individuals to a nation.[1] Ordinary cosmopolitism is made up of the everyday arrangements made by those women and men who are in the 'labyrinth of the foreigner' (Alfred Schütz's expression) without yet having managed to emerge from it, who settle in the border situation, have to deal with other languages, ways of acting, thinking and governing, and adapt and transform themselves by this obligatory exercise. This led me to describe border situations and borderlands more generally, and to exhibit the paradox of the wall, which is at the same time an imitation and a negation of the border.

Persons in displacement may well be in the process of living an experience far more universal than it might appear, beyond the categories, classes and nationalities that are involved today. Even if they find themselves 'on the margin', they enable us to anticipate a way of being-in-the-world that globalization is tending to generalize. In this conception, cosmopolitism is not the monopoly of a globalized elite. On the contrary, it is the experience of the roughness of the world by all those who, by taste, necessity or compulsion, by desire or by habit, are led to live in several places almost simultaneously and, in the absence of ubiquity, to live increasingly in mobility, even in an in-between.

I have also taken advantage of this new edition to bring clarifications, further research and bibliographic data, and new lines of argument that I felt were lacking in the initial version. And finally, I have reorganized the whole book around two topics that may be read either successively or in parallel: 'decentring the world' and 'the decentred subject'.

I am deeply grateful to Rémy Toulouse, François Gèze and John Thompson for their editorial advice, as well as to Marc Abélès, Rigas Arvanitis, Étienne Balibar, Mamadou Diouf, Michel Naepels and Étienne Tassin for their comments and suggestions on earlier versions of the text. And finally I thank Patricia Birman (State University of Rio de Janeiro), José Sergio Leite Lopes (Colegio Brasileiro de Altos Estudos/Federal University of Rio de Janeiro) and Bruno Calvalcanti (Federal University of Alagoas) for their welcome in Rio and Maceio between September and December 2014, where I found both the time and the context to write this new version and discuss certain developments of it.

INTRODUCTION: THE MIGRANT, THE BORDER AND THE WORLD

Since the late 1990s, migrants originating in Iraq, Afghanistan, Pakistan, Egypt, Libya, Sudan or Eritrea, more recently joined by young Palestinians from Lebanon, have found their way to the port of Patras – a small Greek town on the shore of the Ionian Sea, and the point of departure of cargo boats for Venice, Ancona and Bari in Italy. What the migrants are after here is a crossing to Europe. This is what I saw one February day in 2009, a few metres from the border control.

A group of some twenty Afghans are walking along the edge of the road outside the port. They are waiting, as they do every day, for the lorries moving slowly towards the port, to be loaded into the holds of ships that take them and their goods to Italy. When one of these lorries arrives the young people start running, a couple of them try to open the rear doors of the lorry and, if they manage to do so, hold the doors open while still running as one or two others hurriedly try to climb up. Some shouts, sometimes laughter, as this inevitably becomes almost a game. Certain drivers, annoyed by this daily exercise, sadistically play at accelerating and braking to make the climbers fall off. Stationed on the roadside is a police car, in which four policemen continue to chat as they observe the young people running a few metres away. Finally, on the other side of the road beyond a patch of grass, there is a prestige apartment block whose entire ground floor is occupied by a plate-glass window. Behind the glass you can see a fitness centre, its various apparatuses positioned so that while using them you can see what is happening outside. Side by side on the exercise bikes and treadmills are a dozen people pedalling or running on the spot while placidly watching the young Afghans in their chase behind the lorries. In their field of vision they also have the

1

port, the ships and the sea in the distance – and very likely the police car stationed on the roadside as well.

No word is exchanged between the young Afghans and the fitness practitioners, nor is there any direct contact between the police and these migrants or refugees; the police just study their movements, trying to pick out those in the huddled group who will manage to climb up on the lorries so that when these are on the port parking lot they can make them get out, after crossing the barrier that serves as a border but still in a standby situation awaiting embarkation. There are only looks, with perhaps a few glances exchanged. And the acceleration and braking of the lorry drivers, which tell the young Afghans that they have indeed been seen and that their lives are fragile.

This silent scene has three places, three actors and three gazes. What the sum total of this symbolizes above all is a (non-)relationship and a kind of concentrate of the state of the world.

Blocked at the border

Whether running or strolling, in their wandering these young Afghan migrants embody a new figure of the foreigner, zigzagging between prohibitions. For, if the policemen who watch them seem calm, this is because the port is surrounded by a complex system of very high fences, because the lorries are minutely inspected on the parking lot before embarkation, and because on arrival in Italy those who have succeeded in crossing will be seized and sent back on the return boat. They will find themselves back in the Patras encampment. So it is harder for them to cross than for the goods under which they try to conceal themselves – a fact that we already know, though in a rather abstract way, when we compare the free circulation of goods and capital with the much harder, and sometimes even impossible, circulation of persons.

In July 2012, two dead migrants were found at the port of Venice after a forty-hour crossing in a container lorry in the hold of a ship; they had died of asphyxiation after hiding their faces in plastic bags to conceal the traces of respiration that the police 'see' with the aid of breathing detectors.[1] Some crossings are successful, despite everything (a handful by sea, others by land routes that are longer and more exhausting), which sustains the desire and energy of those who remain blocked at the border. And for those who fail in the attempt, months and years can pass here, between the port, the encampment, the squats in the town and seasonal work in the region's orange and

2

olive groves. A whole life is organized in these border places, marked by the uncertainty of the moment and the immediate future, as well as the uncertainty of the gaze directed at them. When they run after the lorries they do not see the middle-class townsfolk watching them with indifference from their fitness centre, or else they make fun of them, as they laugh at the townsfolk who watch them walking along the pavement of the road alongside the port, and joke among themselves without embarrassment when a pretty girl crosses their path. They are easily recognizable by their bodies (tired, damaged, wounded), by their clothing (the impression of dirt encrusted on their clothes by time, by nights spent outdoors, by the smoke of braziers), by their manner of being (slow, almost nonchalant, with a gravity always tinged with humour) and by their odd everyday rhythms – a good deal of waiting and drowsiness until the moment comes to approach the frontier and the arriving lorries.

Indifference and solidarities

As the second actor on the stage we have those townsfolk who spend some leisure time in the fitness centre and while cycling on the spot watch the migrants running after the lorries – apparently embodying the politics of indifference. An indifference to the world that surrounds us and a loss from view of an 'other' about whom there seems to be nothing to think, no relationship to symbolize. This conception praises individualism, the defence of bodies, territories and private goods against a world suspected of being wretched and intrusive. The planet does not seem a common world. Most often present as a supposedly heard and shared 'subtext' in xenophobic and security discourse, this individual combat against a threatening world is sometimes expressed in the public and political domain in the form of cynical statements such as 'Someone else's place, not mine!', or the famous 'Not In My Back Yard' that inspired the NIMBY urban privatization movement in Los Angeles.[2]

This posture harks back to the model of proprietorial politics, defined in the words of Carl Schmitt as the guarantor of delimitations and 'spatial orders of the Earth' along with the sovereignties associated with these: sovereignties and private territories thus found the confrontation between friend and enemy.[3] In this conception, a threat is seen as coming from an 'outside' that is both absolute and empty, figured in the features of a shadow, that of an abstract 'foreigner', demographically surplus, supernumerary, and recognized only in the form of this excess. In every state, space and milieu of the planet that is relatively privileged, this politics of indifference backs up policies that protect privileged groups and dismiss this nameless 'foreigner'. From this point of view, the same scene could have been described on the small tourist islands of Malta or Lampedusa in the Mediterranean, where welcome tourists cross paths with 'clandestine' immigrants, or in the Spanish enclaves of Ceuta and Melilla, or in the surroundings of Jerusalem, now walled in and entrenched from its immediate urban environment, or again somewhere close to the very long barrier between the United States and Mexico, in the towns of El Paso or Tijuana.

Of course, this depiction needs qualification. In actual fact, indifference is not automatically associated with the relatively privileged social and national place of those women and men whom policies of indifference towards displaced persons seek to enlist or claim to represent. Who exactly knows, around the port of Patras, what one of these fitness practitioners may do the next day, or even after going home the same day? In many countries over the last decade, increasingly visible solidarities have been displayed towards so-called 'clandestine' foreigners, either individually or by way of voluntary associations, in the form of efforts to help them, to see that they get their proper rights, and to 'de-diabolize' them simply by establishing contact with them. This attitude has been legitimized in terms of culture, particularly in the world of science and that of the arts (literature, theatre, cinema), where a number of new works over the last few years have aimed to understand and depict the subjectivity of undesirable foreigners.

This hospitable attitude, in a context that is globally hostile towards 'foreigners', is also expressed as a political alternative, even if it remains very much a minority position, in the form of activist mobilizations around asylum, the rights of foreigners, the free circulation of immigrants and their families. These are culturally heterogeneous milieus, whose motives, despite their contradictory character – more or less humanitarian or political, for example – do have effects from the point of view of the protection and integration of foreigners. It is thanks to local mobilization, moreover, and the support of a Greek association in defence of the rights of foreigners, that the Patras encampment has been able to exist for twelve years. Despite being precarious and always threatened with disappearance, its existence has been the result of a compromise negotiated between activists in voluntary associations (students and middle-class individuals from the town) and the municipality. Opened at the end of

1996, the encampment was destroyed by fire and police bulldozers in July 2009. It was like a refugee camp transplanted into the midst of the middle-class apartment blocks and houses of the European town close to the port. At certain times in its existence it sheltered up to 2,000 people, migrants who were not yet refugees (they had simply requested asylum) or were considered clandestine. This is where the young people lived who ran after the lorries every day. Others grew tired of this, and the encampment a few metres from the border became their new place of life.

Borders and walls

The police, then, the third actor on the Patras stage, are charged with technical and routine control of movements and the situation on the Greek border. They 'do the job' of the state that controls spaces, with an objective cruelty that comes from their role of patrolling and filtering at the borders. Elsewhere in Europe, between France and Spain for example, some police responsible for migrants even refer to themselves as 'hunters'. More generally, control at the European borders is conducted by a European institution that functions well and has enjoyed a steady increase in its budget since its creation in 2005 – Frontex (officially, the European Agency for the Management of Operational Cooperation at the External Borders of the Member States of the European Union).

In 2010, after Europe requested that Greece increase its surveillance of migration flows from Africa and the East, the country proposed constructing a wall on its border with Turkey. Ten kilometres of this were built on the land frontier in early 2012, while for the maritime border surveillance operations are planned, to be conducted from boats that would also act as detention centres on the high seas. In the United States, police border patrols have been under pressure since 2005 from 'auxiliaries' that spur them on; while claiming to fill the gaps left by an inadequate state, these stand watch and set up camp close to the thousand kilometres of wall that divides the United States from Mexico, monitoring and hunting 'Latinos' who manage to cross over or under this. Above all, these patrols develop an anti-immigrant propaganda that is very effective in the political and media sphere.[4]

What the situation at the port of Patras displays, like many other border places today, is a hardening of borders and, despite this, the stubbornness of migrants who seek to cross them, since this seems possible and legitimate to them even if it is not legal at the actual place of crossing. Opposing legitimacies confront one another, that of the open world and that of protection against the 'misery of the world', that of national sovereignty and that of cosmopolitism. It is this conflict that explains the transformation of borders into walls – more than 20,000 kilometres of these built or under construction in the world today. Despite appearances, we must try not to confuse the two things. I shall go on to show (particularly in chapters 1 and 2) that there is as much difference between a border, both boundary and passage, and a wall, synonymous with reciprocal enclosure, as between alterity and identity. What I am trying to understand is this double excess, an excess that moves from uncertain border to wall, from relationship to identity enclosure and finally the 'disappearance' of the other, that is, the disappearance of the alterity without which identities no longer have a social existence.

In order to avoid the trap of identity enclosure, we need to give a name to the foreigner, to discover by various examples the person I shall describe in what follows as the *other-subject*. The latter is a priori without identity, having lost this with their departure and exile, and is still in the process of seeking or rebuilding it. But he or she is also the person who appears 'here and now' at the border and disturbs the normal and routine order of things.

If there is no explicit interaction on the silent stage of Patras, there certainly is an underlying and complex relationship between the three participating groups, one full of ambivalence and conflict. It resembles that created and replayed each day between each person on the planet and the 'world around them', whether this world is close ('us') or distant ('others'), or again is 'globalization' in the sense of a global impersonal power, completely delocalized and ungraspable, which the word has acquired today. There are also many emotions and fears, expectations and a priori judgements, between the three groups present. The harshness of the situation does not facilitate contact, but the furtive exchange of glances speaks much about the shared awareness of a co-presence.

Borderlands and their inhabitants: a banal cosmopolitism

A long moment of uncertainty has settled on the world. Precarious life lasts longer and people grow used to it; emergency kits and, more generally, temporary and dismantleable arrangements have become pervasive in architecture, industry and art; mobility is ever more frequent and massive, crossing cities and the planet without a single or definitive direction. In the verses of the Palestinian poet Mahmoud Darwish that serve as an epigraph to this book, 'the north in a foreign land' is the direction to choose, but only the wind shows the direction. We have grown up in modernity asking ourselves in what direction the wind is going to turn. Today we discover that we are living 'on the wind', and have to know who we are without having a definite anchorage ('neither there nor here'). Often we enter labyrinths in which we lose the sense of direction before learning to traverse them and then emerge from them.

We are all living the whole time with borders and thresholds, as soon as we move around to a minimum extent, and we never stop crossing these. The border is a place, a situation or a moment that ritualizes the relationship to the other, and in this sense we always need it; still more, its existence is a given fact. Besides, as we shall go on to see, the border always functions with mediations, such as tutelary and protective divinities, bearers or translators. The latter enable us to understand on the level of language or culture the relationships formed between two persons who do not know one another but meet in a border situation, initially uncertain.

One of the border situations most often recalled, but by no means the only one, is that separating nation-states. Unable either to enter a territory or return to their country of origin, some immigrants find themselves trapped in waiting zones, where the border expands in space as ever more of these zones are constructed, transit camps and encampments, and where time stretches as periods of indeterminate status are prolonged for ever more people. These zones create moments in which people no longer know at all clearly who they are or where they are, moments of social and identity potential.

Seen from the border, the world also looks different. The 'margins' of nation-states are the unthought in the theory of public-order policies, just as urban interstices or so-called informal economies remain unthought. Both things are always defined only in relief, in a residual way. Public order applies a management ideal nowadays called 'governance'. This model, obsessed by the threat of the disorderly practice of politics by an undifferentiated *demos* (the political people), favours divisions and a system of worlds that are watertight, reduced, in which control and adherence to the system are exercised. In this system of fragmentation, each person is allotted an identity specific to them, essential and 'true' – whether this is national, racial, ethnic or religious. The most differentialist versions of these – current in the highest spheres of politics and the media – are caricatures, but none the less effective in their enterprise of separation and rejection. The same discourses, however, reject – and this is indeed their rhetorical trick – all those who, taking up and transforming the very languages that have confined them to the margins ('Roma', 'black', 'refugee', 'stateless', for example), claim or impose their 'presence-in-the-world', because this world is both more accessible and more closed than ever before.

I shall seek to show that an ordinary cosmopolitan condition is being formed beyond so-called 'marginal' lives, beyond the lives of those who at some point are here called 'foreigners'. In a global and hybrid world, where experience of the unfamiliar and of uncertainty is practically everyday, this condition is born *on* the border, that is, in everything that makes for the border. This includes uncertain places, uncertain times, uncertain identities that are ambiguous, incomplete or optional, indeterminate or in-between situations, uncertain relationships. These are border landscapes, in which encounters and experiences bring into relation a here and an elsewhere, a same and an other, a 'local' fact and a 'global' context (simply meaning someone or something that comes from 'outside').

My approach is that of an anthropologist. On the basis of my fieldwork I have come to understand that the border is continuously both remade and challenged. I have thus discovered, by way of this ethnographic 'bias' and bit by bit, on the one hand what one can call the *centrality of the border*. This point is essential, and I shall return to it on different occasions (particularly in chapter 3): by expanding in time and space, the borderland becomes a pole of reference for persons in movement who do not find a natural place within the societies or cities that they wish to reach. But in order to grasp this new centrality of the border, it is necessary to redefine anthropological 'decentring': not an exotic 'detour' into distant countries that are supposed to be radically other, but the study of what makes the border of everything, and thus denotes, for concrete experience, the possibility of an alterity (chapter 4). I have discovered, on the other hand, a terrain of exchange and discussion with certain philosophical writings that have taken borderlands and cosmopolitism as an object of reflection. A common perspective is sketched here: the ordinary cosmopolitism of situations, spaces and people of the borderlands that I have studied on the ground intersects and interpellates the debate on cosmopolitism and cosmopolitics.

The contribution of anthropology to this debate is a double one, bearing on questions of cosmopolitism and on the subject or 'subjectification'. It draws on different figures of a 'borderland man' (a generic term to denote those men and women who arrive and 'settle' at the border). To recognize and understand the condition that they embody is one of the major issues of our time. It is by way of what happens in the borderlands that we are *in* the world and *of* the world, cosmopolitans de facto, without either having intended or conceived this. This is an ordinary or 'banal' cosmopolitism, and it is increasingly shared in a growing number of situations of everyday life. In order to recognize its existence, to understand its meaning for oneself and for others, it is only necessary to extract oneself from the identity-based beliefs and utopias that separate an absolute and intrinsic 'within', symbolically or materially walled in, from an 'outside' that is nameless and voiceless, generating all the more fear in that it is reduced to silence and dismissed. We come back therefore to the centrality of the borderland, both as epistemological operation (that of decentring) and as political issue. Focusing attention on the borderland makes it possible to think the question of the subject as *other-subject*, or decentred subject (as will be done in chapter 6): this subject embodies a word, a creation or a political action that emerge at the border and become a factor of disturbance for an existing sedentary order. The borderland as conceived in the present study, as a prolonged time and a border space, in which people learn the ways of the world and of other people, is thus the place where a new cosmopolitan subject is emerging.

To rethink and reconstruct decentring as the foundation of this anthropological project is the epistemological proposal that runs right through this book. Is it still possible, as anthropology claims, to understand the world that surrounds us and the place or engagement of each person in this world, without inquiring as to the effects of today's 'global' reality on local fields of investigation, and thus on the methods and reasonings of anthropologists? I shall take examples of borderlands, places and communities 'in the process of making', in a situation of mobility, displacement and migration, while freeing this research from the identity obsession that often seizes political leaders, commentators on current affairs, and sometimes even researchers in social sciences themselves. For anthropology, which has always interested itself both in man and in societies, does not set out in my view to present and augment the difference of 'others' as pure and homogeneous cultural totalities, radically different. It can on the contrary reduce distance from practices and situations still ignored, describe these and *think with* them (which is the meaning I give to empathy as an intellectual disposition), and so make them less foreign. As we shall go on to see, the place where the other – the other-subject – is to be found is always closer than people believe: it is in a borderland.

9

This will be viewed here as a place, a moment and, in an expanded conception used in this essay, a border *situation*, in which each person has their own experience of the world and of others.

Two other persons are present on the stage at the Patras border. There is the lorry driver, annoyed perhaps by a situation over which he has no control, or even 'playing' with the young people whom he knows well and whom, a few kilometres back, he might have let climb up without saying anything if a trafficker introduced them to him and compensated him for the risks involved. Discourses of denunciation and moralization are useless, but they are none the less par for the course, constantly trapping the gaze and scarcely leaving room for a reflection both more precise and more political, thus more effective. As we know, moral denunciations about international migration focus unanimously on 'traffickers' and their supposedly 'mafia-type networks'. But if these are still there, despite spectacular 'dragnets' and promises of eradication, it is because they play a role that is not moral but political, more or less equivalent to that of checkpoints: they allow a drip feed across the walls, they organize little escapes that make it possible to avoid the massive and brutal confrontation of persons in displacement against the existence of walls. They also play an economic role for the northern countries (Europe and the United States) by keeping a non-negligible part of the subaltern international labour force in a situation of illegality, and all the more fragile and exploitable as they know themselves to be socially undesirable.[5]

Finally, there is the person who observes and will tell this story. I found myself in Patras in 2009 to conduct a study on migrant encampments in European cities and close to the borders.[6] The scene lasted only a short moment, but I 'scanned' it into my memory. And I have written it down here so that it does not disappear, but serves as an indicator for reflection on the state of the world and its violence, on borders and walls, and on the everyday cosmopolitism that is the perspective of this moment of history and gives it, I believe, its deepest and most lasting meaning.

In 2015, the whole world has been able to see how this scene has shifted and multiplied in tens or hundreds of places in Europe, with too these endlessly televised images of long lines of migrants blocked at the borders of Greece, Italy, Macedonia, Hungary and Austria. Near the port and border town of Calais, night-time attempts to board the Eurostar train at the entrance to the Channel tunnel or, as at Patras, people climbing on the back of trucks on the motorway leading to the port, have been an everyday occurrence. They have made the front pages of newspapers and led to at least eleven deaths in 2015 alone, according to organizations present on the ground, as well as a large number of wounded, who either fell off trains or were run over by vehicles. Between 2005 and 2015 several encampments and squats were established in the town of Calais, in which migrants found refuge thanks to the support of several voluntary organizations of local people. In April 2015, the state opened a resettlement camp seven kilometres outside the town, and organized the forced departure of migrants from the encampment and squats they had previously occupied to the new camp, characterized by the government as the only 'tolerated' settlement, and located a few metres from a reception centre offering food rations and a few showers. Soon known as a 'state shanty-town' or the 'New Jungle', the Calais camp would become the place of shelter for some 5,000 people in September 2015, mainly Syrians, Sudanese, Eritreans and Afghans trying in some cases to reach England, or in others seeking asylum in France. In the political and media context of the autumn 2015 'migration crisis' in Europe, the occupants of the Calais camp became symbols of the desire of European governments to convey to the world the message that national borders had been closed. In the course of that month, the Calais camp became increasingly hard of access for voluntary organizations and citizens showing solidarity, mainly French and British. Given the impossibility of legally crossing the border to England, and facing every day the French and British police, the camp occupants began to demonstrate almost daily between the town and the port: they held up placards, shouted slogans and distributed open letters denouncing the inhumanity of French and British policy, demanding the opening of the border and respect for human rights. The governments of the countries concerned refused to acknowledge this, continuing to treat them as a security and possibly humanitarian problem, and the migrants thereby expressed a form of politics that placed the border and human mobility at the centre of the conflict, giving the idea of what a politics of the cosmopolitical subject might be. As a politics that gives a premonition of a world to come, this scene at Calais, with its street demonstrations of migrants blocked at the border, forms the counterpoint of the scene at Patras, at the other end of Europe.

The present essay is made up of two parts, closely linked. The first of these, 'Decentring the World', offers a reflection on the foundations and actuality of borderlands (spatial, temporal and social), on the crisis of representation of the world in the age of 'globalization', and on the formation of an ordinary cosmopolitan condition, perceptible on the basis of the experience of migrants but likely to become the most widespread social and cultural way of life in a near future already in the process of construction. The second part, 'The Decentred Subject', is a study of the transformation of cultures and identities in this context, and a reflection on the intellectual tools needed to grasp these. The question of the capacity of subjects to act on their destiny and on the world that surrounds them runs through the whole of this second part.

Part I

Decentring the World

— 1 —

THE ELEMENTARY FORMS
OF THE BORDER

'"Customs officers without borders" is something for tomorrow', Régis Debray wrote in his *Éloge de la frontière*.[1] 'You have a Frenchman here, I admit', he continued in this lecture given in March 2011 at the Maison Franco-Japonaise in Tokyo, as if to mark from the start an opposition between identity and border. Then, mentioning natural and political borders, more or less vulnerable, he went on to insularity and its specific effects (homogeneous Japan being different in this respect from Cyprus and Ireland, divided by their 'internal' national borders), and finally denounced the political consequences of '*sans-frontiérisme*'. Régis Debray was seeking to relaunch public debate on the subject of borders, as if the scales had swung too far in one direction, that of a global village without borders; as if, in return, a frightful illusion was born from this collective belief in a world that had already come to form a limitless whole, open to the void; and as if, finally, this fear explained the construction of immense walls and new barriers with the object of identity protection.

It is certainly true that arguments are not lacking for a wholesale process of what Debrary calls '*illimitations*' and an 'oil-and-vinegar globalization'.[2] But by seeking too hard to convince at the level of theory, Debray ends up falling into the trap of seeking out and seeking to preserve the 'truth', the 'heart' and 'matrix' of identity; insisting too much on the opposition between inside and outside, he forgets that the world of today is largely made up, whatever he may say, of mobilities either free or compelled, of absences of 'home' and of anchorages that are ever more uncertain. If we want something other than a conservative and identity-based resistance, we should indeed set out to rethink the meaning of borders in the world, to ask how they may still be 'good for thinking' and 'good for living'.[3]

The border as centre of reflection

What we shall offer here, therefore, is not a 'praise' but rather a more analytical attempt to understand the double state of the border question, which will perhaps give more weight and argument to humanist positions while at the same time posing some other basic problems for these.

An initial formulation of the question concerns the social and non-natural foundations of the border, understood as a condition of being-in-the-world and reciprocal recognition of self and others. A second confronts these principles with contemporary reality, in which the enthusiasm of some people for the abolition of borders is followed by a praise of borders on the part of others sharing the same humanist sensibility. This duality is caricatured in a paradoxical representation of globalization: one of flows that cross borders and walls that seal them. Pushed to the extreme, this paradox involves a theoretical impasse that causes borders to disappear in one of two ways: by replacing them with walls or by ignoring their existence. It is important to shed light on the concepts with which we claim to describe and understand the world that surrounds us. Words are important: in the course of this book I shall establish a distinction between the notion of 'identity' and that of 'subject', a distinction that will allow me to present and test the idea according to which the person who seems 'foreign' to me is the 'other' subject that my identity needs in order to exist and endure. I shall thus place the border at the centre of my reflection.

The geographer Michel Foucher, an acknowledged expert on borders, offered in 2007 a geopolitical survey in which he described 'the global stage of borders ... marked by a double movement of obsolescence and resistance on the part of its attributes'.[4] On a basis of wide and precise documentation, he examined the regional and national histories of borders. Each of these is the result and sometimes still the object of political negotiation, war, separation or conquest, while from one generation to another the issues at stake in border lines tend to change or even disappear (as in the case of walls and partitions in Cyprus or Ireland, where the question of two nations has become obsolete for the children and grandchildren of combatants). Orienting his analysis to the political borders of states, Foucher describes their central role in the legitimation of nation-states that have only recently gained independence (as with the former Soviet republics), or their transformation in the long negotiation of the external and internal boundaries of a regional framework (the moment that Europe has been undergoing since the 1980s). This geopolitical and strategic inventory is remarkably well documented and up to date.[5] However, in order to grasp the human (and not just political) dimension of the border, it is necessary to expand considerably the sample of places and moments taken into account, beyond the boundaries of nation-states alone – to what I shall call *border situations*.

Moreover, I believe it necessary to signal two basic disagreements right away, as these will enable me to spell out what an *anthropology* of borders may mean. On the one hand, the geostrategic approach views walls as simply an instance of borders, depriving them of their radical meaning, that of a physical and symbolic violence, and thus tending to 'banalize' their existence in the name of political realism and the lesser evil. On the contrary, as we shall see, the wall is the negation of the border, even if this requires freeing ourselves for a moment from political actuality. It crushes borders, making them disappear, until the 'walled' (who include, of course, those walled out) overthrow it or transform it and make it disappear by cutting holes in it, putting up ladders or equipping it with gates.

On the other hand, Michel Foucher's approach (which is also found more widely among the champions of realpolitik) consists in taking as given and beyond dispute the reference to 'identitarian projects', national or ethnic identities as the first cause that determines the course, legitimacy, and greater or lesser openness or closure of borders. However, it is precisely the two-fold conflict between 'identitarian' and relationship, between wall and border (the wall being to the border what identity obsession is to relationship), that in my view has to be deciphered and overcome. This will make it possible to challenge the false identity-based obviousness on which arguments of global or national 'governance' are based, particularly what is today known as 'political realism'. For, if we want to be precise, the contemporary fury with which walls are constructed is the expression less of what Michel Foucher calls an 'obsession with borders' than of an obsession with identity. And its spread is the sign of a very current propensity, which Wendy Brown has called, in a rather provocative fashion, a 'desire for walls',[6] and what I shall analyse as an identity trap.

Why not slow down and note that we are still in the final episodes of what Marc Augé has called the 'prehistory of the world',[7] slow down and recognize the complexity of the challenge, at whatever place on Earth we happen to be, to simultaneously think globally and act effectively where we are, locally? The object of anthropology is

17

not to praise borders – accrediting the idea that walls are simply an instance of these – unfortunate for some, inevitable for others. Nor is it to produce 'manifestos', whether favourable to them or unfavourable, nor again to advise defenders of world 'governance', but rather to challenge the false obviousness of borders, world, and the global scale of power and politics. Above all, anthropology can contribute to understanding why and how humans constantly invent new borders in order to 'place' themselves in the world and vis-à-vis others, how they did so in the past and are continuing to do so today.

Temporal, social and spatial dimensions of the border ritual

This will be the first point in my argument: the border ritual attests to the institution of all social life in a given environment; it determines the division from and relationship with the natural and social world that surrounds it. Before describing the moment of crossing at the wall, therefore, we have to go back to the principle of the border. For this purpose, rather than regarding the border as a fixed and absolute fait accompli (let alone the wall as just one of its possible instances), it is necessary to study the border *as it is being made*. What the border displays is both a division and a relationship. Its action is double, external and internal; it is both a threshold and an act of institution: to institute one's own place, whether social or sacred, involves separating this from an environment – nature, city or society – which makes it possible to inscribe a given collective, a 'group' or 'community' of humans in the social world with which, thanks to the border created, a relationship to others can be established and thus exist.

This separation/relationship is the object of an act of foundation and delimitation, it relates to an event out of the ordinary, which needs to be repeated according to ritual rules or a ritual calendar of commemoration or renewal of the boundary. Closely linked to this historic event that instituted it within the world that surrounds it, the border permits recognition of a group in the social world, and the inscription of a place in space. It is this being inscribed in three relative dimensions that it is important to keep in mind, and whose place we shall have to verify case by case: time, social world and space.

It is temporal in the sense that the place and the community have not always existed; they were founded at a given moment, and this relativity of every border between a before and an after also leads us to suppose that the event might well not have taken place: it is thus

18

symbolically effective to recall the event and the division in time that it has realized.

The border is also social in the sense that the threshold where the instituted group symbolically begins is recognized on both sides, which also means that the placing in relationship – and beyond this, the relational framework represented by the border itself – are necessary for the double recognition of self and other.

Finally, the border is spatial, the boundary has a form that partitions space and materializes an inside and an outside. Even when the social separation is not materialized by a border in space, this is never just a metaphor. For example, if we speak, as Fredrik Barth has done,[8] and after him several other ethnologists, of the boundaries of ethnic groups, these are certainly symbolic ones – basically meaning that everyone knows what they can and should do or say, or cannot and should not, in this or that context – but it is rare indeed for these boundaries not to find expression, at least provisionally, in a *space* of contact and exchange that makes a border.

It follows from what has been said that on all these levels, spatial, social and sacred (and here we consider the sacred as one production of the social), a constant characteristic of the border is its intrinsic duality – a point we shall return to; it is itself constituted by two sides or two edges, like a line drawn in pencil whose thickness can be seen only under the microscope. Anthropology *of* the border must then become anthropology *in* the border.

Community and locality: the border as social fact

Whatever their themes and places of study, close or distant, urban or rural, anthropologists have always come across the imposition of a border, even when they have not necessarily paid attention to this, it being so self-evident. Local inscriptions have had to be challenged, sometimes painfully, by territorial transformations (regional delimitation, extension of metropolitan agglomerations, creation of supranational economic zones) or by migration (national, international and, now more easily, intercontinental), for the investigation in return of what were formerly and are today 'techniques for the production of locality'.[9] (The term 'locality' here should not be taken in the sense of the actual place name, but rather in that of the local inscription of individual and collective lives, or even the identification of persons and groups with this or that place.) Taking this path, we perceive, as it were retrospectively, that every ritual is also local, and

19

that every group and place likewise need, in order to exist, the institution of a border. We shall see this with a brief example taken from my research in Brazil.

The sacred space in Salvador de Bahia

Situated in the city of Salvador de Bahia is a site of some 300 square metres known as the 'Vila Flaviana', occupied by a 'saint's house' (temple or *terreiro* dedicated to the cult of *orixás*).[10] An African woman, Flaviana Bianchi, born in 1846, most likely a slave with a family of European origin, the Bianchis, whose name she was given at the time of emancipation, founded this *terreiro* for *candomblé* in the last quarter of the nineteenth century. It was what in Bahia is called a *roça* (literally, 'farm'), an ecological and social compound made up of sacred places (halls for ceremonies and receptions, internal and external altars to divinities, sacred trees or points of water) and places of everyday habitation occupied by various of its followers. The space of the Vila Flaviana occupies close to 1,500 square metres. When the old 'saint's mother' died in 1940, the *terreiro* ended its public activities, the building was occupied by members of her biological family, and the surrounding land was gradually abandoned and sold.

Fifty years later, a new change took place when the great-granddaughter of the founder, herself an initiate of the *candomblé* cult, decided to reopen the *terreiro* for its religious and public activities, and to become its new 'saint's mother'. With the support of a 'community' that included the major *terreiros* of the city and leaders of the black political and cultural movement, she got the house back and gradually evicted Flaviana's other descendants. Activities recommenced in January 1991 with a *padê*, the ritual that opens the annual cycle of *candomblé* ceremonies.

Each year since then this ritual has been repeated a few days before the beginning of the cyclic calendar of ceremonies in homage to the other divinities of the *terreiro*. Dedicated to Exu,[11] this ritual is preliminary and propitiatory, a ritual of opening to the world of divinities and an 'opening of paths' for each participant in his or her personal projects. But it also has a more implicit and broader function, a community one or a political one in the wider sense of the word: that of delimiting the sacred space. If this is particularly clear in the case of the Vila Flaviana, its sense can be generalized more or less across the whole world of *candomblé*, which has this opening ritual as its main common denominator.

Ritual enables the line of the border, still fragile, to be rehearsed in a sacred form. Concretely, sacralization is effected by the copious application of ritual blood (*eje*), by the 'saint's mother' and her officiants, over the three material representations of Exu: one at the entrance, which marks the boundary between the street and the courtyard, another opposite the ceremonial hall, and a third right in front of the building. The blood is also applied to the walls of the building itself. On the basis of this opening ritual and in the ceremonies that follow, the social unit that recognizes itself in this place will refer to the 'saint's house' where she is to be found. The point is that reference to the ritual blood enables the space to be given a sacred dimension, bringing into existence the symbolic community (called 'saint's people') who gather there.

What does this story teach us about the relation between a community (still fragile) and the border of the place where it is formed, a border whose ritualization, as we saw, is particularly insistent? The community of this *terreiro* rests today on a set of factors that converge at a particular moment (their heterogeneity, moreover, removing any legitimacy from identity-based essentialism): individual conversion or adherence, the extent of urban and global networks, the politicization of religious 'identities', as much as if not more so than the family constraint, the disease and the affliction that formed in the past the dominant contexts of the cult of *orixás*. If these contexts have not disappeared, they now form only part of the cult's components, the most intimate and hidden one, whereas the social and symbolic contexts of the rite and the community of the 'saint's people' have changed nature and scale with globalization and urban development.[12]

The followers, friends who have come from other *terreiros*, curious visitors, young neighbours from the district and passing tourists thus form a temporary symbolic community, whose spatial distribution is urban and national, or even, increasingly often, extranational (through the regular frequentation of American and European followers who have come through the channels of cultural tourism). The community is open in the sense that each member can frequent other *terreiros*, or even leave the cult and either return later or not. This fragility of community membership expresses a form of distancing on the part of the participants themselves, which implies all the more ritualization: recognition of the place as a *terreiro* and space of reference of a local/urban/global community will be reproduced as long as this place sees its boundaries and its meaning reaffirmed by way of appropriate rituals. The uncertainties arising from both relative distance and fragility of membership are characteristics of urban milieus and more generally of the contemporary world, more often open to a

21

greater number of cultural alternatives than previously or elsewhere. These characteristics today strengthen the need for this elementary form of border, to institute the separation of a socially sacred place in an environment, natural or urban, that must be recalled and 'replayed' as often as necessary.

The point is to emphasize somehow the drawing of a boundary and thus reaffirm symbolically the existence of the space as well as the connection of the space to the community. It is neither modernity nor postmodernity that is at issue in the rehearsing of ritual, but rather the uncertainty of any border: an uncertainty that is simultaneously temporal, spatial and social. The repeated drawing of the border reaffirms, if need be, its non-natural character, as its social inscription is inversely proportional to its natural self-evidence.

There are copious examples of other rituals of the same order, acting in different spatial and social perimeters from that which we have just discussed, and these can be found in many ethnographic or archaeological studies. The historical and sociological contexts are different, and on each occasion local determinations are important in explaining this need to rehearse the border ritually as social and not natural fact. Beyond these differences of context, however, we can hold on to this formal analogy that shows the importance of what we may call, in a very general way, the symbolism of the border.

The symbolic construction of the border

This is shown for example by the doubly founding role of the ritual construction of the tower of the initiates' house (the *tsimia*) in New Guinea's Baruya society, studied by Maurice Godelier in the 1960s and 1970s.[13] The term *tsimia* denotes the building in which the initiation of the group's young males into manhood takes place. The composition of this building represents in symbolic fashion the 'body' of the whole community, whose centre is the *tsimié* (the tallest pole representing the group's ancestor). The building is the work of the collective of the fathers of future initiates: each of these brings from the forest one of the posts that will constitute the wall of the 'body' under construction, and these are then aligned with others to form a circle that will delimit the periphery of the *tsimia*. On the signal given by the shamanic master of ceremonies, each plants his post in front of him, emitting a war cry that is taken up by everyone surrounding them.

Godelier observes that the house is rebuilt every three or four years to receive a new group of male initiates; and that with each rebuild-

22

ing, the ritual group is formed not as a function of ties of kinship but according to ties of co-residence and cooperation, by village.[14] The comments on this description that Godelier gave later show very well the scope of the ritual and the metonymic connection between spatial and social borders: 'What the Baruya assert and reassert with each initiation is their right to exercise in common a form of sovereignty over a territory, its resources and the individuals who people it, a territory whose borders are recognized by their neighbours.'[15]

Thus, the sacred space is the symbolic support and reference of the group: it is what proves and effects the double foundation of the *tsimia*, both sacred (for the initiates) and social (for the whole Baruya group). In terms of symbolic form, there is a metonymic connection between sacred group and social group, between space and society: the house of initiates focuses the forces and spirits that irradiate the whole of Baruya society. Just as the *terreiro* in *candomblé*, delimited by the tutelary figure of Exu, is the space of reference in Bahia of a wider community that is dispersed both in the urban space and beyond.

What we wish to emphasize here is the importance of the spatial dimension of every social border: this is explained by the necessity of ritual and the fact that, in order to repeat the border as social fact, this always inscribes what it institutes materially and locally.

An anthropology of/in the border

Border of places (here and over there), border of time (before and after), and border of the social world of experience, that is, of everything that comes to exist socially by delimiting within a defined environment an 'own' and a 'different': these are the elementary forms of the border, but also the contexts of its uncertainty, its incompletion in space, in duration, and vis-à-vis others. The social and non-natural character of the border ends up creating a particular situation: the uncertainty of its drawing is expressed in time – of waiting, reflection, conflict – and in space – vague, as if the border was the place where uncertainty had found its most exact recognition. This consubstantial uncertainty explains the necessary repetitions and reconfigurations assumed by ritual, whose fundamental role is not to freeze the border, but rather to make it live in order for self and other to live at the same time. Hence the interest in revisiting this function of ritual in the context of identity-based uncertainties.

Founding, naming, limiting

Anthropological studies have shown that rituals aim to inscribe individual lives in a social organization; and that by doing so, they institute and reproduce the forms of association themselves. This is the particular object of rites of passage (male and female initiation, integration into age classes, celebration of marriages or funerals), which reproduce categories of gender, age classes or family systems while celebrating the integration and place of individuals within them. But it is also the role of rites of institution (creation of new forms of association), and of all those that, in a cyclical manner, ensure the proper functioning of institutions and the proper reproduction of instituted groups (rites of separation, propitiation, purification, etc.), while at the same time inscribing individual trajectories in these collectives.[16] This reminder is important, in order to situate the relationship that the ritual takes charge of between individual and community on the one hand and locality on the other, and finally between these two 'integrating' contexts of the individual – communal, social and local – and the border that makes them exist.

In all these cases, these social rites need a space whose resources they use in order to be accomplished, and that they configure according to the characteristics of the community created in this place and at this moment. Here are a few brief examples. There is the closed space of dance and ceremony, like the *barracão* (or ceremonial hall) mentioned earlier and always necessary, whatever its form, in the functioning of the ritual community of Afro-Brazilian *candomblé*. It may be an ordinary space changed into a ritual place for a limited time, during which it becomes the path for a procession or parade to travel: the case for example of the carnival circuit which, in the city of Salvador de Bahia, is the object of bitter negotiation before and during the parade, between the different carnival associations that participate in it and seek to occupy the street as a function of their own social and local anchorages in the city and their desires to confirm or reverse these ordinary anchorages in the ritual moment; from the official announcement that 'the street is for the people' ('*A rua é do povo*'), certain of the city's arteries lose their everyday uses and suddenly acquire an importance in ritual not comparable with that which they have in ordinary life. The ritual space can also be the ground where material representations of the divinities are deposited or buried; or again, on a larger scale, the forest around which a village population and subsequently a capital have developed, as in the case of the forest of Bè at the heart of the city of Lomé, capital of Togo:

the woodland here was transformed and sanctuarized into a 'sacred forest', the focus and place of episodic gathering of the descendants of the earliest arrivals on the coast and the first occupants of the city, who deposit and regularly honour there the divinities of their lineage.

By using space as support, the social rite (which integrates individuals into the community and reproduces this at the same time) generally gives a specific meaning to the place each time: indirectly, it founds this by establishing its symbolic connection with a social or sacred entity, on the basis of its natural or material existence but going beyond this.

The rite can also be directly local and secondarily (or with an 'expanded' meaning and ritual arrangement) social. This is the case, for example, with the foundation of a town or the inauguration of a house, as we have seen with the repeated and ritual foundation of the house of male initiation studied by Maurice Godelier among the Baruya of New Guinea. It is also what we find in a different context, that of the commemoration of the foundation of Rome, recalled in one of the rituals of the pre-carnivalesque form of the Lupercalia.[17] One of the actions in this performance involves a chaotic round of dancers imitating wolves around the 'primordial furrow' that embodies the first boundary of the city on its foundation. In this ritual, known as the 'run of the Luperci [the priests of Lupercus], the wolf (*lupus*) disguise is a metonym for the surrounding wild forest, and the round chase of the wolves symbolically confirms the digging of the primordial furrow. Then the mad chase continues through the streets of the city with a purificatory function associated with the time of rebirth during the transition to the new Roman year.[18] As the first moment of this rite, also described as one 'of rebirth', the run of the Luperci around the primordial furrow may be viewed as a ritual model of the city's foundation. On the one hand, it recalls the founding gesture (the line of the furrow) that, according to myth, separated the community from its natural environment and made the city exist as the community's space, surrounded by walls and gates without which there would not have been a city as a defined space. On the other hand, the round of the wolves is a ritual that at the same time scares and amuses, in the same way as the many animals of carnival would subsequently do, being there to remind us of our separation from the wild world and the relationship that connects us to it. The fictitious violence of the Lupercalia turning around the boundary of the primordial furrow has a double effect: it recalls the foundation myth of the city of Rome by the separation of a subject (the community) from what surrounds it; and it 'autonomizes' this surround

25

which becomes, by being separated and imitated in the rite, its object of thought and emotions (nature as both attractive and threatening).

From this, we can conclude that the border has an instability that is both theoretically founded and in some sense universal. This also means that the processes of its imposition may occupy chance spaces and times. The more this uncertainty persists and establishes itself, the more the border thickens, occupying kilometres or slowing down time. What will interest us here therefore is this spread of the border's space and time, and from this exploration we shall draw material for a wider reflection on the liminality of border situations, their uncertainty and their transformative character.

Borderlands as uncertain places: Tocqueville at Saginaw

Saginaw, 1831. Alexis de Tocqueville and his companion Gustave de Beaumont are walking and riding along this border of 175 kilometres. Before concluding that the American model of democracy was a fit subject of study on the grounds of being quite new and still coming into being, Tocqueville wanted to conduct his investigation at 'the last limits of European civilization'.[19] This exploration led him from Detroit, already 'on the edge of civilization', to the village of Saginaw that the Americans called the 'frontier': this was 'the last point inhabited by the Europeans toward the northwest of the vast peninsula of Michigan . . ., an advance post, a sort of refuge that the whites have come to plant among the Indian nations' (p. 271). But he was never certain of reaching the other side, that of the imagined Indian, whom he was told every day on his route was further, always further, and several kilometres more so each year.

Slowly, before reaching the Saginaw frontier, the two explorers crossed what turned out to be a long borderland ('*terre de frontière*'), a forest thinly populated by immigrants, pioneers, a few Indians and Métis. From the Flint River, and guided by two Indians, 'we came into permanent solitude', Tocqueville noted, and soon 'we had before us the spectacle we had run after so long: the interior of a virgin forest' (p. 262). It was here that Tocqueville encountered the inextricable chaos of the forest – which he depicted at length – as well as the Bois-Brûlés, 'this singular race of half-breeds which covers all the frontiers of Canada and a part of those of the United States' (p. 268).

The descriptions Tocqueville gives of the 'Indian' are less surprising (since they conform to the image of the Enlightenment philosophers as to the detachment and grandeur of the 'savage' who views with a certain contempt the efforts and conveniences of the European) than the newer and more candid ones that he gives of the 'European of the frontier' and the torments of the Métis. The latter lives in 'a rustic cabin more comfortable than the savage's wigwam and more crude than the house of civilized man [*l'homme policé*]' (p. 74). And, like the forest where Tocqueville met him, his mind was a 'tangled chaos' that 'forms a composite as inexplicable to others as to himself' (p. 74). A century and a half before the philosopher Michel Serres praised the joyful singularity of the Harlequin who has assimilated and superseded diverse and varied apprenticeships to become the '*tiers-instruit*',[20] the Métis was described by Tocqueville as astonished by the new world that he discovers but does not understand. Spontaneously, in words that are transparent and marked by the language of his time, he describes the unease, ignorance and uncertainty of the person faced with tests to his identity in a border situation:

> Proud of his European origin, he despises the wilderness, and yet he loves the savage freedom which reigns there; he admires civilization and is unable to submit himself completely to its empire. His tastes are in contradiction with his ideas, his opinions with his ways. Not knowing how to guide himself by the doubtful light which illumines him, his soul struggles painfully in the web of universal doubt: he adopts contrary usages, he prays at two altars, he believes in the Redeemer of the world and the amulettes of the charlatan, and he reaches the end of his career without having been able to untangle the obscure problem of his existence. (p. 74)

Whatever the quantities of information about the world that may be contrasted today with this short travel diary of 1831, it makes for an interesting read: the author is more motivated by the discovery of unexplored worlds and the 'swaddling of a universal doubt' than by the identity-based view of *métissage* as degeneration (as expressed by the writer Arthur de Gobineau some twenty years later in his *Essay on the Inequality of Races*) or, on the contrary but still in the same register, as improvement by reference to a supposed racial purity (detestable in this case). Tocqueville the explorer has no time for any of that. The borderland is for him the real mystery, in a visit to America motivated by the quest for democracy and equality. What his exploration revealed above all was the violence, uncertainty and creativity that characterized the long space of the border. None of these notions is absent from his final comments: 'It's this idea of destruction, this conception of near and inevitable change which gives in our opinion so original a character and so touching a beauty to the solitudes of America. One sees them with melancholy pleasure' (p. 280).

In these reflections I adopt a definition of the border that is less administrative than is generally understood. But this is because the policed national border represents only one aspect of border situations: more often, the border situation is observed in places, moments or experiences that bring into play a relationship with an 'other', an external subject who crosses or penetrates a space that is not familiar to him or her, themselves becoming the unfamiliar for those who are there. It is this event that creates a relative foreignness in the particular context, which is repeated and observable in other places. It may seem a priori that the kind of border represented by the Saginaw forest in 1831 has since disappeared, given that all available spaces have been conquered and distributed. The policies of landowners, conquerors and colonists have partitioned more or less the totality of global space. Yet, still today, conflicts create 'buffer zones', controlled more or less closely by UN or foreign armies in the case of national borders – borders that may well be political and administrative, but that over time sometimes become places of a civilian, even urban, occupation. This is the case with the movement of the 'bufferers' in Cyprus, who occupy the buffer zone of Nicosia and demand the departure of the UN forces and the end of the division of the island and its capital between Greek and Turkish sectors.[21] A similar uncertainty as to the status of the space is found in other border situations, for example those created by the many movements of land invasion and occupation on rural or urban margins, whose legalization signifies recognition and inclusion in an expanded perimeter of legality. In other words, the border is both object of negotiation and place in the politics of these occupation movements. This solution, which has now been adopted as part of urban policy in several so-called 'emerging' countries, particularly Argentina and Brazil, proves more effective from the point of view of social, urban or political integration than the stigmatization on the basis of identity (racial, religious or ethnic) that is found in Europe, for example vis-à-vis Roma or Afghan encampments or 'ghettoized' districts.

Empty space, no-man's-land, the interstitial is a moving border in the course of negotiation, a moment of conflict as much as a space of encounter.

Interval time: carnivals and deceleration

What we come to now is 'border time', to use an expression as close as possible to that used to describe a border space that can extend to 175 kilometres; this border time can itself stretch and become the long moment of a liminal existence. Shedding light on the margins of social time makes it possible to grasp its prolonged effects on ordinary time. It also enables us to take into account their ritual dimension, which here again means how far they are both necessary and fragile.

If time has considerably accelerated in recent decades, and if the speed of mass displacement (by road, train or plane) and communication is an essential component of globalization, we have to admit that the organization of time is social and not technical (unless the social is subjected to the rhythms of technology, of course, but this remains a decision socially taken). The acceleration of time, moreover, is a model of participation in the hypermodernity of the world, and in such a runaway situation we may think that our capacity for deceleration has become vital. True, the individualization of social lives leads each person to try to make a personal or family calendar coincide with the social calendar they depend on, but adjustments are calculated as tightly as possible. The tasks ascribed to each day, week and month follow in sequences with no interval or 'dead time'. And it is increasingly hard to imagine a generalized interruption in the social organization of time. If speed is one of the major problems of our age, this is also because temporal borders tend to become ever more thin: an end to voids and latency. How is time to be stopped? There is of course a response. This is found on the one hand in the historical place of interval time in calendar rhythms and in its ritualization; it is found on the other hand in the age-old attention that has been paid to this intercalary time, to what happens and what is invented there.

In order to find traces of the birth of an interval time, we have to go back to the beginning of calendars, even before the Roman calendar established by Julius Caesar that lies at the origin of today's so-called Gregorian calendar (established by Pope Gregory XIII in the late sixteenth century), very close to what is today globally accepted. There is no need to go into the long historical meanders of societies that have sought throughout their existence to master time – the passage of days, seasons and years. On the whole, the issue for a long time and in different cultures (Egyptian, Mayan, Oriental, Greek, Roman, etc.) has been to adjust accounts between (annual) solar cycles and (monthly) lunar ones. These adjustments have given rise to many hesitations.[22]

We can thus note the quite general presence of interval time, born initially as a vague moment of transition and limit between a dying year and a new one being born, then increasingly established by rituals specific to it. According to various annual calendar systems and the adjustments to which they gave rise, there was a 'remainder' of five, ten or twelve days, which were close either to the winter solstice or, more rarely, to the spring equinox. A ritual time was invented to mark this scansion of time and even help it to pass from one cycle of seasons to another: rituals of transgression or inversion of hierarchies, also of purification, helped the emergence from one period and prepared the regenerations needed to enter the next. In the late nineteenth century, the ethnologist Arnold Van Gennep found in this transition sequence the principle he would generally apply to the ritual situation: the succession of three phases of the rite: preliminary (separation), liminal (transformation) and post-liminal (reaggregation). It is the liminal moment that embodies the border of time and, by its cathartic overflowing, moves the border between identities.

The end of the annual cycle gave rise everywhere to more or less extended festivities of rupture and renewal, of end (or death) and beginning. This interval time received a special status. For example, in the ancient Mayan calendar (the *tun*, a year of 360 days), there were 'five days called empty or phantom, days of unhappiness that had no name'.[23] In Rome in December, the Saturnalia were 'a moment of general license and reversal of norms, when slaves took the place of masters'.[24] Celebrated in homage to Saturn, master of time, these were ten days of reversal, with their characteristic masks, their transgression of authority and their burlesque king, chosen by lot, who held power and freedom of speech before being sacrificed on the final day. And on the first days of the new year, masquerades of deer, donkeys and men disguised as women paraded on the Roman calends (*calendae januariae*), which marked the hesitant and slow transition from one annual cycle to another. Later on, in the Julian calendar as revised by the Catholic church, the twelve days of the pagan cult of the winter solstice were placed between the day after the last day of the ancient Roman Saturnalia (25 December) and Epiphany (6 January), forming a 'junction time' of twelve days that is also found in the Orient and in medieval Europe. Through to the Middle Ages, these days of annual rupture would become the moment of a ritual profusion: the Feast of Fools or of drunken deacons (reversal of the clerical hierarchy), the Feast of the Innocents or children, the Feast of the Ass, burlesque celebrations and festivities, as well as masquerades.

All these rituals proclaim the time of carnival. But the beginning of the intercalary time of carnival is itself the object of several versions: on the day after the Saturnalia and at the start of the Feast of Fools (25 December), or at the end of this (6 January), as is still the case today for certain carnivals in the West Indies; or 2 February (the day of Mary in the Catholic calendar, the month of February being formerly considered the month of the dead and of 'purification' in the Roman calendar); or finally, from the eleventh century, the three (or five) days that lead up to Shrove Tuesday, the eve of the forty days of Lent that herald and prepare the celebration of Easter. Thus, in the late eleventh century, carnival was more or less fixed in the church calendar on the days of carousing that preceded Ash Wednesday, asceticism and abstinence. But carnival could overspill its limit, from the European Middle Ages to contemporary Brazil; it also happened that, detached from its medieval Christian inscription, it was re-created on other dates more propitious for street festivals (August in Europe) or closer to its original calendar (as the New Year carnival in the Cape province of South Africa).

The medieval Christian calendar effected a kind of politico-religious recuperation of the Julian calendar and the pagan cults that celebrated the death and rebirth of nature and the cycles of time in the winter solstice. Simply by so doing, it effected a recuperation/integration of pagan and political disorders into the time of carnival. But uncertainty remains, both as to the start and end of this interval time and as to what goes on in it.

Its out-of-synch tempo is proclaimed by a sharp signal: the throwing of water or flour, thrusts,[25] whistles, the beating of syncopated drums, the 'carnival shout' or the appearance of an imp. Against the everyday order that it interrupts, it opens for a given time a space for the deployment of various forms of parody, buffoonery, poetic or political demonstration freed from the constraints of social time. In this way an other space-time is created, outside the everyday, which will form the situation in which a duplication of self can be effected, as it is necessary to be 'outside oneself' in order to exist under another mask than the social one through which the person exists in his or her everyday life. Finally, it is here, in the moment opened by this irruption, that the gap and with it the carnival spirit produce another force, 'in duplicate', that can extend beyond the temporal limit of the rite and more widely irradiate the ordinary and everyday forms of popular culture. The medieval carnival, which the Russian literary historian Mikhail Bakhtin showed was based on laughter, derision, and the challenge in parody to official powers and their cultural codes (in particular, the superiority of mind over body).[26] Also that of Creole speech, jubilatory and aggressive, a 'speech that carnivalizes the world and verbalizes its chaos', as Christine Ramat noted in a reflection on the literary and poetic culture of the Caribbean.[27] Or again, that of racial contestation and the reinvention of Africa in the carnivals of Brazil, Colombia and the Caribbean over recent decades,

31

the final avatar of a carnivalesque invention that breaks with the world of ordinary dominations and is capable of transforming it.

Since carnival has a temporal existence beyond the actual ritual, it was viewed from the start by the public authorities as a problem, and was the object of a constant attempt to rein it in. It was a summons to disorder and an invitation to break with the ordinary, a summons to games of reversal, excess or derision that were always risky. If carnival is often discussed in terms of catharsis, history both ancient and modern shows that it is also a time of sedition, which sees ritual parody spill outside its calendar into a real inversion of order; for example the carnival uprisings of 1881 and 1884 in Trinidad, the riots of the *Cannes brûlés* (literally 'burned canes': the Canboulay riots), which saw violent confrontations between revellers armed with sticks (commemorating the abolition of slavery in 1838) and the police.[28] In Guadeloupe, it was percussion bands known as *groupes à peaux* (skin bands) who relaunched this carnivalesque spirit associated with rupture and sedition in the 1970s. Inspired by the *gwo-ka* drums of the colonial era, they took an increasingly prominent place, in the image of Akiyo and what was more generally called the Mouvman Kilitrel Gwadloup (Guadeloupe Cultural Movement). The rapid dance accompanied by percussion imitates the struggle against oppression and marks the arrival of the band in the carnival streets. It was this 'overflow' of ritual and its contestatory character, for example with the *déboulés de mobilisation* (mobilized revellers), that led to the major role played by carnival bands in the formation of the cultural movement, one of the components in the social revolt of 2009 led by the Lannyaj Kont Profitasyon (against profiteering).[29]

This is a moment when time is interrupted, a moment that stops the calendar – a characteristic of ritual time in general. But for all that, we are not out of the world, but on the contrary very much present-in-the-world, in the concrete, physical and fleshly, to the point of the grotesque that caricatures the presence of the body vis-à-vis those dominant forces (political, clerical or others) that render it obscene. It is an interval time that is both ritual (there may be several days of parade) and political, in the sense that the everyday is reflected in it. A time therefore of deceleration, reflection, cultural innovation and action, which infiltrates into an intercalary 'dead time'. The big business of carnival in many cities of the world, with its commercial recuperations or political uses, should not make us forget this primary and always essential element, even if it is covered by other more recent functions: the ritual time that it embodies helps the passage of time, individual passage (the ages of life) and social passage (formerly the seasons, today political or urban integration).

Carnival and the feasts that preceded it, as also those inspired by it, form a border moment between a before (that is cast off by purifying oneself) and an after (in which one gathers oneself together). Carnival is a border, itself marked by two edges, those of its beginning and its end. The interest of the study of rituals lies in the fact that they lie at the heart of this liminal moment. Everything that happens here reminds us that no passage is easy to live. This is the reason that so-called 'rites of passage' were invented.

Everything that the border is the place of

To close this reflection, at least momentarily, I shall sum up the main theses developed in this chapter. First of all, the establishment of social and spatial borders is a deeply human action, whose ritual institution is all the more necessary in that it is not natural, being inscribed in relative social temporalities. Secondly, the incompletion and instability of social processes lies at the origin both of the establishment of borders and of their transformation, their instability and their incompletion. Thirdly, and surprising as it may seem when we think of the actuality of recent decades – with its cleavages between national identity and immigration, its strengthened controls at national borders and the media coverage of expulsions of foreigners, or with fabricated oppositions between the ancestral purity of the indigenous and the cultural degeneration of the 'alien' – the border is set against the idea of indigeneity. It is fundamentally opposed to it, if by indigeneity we understand a state given by nature. And it contradicts it in fact if the limits of indigeneity are supposedly inherited and not immovable. Borders are socially 'constructed' and shifting. We shall return to these themes, after tackling more directly the critique of the identity paradigm.

Borders and identity

In fact, as distinct from all identity-based beliefs in human indigeneity, ancient or contemporary, as the principal or universal model of identity and the natural framework of existence, we see that every *em*placement was preceded and will be followed by a *dis*placement. The history of identities, that of humanity as a whole, is a succession of migrations, chances and accommodations. And in the end,

33

an always arbitrary relationship formed between a being in motion and an indefinite place 'on the surface of the Earth', at the end of an encounter that only a priori can give itself the airs of self-evidence and axiomatic truth.

In fact, no human has ever been 'indigenous', and all borders have always been unstable. All the histories of settlement studied by ethnologists show this: the first arrivals, 'already here' when others arrive, transform themselves into an 'always here' on the basis of a relative and strategic point of view vis-à-vis the followers, at the cost of an operation that freezes and essentializes a being in motion, an operation that today would be called 'freeze frame' and that fixes the identity of space ('territory') in an arbitrary way.

No human has really 'arisen from the land' (the more or less literal meaning of 'autochthonous'), and the displacement of humans (in groups, families and individually) over the surface of the Earth has been part of the history of humanity since its beginnings. It is under-standable, therefore, how 'production' of one's own place is a univer-sal event inasmuch as it is not natural: it has to be rehearsed, and in the course of this rehearsal the place itself is constantly transformed in time and space in order to exist. The close relationship between the two ritual institutions of community and locality, which I have sought to describe and illustrate in this chapter, confirms the connection that these have both had with human mobility since the earliest times.

The invention of myths of origin is part of the identity-based fictionalization of this relative anteriority. These myths themselves, moreover, are not fixed in time, they can assume various versions depending on the place where they are uttered, the person who utters them, or the strategies and conflicts that motivate them. We may wonder whether every myth of origin is not always identity-based from the moment it is created and uttered, and so whether it is not always a 'myth/ideology',[30] but also and complementary to this whether it does not constitute the very principle of the heteroclite accumulation that forms the memory and culture of places in general, constantly 'worked' by identity assignment and the critique of this.

Border situations and liminality

By placing my gaze 'within' borders – both those that are palpable or come to exist socially for others and for oneself, and the expanded borders of space or again those of time – I have sought to bring to light an object of study and reflection concerning everything that takes place on the border. Width in space, social thickness, or the long duration of the border make it possible to inventory a certain number of its characteristics, which we shall return to later. To be precise, avoiding hollow metaphors and indicating observable facts, we can make a list (or at least start one) of what characterizes border situations. Here is a first attempt.

In border spaces we have seen conflicts, colonization under way, hybrid material forms (buildings, cities) and again the 'inextricable chaos', to use Tocqueville's image, which indicates both the discovery and the clearing of the space encountered. This latter aspect also corresponds to the social dimension of the border, and the individual sense of shock arising from the gap between the cultural referents of the first socializations and the new local anchorings revealed in displacement. On this level, that of social experience, fear, misunderstanding and self-questioning are aspects of the discovery of the other and their relative foreignness before the situation is understood. From the point of view of the temporal border, finally, we have seen that the interval between a before and an after is a moment of disorder, but also of purification, regeneration and cultural creation. Viewed as 'dead time', potentially extinguishable in the hypermodern conception of time subjected to speed, it is a place of catharsis, of relative freedom associated with an in-between state, thus a moment of possible duplication of self in which new masks are invented, and finally, one of possible transformation of context, even of sedition.

A 'fallow' that interrupts spatial continuity, an uncertainty floating in the initial experience of an encounter, an interval time that stretches in the transition between two periods or two states, the border situation always maintains an exceptional character, which is the very principle of spatial boundary, no matter how 'thin' and brief, when it becomes a place outside of all places, an out-place. The meaning of this 'exception' can be expanded by focusing on its 'liminal' character. Literally denoting the threshold (*limen*) and the in-between, liminality defines the border in its ritual aspect, marking the crossing of a threshold and the entry into a different 'law' for any actors who find themselves there and take on new identities. This is the original sense of the term, but it can be felt when, at the moment one arrives at the actual place of the border, one 'becomes' a foreigner and even momentarily – but sometimes for longer – without status.

This liminality is also social, concerning everything that is generally denoted by the 'margins' and that we can situate more precisely in the state of uncertainty about existing socially and being recognized by others: a liminal condition, therefore, which does not have the status of a social category but can sometimes correspond to what is denoted by 'liminal', that is, a state hardly perceptible, hardly audible and 'voiceless'. It is by visiting camps of refugees, internally displaced persons and clandestine migrants that I have most directly grasped this *social* liminality, which it then seemed to me possible to expand to all 'out-places'. Their suspended temporality and interstitial place (outside all places, yet for all that real and localizable) produce the experience of a gap with the official social world. A latency and an expectation install themselves in this gap, a life in which people seem to do nothing but 'pushing time', as certain refugees say.

Finally, the liminality of border situations is political, in the sense that it is a moment of exception whose exceptionality extends in time. It may be imposed by a power that decrees the maintenance in 'banishment', that is, outside the boundary of the common law, of a person (a *sans-papier*), a place (a 'waiting zone') or a period (a state of emergency or of exception). Conversely, however, or even against this very decree of exception, exception may also be created or turned to profit as an extraordinary moment and space of emancipation and political sovereignty of subjects against their assignment by identity and locality.

Thus, seeking to understand everything that happens at the border leads us to recognize its thickness and to identify, in all its occurrences, the presence and scope of a liminality – at the same time in-between, exception and uncertainty – that is certainly, beyond the administrative and national specifications with which it is generally associated, the most universal characteristic of the border.

THE WORLD AS 'PROBLEM'

The violence that states have deployed against migrants arriving from Africa, Latin America, Asia and the Middle East fosters the myth of a security attained by establishing an artificial insularity, a self-enclosure. This myth of identity is a deadly ideology. According to the data of the NGO platform Migreurop in 2012, 'the closing of legal paths of access to the European territory has been accompanied by the establishment of repressive measures that prevent immigrants and refugees from reaching European soil. Between January 1993 and March 2012, more than 16,000 persons have died at the EU borders.'[1] This estimate is in fact highly conservative, as it only includes bodies actually found in the desert or washed up on the beaches, and the estimates given by survivors. It is exceptional for bodies to be recovered, in the way that they were with the shipwreck of October 2013 off the coast of Lampedusa. Emotion then directly confronts the face and body of each of the drowned, who even without words force recognition of the subjects that they are behind the administrative or media labels attributed to them ('clandestine', 'illegal'). Dead and recognized as subjects. Victims and heroes. What has taken place at the North–South borders since the end of the Cold War is a scene of war.

War at the borders

Lampedusa, 3 October 2013. Three hundred and sixty-six dead, a hundred survivors, was the balance-sheet of the shipwreck in the Mediterranean of a boat on which 504 migrants from East Africa had risked their lives, mainly Somalians and Eritreans who had paid an exorbitant price to a trafficker. The pope expressed indignation, the mayor of Lampedusa, in tears, insisted that the tragedy should be recorded in images, otherwise people would claim it had not happened, and the Italian government took the measure of the drama by announcing a day of national mourning. The following year, a few days from the anniversary of this event, another shipwreck, this time off the island of Malta, provoked the death of at least 500 persons. The International Organization for Migration (IOM) then announced that 3,000 migrants had died in the Mediterranean between January and September 2014. But the same organization also noted a more extensive violence at the borders: according to retrospective data collected by the IOM, a world total of 40,000 persons died between 2000 and 2014 crossing either maritime or land borders, 22,000 of these trying to reach Europe and 6,000 on the border between Mexico and the United States.[2]

In the course of 2015, the limits of the intolerable seem to have been breached, first of all with a thousand deaths in three boats that capsized between 12 and 19 April, followed by others, until these became almost a daily occurrence in the month of August. By October 2015, there had been a total of at least 3,500 deaths on the borders of Europe (in the Mediterranean and in the Balkans) since the start of the year. This year more than previously, the images have often been reminiscent of a human catastrophe, and the number of migrants flocking to Europe via the Mediterranean and the Balkans (around 800,000) has reminded European nations that they are not apart from the world. On a planetary scale, they are close to those places most involved in the wars or enduring crises of the early twenty-first century: Syria, Iraq, Afghanistan, Israel/Palestine, Eritrea, South Sudan, Libya, Mali. Yet European governments, particularly the French, have stubbornly remained caught in a language and politics of security, fostering the illusion of a possible national enclosure of Europeans and thereby justifying a politics of indifference towards the world. And yet, citizens and voluntary associations have mobilized, bringing help and hospitality to the migrants and strongly calling for solidarity and respect for human rights. A conflict is steadily growing in which borders are the stake and often the place, generating ever more violence.

'These nameless bodies must be found, their corpses must be brought to the surface to be returned to their families', was the demand of the Lampedusa rescuers in 2014, as they knew, being closest to the truth of these bodies, that each was unique, a man or a woman, an adolescent or a child . . . and that no one is reducible to the assigned identity by which they are denoted. Neither 'immigrants', as they did not arrive, nor 'refugees', as they had not been able to request asylum, nor even 'clandestine', as there was no legal verdict on their condition; they *died on migration*, during their displacement. Now, it is this mobility, despite being cherished and valued as the mark of a modern and fluid global world when we speak of 'our' lives, that is the target of police and national governments when we speak of the lives of 'others'. And mobility is again the key question, associated with that of equality – equality in mobility – when we inquire as to the form of a 'common world' shared by all on a planetary scale.

There is both tenacity and fragility in the forward course of the migrant, who resembles Giacometti's 'Walking Man'. He tears himself away from the ground of his identity and launches himself towards the world and others, towards the blank page that begins immediately after he crosses the border of the country or place from which he comes, then towards the 'margins lost in the dark night',[3] the unknown that he will one day manage to render familiar.

The very existence of women and men in displacement, in migration, when they are not yet either here or there, neither arrived nor clearly left, since they cannot give a signal from elsewhere to those they have left – their sole existence is their politics. A politics of life against the politics of indifference. It symbolizes alterity and mobility with an insistence, even obstinacy, vis-à-vis a world that sees them as a problem, and thereby also sees itself likewise.

Is the world a problem? Cosmopolitical reality and realpolitik

In the previous chapter we saw how the border is what makes and marks the foundation of a group in its social environment, of a place in a natural or inhabited space, and of an account of oneself in history. The border establishes a relationship between two entities that it both distinguishes and separates, and this is how it permits and renews the social existence of individuals, places, communities. This simple 'self-evidence' seems less evident to us today, even anachronistic, given the extent to which globalization – whether economic, political or cultural – has imposed two contrary self-evidences, each seemingly the reverse of the other: that of generalized translocality, of which transnationality is only one aspect; and that of the multiplication of walls, more generally of a hardening and violence of borders. If the first self-evident fact (translocality) seems to make the border disappear, the second (violence) crushes it beneath walls. The phenomenon is a complex one, which is why it deserves profound reflection both on the *problem* of the world – in what way is the world a problem? – and on the various forms of violence of which the border is today the place and the Mediterranean shipwrecks of the last few years the most intolerable expressions.

When people talk of the 'closing of borders' they generally have in mind the hardened jurisdictions, police practices and xenophobic propaganda that have developed in the most powerful countries (the 'First World' headed by Europe and the United States) towards foreigners coming from the countries of the South, whatever their status (migrant, refugee, clandestine, etc.). In actual fact, what we have is a more general and widespread reaction to the greater possibility of exchange and circulation on the planetary scale, and to the sensation that borders are more readily crossable by human beings than they are by goods, capital and images. The border, its meaning and its uses, are thus the object of a conflict.

Two forms have particularly prospered in the last twenty years as reactions to global opening. The wall: in the *war of walls* against migrants, or against 'the other' in general, we find traces of what defines the border, and we also find what it is that negates it. And the expansion of the border: from a spatial, temporal and social point of view borders are more extensive and people spend more time there, in an uncertainty or ignorance of social rules greater than elsewhere, an uncertainty that tends to become the context if not the rule of a life 'in' the border. For all that, as we have just seen, the thickness of the border (in time and in space) is not an absolutely new fact. The co-presence of these different and sometimes contradictory aspects (long walls and enclosures alongside dense border situations, violence alongside encounters) necessitates a contextualization on the most common scale, that of the planet, and a deciphering of the different 'problems' of the border.

Economic globalization and the weakening of nation-states

With the end of the East–West conflict and the opening up of markets and territories, the 1980s and 1990s saw a spreading sentiment that we could and should share one single world, whose final impassable border was the natural boundary of planet Earth. It seemed possible to translate the discovery of the Earth's unique ecology into a political and sociological uniqueness, also made possible by the end of the Cold War. Conceptions that were more or less enthusiastic, utopian, happy or disturbed were formed on the basis of this problematic of the planet as a unity. It was perceived as a finished ensemble (its whole composition could be embraced, no people or place being excluded), a round surface (people could not escape one another) and a potentially common world (a world thought or even a world politics could be envisaged and became realistic, since it had found its 'reality').

What took place then was a profound rediscovery of the world. In fact, if we view the turning point on a larger scale, taking the years 1960 to 1990, from decolonization to the fall of the Berlin Wall, with the development of technological and economic means of transport and mass communication, and more generally of human mobility – we see how an updated reading of Enlightenment thought was possible. The Earth had acquired a human size, it had become the material form of universalism, its reality more conforming and contemporary. The Kantian principle of 'cosmopolitical right' as a 'natural visiting right' and a right of people to circulate on a planetary scale acquired the meaning of a reality that was accessible from almost any point on the planet. To circulate, to share the same world, became technologically realizable. It remained to render it applicable between men, 'in virtue of their right to the common possession of the surface of the Earth, to no part of which anyone had originally more right than another; and upon which, from its being a globe, they cannot scatter themselves to infinite distances, but must at last bear to live side by side with each other', in the famous formula of the Enlightenment philosopher Immanuel Kant.[4]

Frequently evoked in recent years as the foundation of a new theory of 'unconditional' hospitality (understood in the sense of universal and on principle, notwithstanding the concrete conditions for its application), this principle made it possible to elaborate a cosmopolitan alternative for living and thinking the planet as a 'common world'.[5] 'The strength of this conceptual approach', the philosopher Antonia Birnbaum writes in her commentary on Kant's work,

> is that it deactivates the nightmare of a total state, with the abolition of borders, and affirms the circulation of all as universal hospitality. All this with one and the same gesture, without adding any condition whatsoever, a condition of reciprocal economic exchange, identity-based integration, or national origin. At one stroke, with elegance and simplicity, the whole complex apparatus of international right is made synonymous with a concept brought in from a quite different sphere, that of hospitality. What is universal is hospitality and nothing else. All the rest is simply particularity, and thus stained with arbitrariness. States that are not at war cannot close their borders, the permeability of borders is the criterion of peace.[6]

41

This point of view, little present in national and international political milieus, is generally viewed by these as humanist but unrealistic, as opposed to a 'politics based on reality' (realpolitik) that should necessarily prevail. The anthropologist, for his part, always swinging between his study of what is universal for all human beings and his ethnographic basis that consists in sticking to propositions anchored in the field of investigation, has the professional assurance of only producing what certain sociologists have called 'grounded theory'; he is thus tempted to avoid being impressed by discourses of authority, and to cross swords with the champions of a politics of so-called 'reality'.

What after all is this 'reality'? Several sociological and economic analyses, developed since the 1990s, make clear to everyone that the world as a common context does indeed exist in a very large sector of economic, financial, communication and media activities – even, though to a lesser extent, political ones. States have already 'ceded' a large share of their sovereignty over economic, industrial or political functions, or have seen, without wishing or being able to do anything about it, sectors such as labour or finance escape national spheres of influence and control. According to the Dutch-American sociologist Saskia Sassen, economic globalization has taken the form of a partial 'denationalization' of the economy even within nation-states and under their impulse and control.[7] This brings into being a whole social world of an economy that conceives itself as 'global'. Sociologically, this is a supranational minority.[8] In theoretical terms, it means that only capital is absolutely 'global': it circulates and its leaders think on this scale, without depending on national sovereignties, and there only remain problems of borders, national identity and minorities.

States, businesses or national groups recuperate a part of this economy whose overall tendency is to 'denationalization'. But this partial recuperation is the particular object of political strategies reaffirmed in electoral periods and then just as quickly forgotten, or else too difficult to apply, which would tend to confirm a gap, already indicated by the work of Saskia Sassen and Wendy Brown: on the one hand, an emotional tendency to national assertion or even nationalist withdrawal in the political sphere; on the other hand, a powerful and effective tendency to denationalization as the dominant feature in the economic domain, in the realm of work, exchange and communication. This permanent hiatus is a source of conflict, in which national sovereignties bear on those links in the social structure viewed as 'weakest', whether culture or identity-based rhetoric. In the end, they bear on the human part, another 'weak' link of globalization, investing time, much money and a great deal of meaning in the control of migratory 'flows'.[9]

Landscapes, routes and networks: the shape of the world

Do these 'denationalized' activities and networks form new worlds and new borders? This is a complex question, and if we want to avoid apologetic or agonizing metaphors, they require qualified responses. In an innovatory essay seeking to shed light on global 'nomadic' flows, the anthropologist Arjun Appadurai systematically traces the 'landscape' of a supranational globalization.[10] He starts from metaphors and defines various 'scapes' analogous to landscape in the strict sense, as both the contexts of practices and horizons of subjectivities. In this description, people, machines, money, images and ideas are set in motion and perspective within global landscapes, in more or less harmonious relationships with one another. In what he calls the 'ethnoscape', it is individuals that are in movement: tourists, migrants, refugees, exiles, expatriate workers, and other mobile groups and individuals who transcend the power of nations and have a negative effect on this. By way of the 'technoscape', it is businesses and their technologies that are very rapidly exported and delocalized in a supranational world. 'Financescapes' represent flows of global capital and financial exchange, likewise endowed with a great rapidity of supranational circulation and decision. With these three 'landscapes' that form the material base of global interactions, Appadurai associates two 'landscapes of images': 'mediascapes' (the circulation of TV and cinema images, joined nowadays by 'virtual' ones via the Internet), and finally 'ideoscapes' (flows of ideas, propaganda discourse and concepts).

In order to understand the formation of this theory of five global landscapes (those of individuals, machines, money, images and ideas), we need to go back to the basis of Appadurai's argument: his anthropology of cultural globalization arises from awareness of a *crisis of locality*. He then examines in return, in a very reflexive way, the ritual forms of 'production of locality', drawing on anthropological literature with social and local foundations. But what drives him towards these 'global landscapes' is above all the bitter and disenchanted observation of the growing disjunction between, on the one hand, an increasingly global production of the contexts of existence and self-projection to others – what he describes with his 'scapes' but also more vaguely with clusters of contacts that he calls 'neighbourings' and which are the more or less virtual and flexible relational contexts – and, on the other hand, the strengthening of localist or even nationalist rhetorics. This tension leads him to de-anchor his thesis, to dematerialize it in a certain sense, perhaps for fear of falling into what he calls the 'territorial imaginary'[11] that obsesses both the nation-state and classical ethnology.

This is where we find the failure and ineffectiveness of long-term reasoning, despite the apparent legibility of the five global landscapes. In the end, the pattern and form that all these 'scapes' imitate have disappeared: what is missing in his inventory is a 'global landscape' in the precise and empirical sense of the term. This raises the question of the metaphorical fashioning of concepts when metaphor is pushed to excess, through to the disappearance of the reality of reference. And this introduces the real challenge to anthropology presented by the need to take new world scales into account, when its reflections still seek to be ethnographic, anchored in the here and now. It is this anchoring of the global that we need to grasp, by returning to the question of the drawing of borders.

In fact, the instability of borders, their shifting (between local, national and global contexts) or constant renegotiation is an immediate cause for rejoicing, since this is what constantly 'replays' the relation to others and makes possible the double recognition of self and others in changing contexts. In a word, it is what participates in the social dynamic in general. This dimension, whatever one's feelings about it and whatever the present dramas and dramatizations of violence at the borders, is indeed present in the same 'reality'. It concerns all those social relations that borrow, today with very great curiosity and sometimes a certain apprehension, what we can call the global path or 'route', thanks to the opening of means of transport, on land and air – for example, thanks to the rapid journeys of tourism and humanitarian missions and the 'unprecedented' discoveries that these permit and sometimes nourish, when there are sudden changes of context, personal experience of the perception of the diversity and, in general, the inequality of the world.

Global routes also develop thanks to the technical performance of communication through the Internet. This makes it possible to feel oneself 'in' the world thanks to a personal connection to multilocalized networks. It is then the technical networks (optical fibre or satellite relays) and the communications that travel on them which form new social networks, some of which become new social worlds. These trace fine borders thanks to access codes, communication conventions, norms of behaviour, possibly masks ('pseudos' and other 'avatars'); and they lead to the crossing of other borders, those of cities and nation-states. Yet they still do not form communities, at least so long as they are individual experiences before a solitary screen. Hence the improbable but very logical invention of 'flash mobs', in order to be seen together for the first time and discover that this meeting makes a momentary community, with thin borders but with multiple localizations and discontinuous temporalities.

In these still hesitant experiments there is the dynamic and transformative dimension of changing perimeters of social life, even if this appears only in an underground fashion and sometimes, in certain countries, a clandestine one. In a reflection on the changing conception of time today, Marc Augé observes that anthropologists, who have already confronted key moments of history such as decolonization, have sometimes been more moved by what they saw disappearing than concerned and genuinely challenged by what they saw being born.[12] The same holds for the 'construction' of the world as common context. To be able to grasp both what is dying and what is being born is the advantage of the advanced, implicated position of the explorer and experimenter in contemporary social worlds that is the ethnologist. Thus, the revolutionary place taken up in recent years by certain political actors who have emerged from Internet networks, for example in challenging oppressive national governments (in China and the Arab countries), was not so 'revolutionary' in terms of the demands made. It was so rather by the perimeter of their communication, the abolition of certain local or national borders, and the creation of new networks with extendible borders, effective on several scales at the same time – local for the organization of street mobilizations, global for their publicity in the media and the responses of solidarity conveyed in return. That is why, against the naïve belief in the advent of a 'global village' or in the power of supra-local and even more so global flows that they are 'off-ground' [hors-sol], we have to consider the anchorages, 'here and now', of social activities that all unfurl in a network, with unpredictable extensions and intensities, but which can always be observed locally, even if this is in a multilocality.[13]

To sum up, in order to understand the world it is necessary to take into account at the same time the reality of this global circulation – the 'flows' and relationships that 'traverse' the planet (which makes them in part transnational but not supranational) – and the existence of the reverse narrative, territorial and 'indigenous'. The latter holds the front of the international stage and of a large number of local situations, its main operators of reality being the building of walls and the stigmatization of others as a problem, even a danger, through to their expulsion or death. And this account, supposedly one of 'real-politik', is developed in a spectacular manner, which is far from being secondary or occasional. On the contrary, this spectacular dimension indicates the necessary visibility of this political strategy in the different registers of violence that we shall now examine.

Violence at the border: the outside of the nation

Even if human globalization lags way behind the voluminous and easy circulation of capital, goods, political ideas or images, it is still the case that globalization in general makes existing borders more uncertain, and future ones more fragile. In 2010, the number of international migrants was estimated as 214 million (or 3 per cent of the world population), a number that had tripled since 1970. A third of these migrations were directed from countries of the South to those of the North, and another third was between countries of the South. This is the second great wave of migration in the world in the modern era, following that of the late nineteenth and early twentieth century, which was essentially marked by major movements from Europe to the Americas. These figures are likely to grow considerably in the coming decades. Europe, North America and the Gulf states are today the three main regions of immigration, even if almost all regions of the world are involved. On top of this, a further 740 million are displaced within their own countries.[14] All studies underline the multidirectional and diversified aspect of present displacements. Reference to the planet in its global dimension is increasingly replacing a postcolonial conception of spaces of international migration (when migrants from the South headed for their former metropolises), and migrants no longer see the country of reception as the only country for their establishment. We can thus believe that the social form of the world is itself in a process of recomposition and that, from an anthropological point of view, the cosmopolitan dimension of life will spread still more in the years to come.

The 'border police', or what remains of nation-states

One reaction to this great human mobility – analysed by Wendy Brown, as we shall see, as a 'desire for walls' – itself needs deciphering. What are these impressive walls that provoke the indignation of humanists, that many migrants come up against, where some even die, while others learn to live with them, dig holes or tunnels to get round them, or queue up morning and evening at checkpoints (which are the only gates) in order to work on the other side?

We have seen the meaning that the thickness of borders in time, in space or in social relations can acquire, as well as the meaning of its disassociation and multiplication. But a special reflection is needed on the question of the violence, even wars, of which borders are now the place, and on the profusion of walls. For if the presence of borders is constitutive of the human and the social, understood as separation and relationship with nature, with the inhabited environment and with others, the wall is also, as I indicated in the previous chapter, the imitation and negation of the border. This is shown by the conflicts and polemics of the last years of the twentieth century and the first decade of the new century, a historic moment of which the profusion of walls is one of the most remarkable symbols.

The management of migrations, the control of migratory flows, global governance, contradictory globalizations, regulation of borders, migratory risk: these are some of the terms in an international lexicon that illustrates a new thematic, which emerged in international relations after the end of the Cold War and bears on the control of mobilities and the future of the borders of nation-states. This lexicon is mobilized, sometimes debated or criticized, in the previously cited study that Catherine Wihtol de Wenden has made of migrations in the world, making these a question of international relations. In her analysis of the jungle of international discourse on migration, she detects a major opposition between the individual and international institutions, the latter having great difficulty in 'capturing' the former. And de Wenden asks whether nation-states are not themselves confused by this phenomenon of individualization, that is, by the imperceptible and inaccessible character of individual itineraries from the perspective of the national forces of order. It is clearly possible to reverse this observation and note the inaccessibility of the state for persons in displacement, both from the point of view of their security and that of citizenship. Migrants do not desire to be 'clandestine', and no one comes into the world as an 'illegal'. Today it is nation-states, and they alone, that trace the boundaries of illegality. The relation between individual and the state is one of unequal forces. This is seen *a contrario* in the capacity that states have to legalize certain migrants 'in an irregular situation' while maintaining others in legal precariousness: the example of massive regularizations of such migrants in the last few years in the United States, Spain or Italy shows that it is indeed nation-states that have the power to define the situation, and transform from one day to the next the legal and political relation between individual and state for hundreds of thousands if not millions of migrants.

The social and political uncertainty bound up with the prevailing global scale, combined with the individual awareness for an increasing number of persons that they belong to the world as a whole, leads in response to a fearful thought and politics based on the biopolitical control of 'flows' of humans. In Europe, particularly since the late 1990s, the governments of those nation-states most 'denationalized' in the management of flows of goods, images or labour have seemed to place their whole foundation of legitimacy in the ideological and political opposition to human globalization. They have made themselves 'protectors' of their populations against the harmful effects of this globalization, targeting its weakest expressions: the bodies of the least protected migrants (economically and legally) and of refugees, or again their descendants, considered increasingly often as 'foreigners' even within national boundaries. With unequal weapons, the public authorities track and harass individuals in a 'clandestine' situation, or whose appearance and phenotype (what in France is called their *faciès*) evoke this underground foreign 'infiltration'. This wider sense of 'border policing', mobilized against individualized targets, acquires a major place, even if it contains all that remains of the meaning of the nation-state in terms of protection of citizen.

The fiction of 'national indigeneity' and its naturalization

A hiatus that has now been established between nation, state and world operates in a comparable fashion in Africa and in postcolonial states in general. In postcolonial contexts, in fact, the legitimacy of the nation-state form as the boundary of political existence is doubly challenged. It is so first of all by a long history, in other words the fact of colonialism itself and what remains of it, the domination still maintained by the former metropolises as well as the support abandoned by them. This is what makes citizenship particularly fragile in the context of the nation-state inherited from colonization, one expression of which is resentment or nostalgia, literally postcolonial sentiments towards the past of an authoritarian and violent state that is always recalled. But citizenship is also most recently made fragile by the inclusion of these postcolonial histories in the context of the accelerated globalization of the post-Cold War period: the legitimacy of the nation-state and the actual place it occupies in the life of citizens are now put to a severe test. In a posture that is not very far removed from that of the nation-states of the First World, 'the regimes of

[African] governments have recourse to theatrical means to institute state power, encourage national unity and persuade citizens of the reality of each of these', write the South African anthropologists Jean and John Comaroff, summarizing long years of study in their own country.[15]

If 'strong' states are to exist, given that their construction today is challenged or even delegitimized by neoliberal globalization, an institutionalization is needed that can frame the material, legal and economic life of its citizens. Despite being inscribed 'within' nation-states, they do not feel citizens 'of' these states. All the more so, given that, on top of the difficult emergence from the colonial context, recently independent nation-states lose a further part of their possible 'symbolic pre-eminence' in the face of the effects of globalization, which acquires unprecedented significance from the standpoint of 'policies of identity-based regulation' – 'not only of ethnic or cultural policy', as the Comaroffs make clear, 'but also policy in the realms of gender, sexuality, age, race, religiosity and style' (p. 80). We should note in passing that this phenomenon further extends the scope of the 'denationalized' spheres of life that we have already discussed; and it also promotes the reprise and spread of the identity paradigm.

What may seem to relegitimize the nation-state in this context is again, in Africa as elsewhere, the 'weak link' mentioned earlier: the world of political ideas and languages, of culture and identity. One of the major interests of the Comaroffs' reflections on the borders of the nation in Africa is to show the place this has acquired in post-apartheid South Africa (though these reflections may be extended to many other African states, as well as to certain tendencies in the countries of Europe or the Americas), a genuine 'naturalization' of national belonging in the language of indigeneity. This becomes a 'national indigeneity': the formula is a fiction, artificially superimposing a supposed fact of nature and another pertaining to geopolitical boundaries. As the Comaroffs point out, it 'seems to increase in direct proportion to the attrition of the tie between state and nation, to the porosity and impotence that populations equate with this regime of sovereignty, increasingly disjunctive' (p. 81). Along an identity-defined gradient with the extremes of the foreigner located at one end and the indigenous at the other, therefore, we discover the truth of identity in indigeneity, the final focus 'of allegiance, affection and attachment'. The tie between this sociological and political border of identity and its naturalist equivalent is never neutral; it serves to legitimize a violence, as is found elsewhere in the world.

The South African example of this process that the Comaroffs give deserves a detailed description and commentary. In the 1990s, a struggle that mobilized the country was fomented against a supposed 'invasion' of 'foreign' plants in the Cape Province. The authors describe how a policy of 'national indigeneity' and xenophobia was constructed on the basis of a 'natural' imaginary, by analogy with the battle against the invasion of foreign plants, supposed to denature native plants. These foreign plants (the jacaranda in particular) were suddenly seen in the mid-1990s as 'invasive', despite their presence being attested for a very long time without this having provoked any particular stigmatization by scientists. A whole analogous language of foreign invasion was developed, at just the same time as a movement arose against 'clandestine' (human) immigrants, treated as 'vultures' who 'spread uncontrollably' in the country. These movements would lead in the 2000s to xenophobic violence, to the (temporary) confinement of foreigners in detention camps, and to the building of a 'wall' (made up of a series of walls, electrified security barriers and checkpoints) along the border with Zimbabwe.

During this episode, the eradication of the 'vegetable foreigner' was the occasion for a presentation of the 'national community', going as far as the national integration of marginal people, since, as the Comaroffs note, 'women and unemployed youth, reformed criminals and even the homeless were supposed to facilitate their rehabilitation by working in eradication teams. The foreign nature, in other words, became the raw material for a collective renaissance' (p. 89).

Basically, these events display the 'paradox of the porosity of borders', that is, the contradiction between 'national protectionism and the division of labour on the world scale' (p. 94). This political uncertainty vis-à-vis the 'problem' of international migrations in South Africa, according to the authors of a recent book on the question, reveals a change in the axis of post-apartheid South Africa, from the racial matrix to a national one.[16] The 'problem' of undocumented migrants, coming from either Mozambique or Zimbabwe, is ideological as much as social or legal, based more on mythologies than on risks or, more precisely, based on risks that are indeed real but produced by xenophobic mythologies, such as that of invasive foreign plants.

Expulsions trace the boundary of national identity

In Europe with migrants from West or North Africa, in the Middle East with the contracting of workers from the Philippines, Ethiopia or Sri Lanka, in the United States with Latin American migrants, in China or Malaysia with Indonesian workers, immigrant labour-power is seen as indispensable to the functioning of local, sectorial or national economies. Construction, domestic work and seasonal agriculture are sectors that employ foreign workers of both sexes on a massive scale. The preference of employers is for migrants in an irregular situation and thus more fragile, exploitable at less cost and easily expellable. The disassociation of borders is manifest: in this case between those of the labour market (in part clandestine, so as to reduce costs and facilitate fluidity) and those of the nation.

As we have just seen with the South African example, the violent rejection of the foreigner is one of the effects of the discourse of identity-based truth, a 'truth' constructed on the idea of national indigeneity. The physical violence deployed in order to expel the foreigner marks the limit of social exchange. Expulsion (by return to another country or by confinement in a detention camp for foreigners as a temporary measure) plays an essential role in this symbolic construction of indigeneity, artificially creating its 'outside'. It brings to light the logic of its construction, supporting the naturalist discourse of indigenous identity. Hence the interest of a decentred reading of those social and political processes that place identity at the centre of their discourse. From a pragmatic and situational point of view, it is the operation of expulsion that attests to the 'indigenous national identity', this anthropological monster.

Expulsion, in fact, is a direct and palpable way of making the border exist by way of its 'outside'. This is shown by Clara Lecadet's study of the world of expellees after their arrival and regrouping in Mali.[17] Tackling nationality from the perspective of expulsion makes visible, first of all, the border stake of this violence. Expulsion occupies the place of national boundary, defining *a contrario* the 'inside' of the nation as the ensemble of those who are not expellable. This question occupies us today because it is fundamental for redesigning borders where these are disassociated from one another, shift or change scale, revealing a crisis of the nation-state as political boundary and englobing and unifying totality. Whether this is willed or not, parts of sovereignty escape it, either passing into the domain of international legislation (rights of refugees, migrant workers, children, labour, etc.), or under the control of economic forces, and sometimes migration networks of informal work.

In this context expulsion acquires two meanings. On the one hand, as Clara Lecadet shows, everything that determines expulsion defines the border: discourses, laws, administrative measures and the police interventions that put it into operation make a division between

51

inside and outside. On the other hand, expulsion pertains to an individualization of the border experience: case-by-case verification, relations with police or social workers charged with drawing up dossiers of regularization, or derogation obtained thanks to support, form a face-to-face ensemble that individualizes the border.

The migration policies expressed in expulsion create an outside of the nation: the vacuum of 'thought from outside',[18] born in the self-centred representation of the nation-state, is transformed into a social reality experienced by the persons who are the 'expellees' of this particular negative story of the nation. 'Expellees' then becomes the name of a possible political subjectivity. What happens just the other side of the border, in the 'ghettos' of Kidal, Tinzawaten or Gao in Mali, where expellees gather and reorganize to prepare other attempts to cross borders or organize public protest against them? Their lives, slow to develop, form part of a stretching of the border in time. The places where they settle ('ghettos', migrant homes) become border places where they cross paths with other wanderers, as we shall see in chapter 3. They lead us, therefore, to the problematic of the expansion of the border, its spaces and its time, which is one of the general characteristics of the present time, as opposed to belief in a globalization that abolishes borders.

Humanitarian spaces as partial delocalization of sovereignty

Humanitarian space establishes its space and finds its legitimacy in the interstices of national borders, the 'outside' of nation-states. The contemporary humanitarian movement, which arose from humanist representations and traces its domain of action in a terrain 'without borders', has followed a history parallel to that which links decolonization and globalization. Starting from a posture both 'marginal' and 'moral', contestatory and anti-political, it has been gradually integrated, morally redefined and politically instrumentalized in the post-Cold War world, as the means for a government of undesirables acting in the hollow of nation-states and the 'outside' of the democratic societies from which it itself arose. This intervention of the delegated humanitarian in an out-place – *between* all borders and *outside* nation-states – represents an extension of the conception of globalization as 'partial denationalization' already proposed by Saskia Sassen for the economic domain. A denationalization that is also a partial delocalization of political sovereignty, in the form of a transfer of sovereignty to humanitarian government, the indirect government of residual and supernumerary parts of the new world organization. Camps and, more widely, the spaces of humanitarian intervention today represent the spatial form corresponding to this removal. They have engendered their own violence, creating the hybrid context of a social life that is lastingly *encamped*, localized in border spaces marked physically by barriers, checkpoints, fences or walls that surround camps of all kinds (those for so-called 'internally displaced persons', for 'refugees', for 'regrouping', or so-called 'zones for persons awaiting decision', detention centres, 'transit zones', etc.). In these in-between spaces, the condition of the occupants is defined by extraterritoriality and exception, which are the legal instruments of their removal.[19]

Up to now we have presented the violence, expulsions and spaces of removal as aspects of the transformation of the border, but also of a certain stabilization of its occupants in an in-between. We shall now dwell a bit more on the question of walls and the paradoxical function that they hold in the definition of borders.

Walls of war

It is generally accepted that walls have proliferated in the world after the fall of the Berlin Wall and the end of the Cold War. According to the geographer Michel Foucher, if all present construction projects throughout the world are completed, more than 20,000 kilometres of walls, fences, and metal or electronic barriers will seal national borders, or more than 8 per cent of the total length of borders between states.[20] Wendy Brown published a key work on this phenomenon in 2009,[21] and I shall draw on some of her conclusions for the argument developed here, as well as new questions.

Colonial war, war on migrants

The building of walls is bound up with a lasting violence, even a state of war. The wall is the sign and instrument of a war. In the case of the Israeli wall, this is a territorial or colonial war. This wall is presented by Israeli authorities as a 'security barrier' in a context of war against an enemy that is made anonymous and socially non-existent by the opacity of the wall. But it may also be viewed quite differently, as the instrument of a war of conquest: it is the 'moving colonial border' that has advanced further into Palestinian territory than had been decided by the Oslo Accords of 1993 on the line of separation.[22] According to the architect Eyal Weizman, the wall is the 'plastic' instrument

53

of a war of conquest, advancing and conquering new enclosure in a military strategy of attrition – it can even happen that Palestinian villagers win the day and manage to divert a portion of the wall under construction that encroaches on their agricultural land. This strategy is indifferent to political validation, no one is duped that the 'protection' argument is only a small part of the real scope of this device.[23]

Even if there is an accommodation with the Palestinians at the checkpoints, this in no way negates the warlike function of the wall, or the everyday violence that it fundamentally introduces for each local inhabitant, forcing them to detours of several kilometres to go from one point to another a few dozen metres away, or prohibiting access to certain parts of the city formerly visited on a daily basis. In certain cities such as Bethlehem or Jerusalem, the 'monstrous' sight of a concrete wall more than three metres high around these everyday urban trajectories is the instrument of a 'psychological' war of immediate humiliation.

In this same colonization, however, there are settlements of new population alongside the wall: the subject is contested in Israel, the settlements are now little loved and settlers are lacking. Immigrants who have declared their Jewish identity have found here an opportunity to receive land, housing and a guaranteed income. Their settlements are advances into Palestinian territory protected by the Israeli army. But a good number of Palestinians have worked on the construction of settlements, and others work as domestics for the settlers (some of whom have requested a diversion of the wall under construction to allow their Palestinian domestics to continue coming to work for them . . .). Besides, a so-called 'non-ideological' colonization is conducted by private builders for settlers who do not support the Zionist cause.[24] This is an embarrassment for the government of the 'Jewish state', which, despite supporting them, finds them lacking the identity reference of the nation, presented as mono-ethnic when it has long since ceased to be so. It makes settlements places marked by the general ambivalence of the colonial border in its extension phase. In the shadow of the wall as means of colonial war, the social thickness of the border is secretly re-created.

The war is also the symbol of a 'war on migrants', as in the case of the 450 kilometres of walls and electronic barriers separating the United States from Mexico, or the high fences of the Spanish enclaves of Ceuta and Melilla in Morocco.[25] Close to these fences, which can be deadly, encampments and 'ghettos' have formed, of people waiting to cross. More generally, transit countries, such as Morocco, Turkey, Greece or Mexico, have become countries of settlement for migrants as an effect of their blockage by walls, the repeated attempts to cross, then the organization of survival. Migrants settle close to the fences themselves, or in cities that become increasingly cosmopolitan, such as Rabat in Morocco or Tijuana in Mexico.

Other walls again, less well known, have been built by certain states in the context of territorial conflicts (between India and Pakistan in Kashmir, between Saudi Arabia and Yemen, etc.), but the detention of migrants or refugees from the other side of the 'barrier' is never absent from these strategies.

Beyond material or concrete walls, the most spectacular of which have a prominence in the media greater than their actual operational effect on the human circulation they are supposed to stop, there is a spread of other walls that are technically more effective. Virtual walls, of electronic software, or literally 'liquid' walls such as the Mediterranean Sea is for migrants seeking to reach Europe, as we have seen. The sophistication of the wall reached an extreme point with the individualization of security, when each undesirable, transformed into a new, radical 'foreigner', is immediately detected and blocked automatically by the barriers best adapted to this purpose. Extended mechanisms of biometric surveillance, which establish the wall and the checkpoint (in other words, the filtering operation) everywhere that it is necessary (airports, stations, urban routes, etc.), while remaining invisible for their regular users, make concrete walls redundant[26] – except for the intention to make them play the role of visible and essentially symbolic protector, as is likewise the case with the 'gated communities' found also in Latin America and South Africa, the United States and the Middle East.[27]

Questions about the 'desire for walls'

What then do walls do? What is their effect? What do they mean? Let us take the best-known examples, those of the border between Mexico and the United States, the European wall of the Spanish enclaves of Ceuta and Melilla in Morocco, and the Israeli wall on the West Bank. We can note, in an approximate order, the information and ideas associated with them.

They provoke indignation. They reassure. They prevent seeing what happens on the other side. They are the mark and means of a 'war'. They are visible, photographed, and in a cynical way photogenic. They lead to deaths (police or militia firing on those trying to cross). They are permeable and spur people to study informal ('clandestine') ways of crossing them (ladders, tunnels, holes, traffickers).

They make life unliveable for those women and men on whom they force a constant presence (the wall in the middle of the street). They produce new political subjectivities: this is an almost immediate ideological effect, the wall brings into existence the 'clandestine', denoting them as such and thus as enemy – 'Arab', 'African' and 'Islamic' migrants in Europe, 'Latinos' in the United States, Palestinians from the other side of the wall between Israel and the West Bank. Anachronistic in a world of flows and networks, impotent vis-à-vis the de facto supranational interdependencies and interconnections, concrete, material walls are an *excess spectacle*.

This spectacle, according to Wendy Brown, is the response to a demand for walls, which this author was the first to indicate and seek to explore by going in search – behind the apparent anachronism of the wall – of the sentiments, emotions and fantasies that make up what she calls the 'desire for walls'. These popular passions, according to her, are embodied in four fantasies: that of the alien, dangerous and unrecognizable foreigner who takes the form of a 'many-headed dragon';[28] that of the 'protective contention' whose guarantor against the excess of globalization is the state; that of impermeability vis-à-vis the 'pillage' and 'porosity' of border, hence a demand for 'insulation'; and finally, that of purity in both the moral and the identity sense.

Based on these four fantasies – of the alien, of protection, of insulation and of purity – a 'desire' for walls exists within individuals. Arguing this point of view, Wendy Brown describes a certain 'spirit' that is not hard to read in media and political discourses. The reason that their messages are effective is that they transform each person's 'existential tremors' – for example, feeling alone and defenceless in the face of danger, death or disease – into 'social fears'.[29] The latter end up giving the illusory impression of being self-perpetuating and self-reinforcing (it is enough to activate this 'program' regularly); artificially decontextualized in this way from the sphere of individual psychology, transferred and recontextualized into the collective political sphere, they can be represented as passions (desires and repulsions), and finally as 'demands' for immunity and security.

This leads Wendy Brown to make what I believe are two errors in her analysis. First, she takes up the idea that politicians offer a response to popular 'passions', as if the latter had their own existence, not only psychological but also cultural. Negative passions that lead to the statement, in other contexts and generally by political figures, that expulsion is better than pogrom, that a wall is better than a confrontation between communities, etc. Politicians supposedly 'offer' their voters walls, as it were, to reassure them and give them the impression of finding their 'ontologized political and economic identities'.[30] This is what is suggested by the phrase that the author put as an epigram to the chapter of her work on the desire for walls, a quotation from the US Republican senator John McCain, who said about the wall between the United States and Mexico in February 2007: 'I think the fence is least effective. But I'll build the goddamned fence if they want it.'[31] Secondly, this interpretation establishes a direct connection between the state and the individual, a duo or duel from which mediations – social and cultural, political or urban – have strangely disappeared. If a psychoanalytic reading took the 'desire' for walls literally, it would see in it the masculinized power of the state, called on to protect the feminized nation.

This assertion is an unverifiable conjecture, to say the least. On the other hand, we can observe from the point of view of analytical method that what is lacking in this study is everything that might make a connection: relationship, community or society. In other words, it is the anthropological dimension of the relation of individuals to the state that must find its due place in the political and philosophical study of what the profusion of walls means today.

Starting from this observation, the existence of a 'wall politics' at the place of the border, it will be more effective, I believe, to work on the hypothesis that the wall is to the border what identity is to alterity. We shall keep here the two features of this relationship, exploring them more deeply later on, in other words that the wall is both the imitation and negation of the border, symbolizing the rupture in the relation between identity and alterity. An expanded and deepened reflection is thus necessary on the meaning of the identity-based thought that prevails today among commentators and political strategists about the world, border, the circulation of migrants, and that leads, as if this were self-evident, to the wall as 'response' to 'protect' identities. They thus attribute to identity the virtues of a basic truth, closed to any representation of the other, who finds himself or herself placed from the start on the other side of the wall.

— 3 —

BORDER DWELLERS AND BORDERLANDS: STUDIES OF BANAL COSMOPOLITISM

Globalization, we conclude, has not suppressed borders: it transforms and shifts them, disassociating some borders from others – certain economic activities, for example, no longer have the same boundary as political activities or communications. It multiplies and expands them, while rendering them more fragile and uncertain. Then it makes them disappear beneath walls. The profusion of walls and, beyond this, the spread of the model of wall and of confinement modify the problematic of the border in the contemporary world. For the wall and with it the regulations and ideologies that aim to block the crossing of borders, borders of all kinds, have a paradoxical effect: they cut off the relational aspect of the border by making the other invisible, but at the same time they contribute to prolonging the time and space of the border, and thus make for a longer life in the in-between, on the threshold, in liminality.

The de-identification of the woman or man who arrives at the border (by loss or removal from those places, ties and goods that made up their identity) then seems incapable of transformation into another existence – a life that would be anything but precarious. All persons who find themselves there are caught in the border trap, unable to cross it completely and find a place, a status, a recognition, a full 'citizenship' in the place of destination. We find again the question of relationship posed earlier, apropos of what founds the meaning of the border and the alterity of the foreigner. Is the expanded 'borderland' a place of anomie or a place of relationship? The place of an absence of identity, sociality, culture and politics, or that of a presence? We shall tackle these questions on the basis of what we learn from studies on the ground.

These have led me to three major figures of 'border dwellers'. They

58

are the *wanderer*, the *'métèque'*[1] and the *pariah*, each of which I shall describe by relating their social condition and their story to the places where they are found. Beyond each particular case, these borderlands fuel the hypothesis of a wide 'borderscape'.[2] For the wanderers, African or Afghan, who seek somewhere around the Mediterranean an entry to Europe, the borders are the desert, the sea and the ports, where they are sometimes found in makeshift encampments. For the Sudanese, Eritrean or Sri Lankan *métèques*, working without documents in Beirut, the whole city is a border and they logically find their place in clandestine occupations; squatted buildings can then become their regular place of existence. Finally, the figure of the pariah is associated with that of the camp considered as border. These different places – encampment, squat, camp – are settlements conceived as temporary and precarious, but they also represent a certain stabilization in border situations. These are situations in which each person discovers their relative foreignness in the gaze of others, these 'others' being for them those who live in the cities to which they themselves have only limited access, but also those who live with them in the same borderlands. These are new contemporary worlds, initially incomprehensible but where each person must slowly engage in a kind of cultural work in order to understand the place in which they live and the 'others' whom they meet there. From this experience each takes a certain distance from their own supposedly 'original' identity and gains a certain comprehension of the 'global'. I shall conclude this exploration of borderlands and their inhabitants by investigating the existence of an everyday or ordinary cosmopolitism, which leads us well beyond the identity paradigm and multicultural policies.

The border dwellers: figures and places of relative foreignness

Three portraits of border dwellers, relating to different places, will help us analyse the figures of the foreigner. These are all cases of *relative foreignness*, and I shall make clear right away what I mean by this expression. So long as a relationship is not established, it is indeterminate and imagined, abstract and absolute; then it becomes relative, in a particular situation, and the alterity that was 'absolute' or 'radical' (in the sense that my way of being and thinking is described by others as 'radically' other) tends to reduce, if not disappear, since the discovery of singularities now becomes possible. There are different degrees of foreignness depending on the border situation and the moment in the situation.[3] It is this border universe that we are going to traverse.

We shall then see that many other dimensions of foreignness are superimposed on the national one.

Wandering as adventure and the border encampment

Let us start with Mamadou, a so-called *sans-papier* in Paris, who left Guinea for Dakar in 1997, at the age of seventeen, to train as a bookkeeper. This led to the very rational desire to continue his studies in the United States or France, but he did not manage to leave. He then returned to Conakry, and later reached France by plane with a false passport. Arrested and placed in the waiting zone at Roissy, then released by the police at midnight in the unknown city of Paris, he slept in a bus shelter, then in a squat, later in a Red Cross centre and then in the Maison de Nanterre (a refuge for homeless persons). Subsequently he went to Germany and Holland, to hunt out friends and look for ways of 'regularization', or just 'to see', then to Brussels where he started working in the black economy, which he continues to do sometimes in Paris ('It's day to day. I wash dishes, I clean, I do deliveries, it works by contacts'). He had been back in Paris for six months when he told his story to a documentary film-making team in 2003. He told them: 'We are in the border.'[4]

He was then twenty-two and staying in the Emmaus building on the rue des Pyrénées in the 20th arrondissement, an 'emergency shelter' closed from 8 a.m. to 6.30 p.m., just a place to spend the evening and sleep; the shelter allows a two-week stay which is renewable only once. The film-makers wanted to learn from the occupants the singular experiences that started with their departure from home. Their stories sketch a 'subjective geography that does not coincide with state borders', a 'long wandering of body, emotions, identity'. But also 'something very concrete: the need to hide in a boat or a lorry, to be constantly changing place'. The shelter is an extension of each person's trajectory: 'the same indefinite waiting, the same confinement, the same wandering continue in this shelter, which in the end resembles many other places where they have stopped'. But it is also a miniature 'observatory on the world'.

The vagabond or wanderer is an old figure, who in other times, or in some places still today, is relatively 'thinkable'. Fairly close to the peddler or nomad, this is a foreigner who never gives up the 'freedom to come and go'. Arriving today, he can leave tomorrow, even if he chooses not to. He is more someone without a fixed dwelling, possibly temporarily 'homeless', rather than 'undocumented' – which he is too, but this has less importance than his mobility, the personal discovery of a state of 'clandestinity' being by chance and almost secondary.

This theoretical figure of wandering has today become something wider and more complex. The 'figure' does not denote a particular person, or a typological category, but rather a moment lived by many displaced persons, including those we call migrants when they cross or try to cross a national border.[5] A survey of the borders around Europe gives the impression of a contemporary world of wandering. Starting from the eastern marches, at Patras in Greece, among Afghan migrants met at crossing points on the border, as presented in the introduction to this book, wandering is the most visible of these ways of being foreign. These people represent a new figure of the vagabond, with no 'indigeneity' to claim, since if they have Afghan parents, they have mostly been born in Pakistani camps or in Iran. Nor do they have a definite place of arrival, being in this way already more 'globally anchored' than many adventurous lives that are proclaimed and presented as 'global' on the advertising spots for globalization. At the other, western, end of the Mediterranean, in the Andalusian province of Almeria, the moment that follows the border crossing (from Morocco by way of Gibraltar, or via the Spanish enclaves of Ceuta and Melilla) places the migrant in a situation of relative 'vulnerability' and uncertainty, a time of latency and search for solutions.[6] Between the actual journey and the prolonged waiting at the border, a whole world of 'clandestinized' migration is formed.

On the other shore of the Mediterranean, in the Moroccan city of Rabat or the woods around Ceuta and Melilla, *foyers* (collective urban lodgings) or encampments (in the forest) become places of social regulation and a certain 'stability in instability'.[7] Their social organization, their relationship to identities of origin, national or other, become in this context important subjects, practical questions that the migrants have to resolve, since each encampment or 'ghetto' through which they pass becomes, like the Emmaus shelter in Paris, a little cosmopolitan world.

A bit further east, in the Sahara, a 'delocalized territory' has been formed by the trajectories of migrants who cross it, from Niger to Libya or Algeria.[8] Thus, at the Dirkou oasis – which now serves as a 'regional transit centre' – as in the community formed in the lorry that crosses the actual desert, a mode of existence (and waiting) is stabilized. According to Julien Brachet, a 'real migratory field' from the Sahel to Africa's Mediterranean shores is formed along these networks and routes, giving rise to a 'cosmopolitan desert'. These migrants show little a priori inclination to know the transit region and its population; they are rather found in ghettos (a term used by the migrants themselves) where they rub shoulders with migrants expelled from Algeria and prepare new attempted migrations, as we have seen.

Whether in Africa, America or Asia, these people are never sure of reaching the end of the path that they embarked on, and that they reconfigure in their imagination as an 'adventure'. Of course, this imaginary of an 'adventurer' cannot be separated from the conditions in which, against the background of deeply unequal North–South relations, the clandestine migrants seek to control their wandering: desires or strategies that are interrupted, diverted, constantly reformulated. In this attempted control that characterizes the adventurer, there is all the energy of those women and men who cannot say exactly where the path they are on will lead, but who adapt to this wandering by making it the context of their social organization and their subjectivity. What we have here is a 'movement thinking', which helps people imagine the possibility of going forward in a completely hostile context. 'At the moment, I'm not living', says Mamadou in the Emmaus refuge in Paris. 'I'm blocked at this point, and time is getting on for me. The battle I've started is sleeping but not dead . . . At this point I'm in a weak position, I'm retreating. As soon as I have the strength, I'll be able to continue.'[9] Everything indicates that adventure is one of the languages of uncertainty, one of those that give the 'subject' the capacity to think and act towards a horizon of life in an always dangerous context.

After conducting a study of Senegalese migrants in transit in Morocco, the sociologist Anaïk Pian investigated the possible 'outcomes' of their adventure – one marked both by the uncertainty of trajectories and by the daring, experience and improvisation of the migrants. She sees four possible endings:[10] successful crossing to Europe (but that is just the start of other 'adventures', as we have shown); the failure of those 'lost along the way', with its effects of material and psychological destitution; the hard decision to return to Senegal; and joining the Senegalese trading networks in the transit country, which is also a way of not completely abandoning the perspective of 'adventure'. In the last three cases, the movement itself becomes the end of the road.[11] The transit country and the life that they lead there become an in-between space, the actual place of the 'adventurers'. And if they find it hard to leave it, that is also because the perspective of the journey remains present so long as they remain in this place, on the border.

A particular border space, that of the encampment, corresponds to this modality of migration. Between 1997 and 2009, the Patras encampment in Greece was home to between 500 and 2,000 occupants at various times. The Calais encampment existed from 2002 to 2009 and sometimes sheltered up to 600 people. Other encampments have developed in the major 'bottlenecks' close to borders, such as those in the woods around the Spanish enclaves of Ceuta and Melilla in northern Morocco, or along the border separating Mexico from the United States.[12]

When a new migrant arrives at Patras, he goes first of all to the squatted building alongside the huts of the Afghan encampment (a few years earlier there were Kurds here). Then he looks to see whether there is room for him in the shelters. Or else, if there are several new arrivals, they build a house. When Yassir, an Afghan Hazara, arrived, he found someone who came from the same town as himself – the same town in Pakistan, not Afghanistan. This person invited him to share his room. Now he is host to another man who arrived a few months after him, a fellow Hazara and again from the same town in Pakistan. Despite not knowing one another, they have people in common, 'so I said to him, "Come here!"'

Mahmoud is presented as the 'leader' of the encampment. He is a social worker by training, but here in the migrant community he moves between Patras and Athens. He keeps one of the encampment's small shops. 'Patras is an outlaw town', he says.

It is a paradox of these non-places that after twelve years of existence the Patras encampment has become a bearing, a fixed point on routes that are many in number but all similar. Patras is known by all who attempt these routes; as well known as Zahedan (on the border between Iran, Pakistan and Afghanistan) or Calais. These places have become to an extent cosmopolitan crossroads: they are staging posts on a worldwide journey, one that is always risky and unpredictable, and for them now runs from Afghanistan (or Pakistan, or Iran) to Europe; but the boundaries of exile can change – as they have changed for African exiles who still head for Europe, but also, more recently, for the Middle East, America and the Far East.

Becoming a pariah and living in a camp

Let us take another African migrant, Bobo N'K, from Liberia. He was twenty-nine when I met him in 2003, in the Boreah refugee camp in Guinea. He has two children with him, aged seven and nine. His wife fell ill after the birth of their second child in the refugee camp of Jui in Sierra Leone, in 1996, and subsequently died. He also has

63

with him three younger brothers (they go to school in the Boreah camp) and a sister who herself has two of her children with her. This is a family of nine people whom Bobo manages to keep, thanks to a so-called 'incentive' (rather than a wage, as the refugees are not officially authorized to work in the country of reception) from the Belgian section of Médécins Sans Frontières, for working to register sick people who come to the camp's clinic, and thanks to the ration provided by the World Food Programme.

One day in September 1990, he explains, 'at four in the morning, the forces of Charles Taylor's NPFL [National Patriotic Front of Liberia] arrived in the town; they dug in there, people heard gunfire and fled'. Between surprise attacks by the Liberian army or the rebel forces, then from the Sierra Leonean army, violence and arrests in Guinea, crossing the forests, and several times the borders of all three countries (Liberia, Sierra Leone, Guinea), he passed through a whole network of camps, becoming so used to them that they are now part of his ordinary life. After twelve years of this rather peculiar wandering, both controlled and forced, Boreah in Guinea is the ninth camp in which he finds himself.[13]

Bobo is very nervous and has difficulty continuing a long conversation, a difficulty that is expressed by nervous tics, disturbed looks, hands that hide his face or rub it vigorously, as if he was washing himself after every sentence. He fears for his safety. Like several hundred other people living in this camp, he has made a request to the Office of the UN High Commissioner for Refugees for 'resettlement in a third country'.[14] But the UNHCR agent told him that he had to produce a 'recommendation' from a humanitarian NGO. This strategy aims to discharge the UN agency from the responsibility for screening the thousands of refugees in the region, who, given what they have experienced, very likely all have a right to international 'protection' as defined by the Geneva Convention of 1951 on the right of asylum and the right of refugees. They would then be able to leave the camps for another life that many still idealize, free and in peace in the 'First World'. Introducing an additional, supposedly 'humanitarian' criterion is not inscribed in the conditions for obtaining the right of asylum as per the Convention, but asking the NGOs to undertake this initial 'screening', and passing on to the UNHCR only those applications considered justified from a humanitarian point of view, amounts to 'vicitimizing' the refugee 'identity' still more, and acknowledging only those women or men recognized as more 'vulnerable' than others, closer therefore to the victim identity of refugee. Even if the refugee may at a given moment receive life-saving assistance in the camp, this 'solution' of a permanent distancing leads him to discover that the life he lives is undesirable and extraterritorial.

Not all the refugees live in camps, far from it, but the camp is today the ideal-typical figure of distancing.

A total of some 75 million people across the world find themselves in a situation of so-called 'forced displacement' – refugees, internally displaced, displaced because of natural catastrophes. A large section of them, between 15 million and 20 million in 2014, spend a longish time in places separated off – camps, encampments, detention centres, waiting zones or zones of temporary reception.

The 'radical' character of their foreignness in other people's eyes is not a function of their nationality or ethnic identity, but rather of their lack of citizenship and the place that they occupy. For their lack of rights and distancing from the human community casts them on principle into the 'human superfluity' already described for the stateless by Hannah Arendt. In this context, whether temporary or not, it is the distancing that characterizes the condition of the foreigner as pariah; the rest of his 'identity' for others follows from it. Extraterritoriality is the first illusion of this type of foreigner: what founds his 'radical' foreignness is a biopolitical alterity, produced by the 'technical' government of a separate population category. This radical alterity imposed by the building of walls and barriers ever harder to cross is primary in relational terms, rather than a cultural difference that is not always existent or put to the test. The 'pariah' is voiceless and faceless from the standpoint of alterity. How can I get on (or not) with an Afghan migrant if he is placed in a detention centre? How can I know whether Bobo N'K is Malinke or Mende, and in what way this is important or not for him, if he remains inaccessible to me, 'enclosed outside' for years on end?

This more or less extended experience that the 'encamped' have brings about a rapid cultural change for them in their contact with refugees from other regions or countries, whom they would never have met if not for this violence, a contact also with a humanitarian system both global and localized. Some learn other languages (including a basic international English), and of course other modes of life, whether in terms of clothing or eating. Above all, they learn to 'get by', and survival strategies in the humanitarian system: the various registrations with the administration to get a larger site on which to settle, duplicate residency (in camp and in town), work in the black economy, the purchase (or resale) of supplementary food ration cards, etc. If the refugee camp is indeed the hardened form of a spatial and temporal 'border' between citizenships and localities that have been lost and are not yet refound, it is also the test of a little cosmopolitan world. And its occupants end up accustoming themselves to this, by necessity, as they are not sure of finding elsewhere a feeling of locality and a relation of citizenship.

Four métèques, *and the squat as border*

Let us now take a couple of emigrants in Beirut, Hashani and Peter, with their two small children. She is Sri Lankan, he Sudanese. They met in Beirut in 2005 where they attended the same Catholic church, a 'church for foreigners', they told me in 2012, where at certain times of day, in the mornings at the mass for foreigners and in the afternoons for recreational activities, Sudanese, Sri Lankans and Filipinos meet up, sometimes joined by Lebanese husbands of foreign women.

Hashani arrived in Beirut in 2001 with a 'contract' that an 'agency' had given her before her departure from Sri Lanka, covering travel and work. She began work as soon as she arrived, as a domestic for the household whom the agency had set her up with. But like many foreign women in her situation, she went a whole year without being paid (to 'refund the air ticket', she was told). Also like many others, she slept on the balcony of her employers' apartment, with a rent for this being deducted from her pay. As official guarantors of her stay in Lebanon, her employers had taken her passport when she arrived, to make sure that she wouldn't run away, she says; she had no other documents, not even a resident's card. After two years of this 'slave's life', as she called it, she left, but was unable to recover her passport, the 'madame' asking $1,700 to return it to her. She now works by the hour on request, with various part-time employers. She seems at ease, 'controlling' her existence and actually receiving the wage (US $4 per hour) that she works for, yet even having found this 'freedom' she is still in a completely illegal situation.

Peter also arrived in Beirut in 2001. Forty years old, he left South Sudan, his native country, when he was seven. He went to his uncle, who lived in a displaced persons' camp on the outskirts of Khartoum that was run by the Sudanese council of churches. Then at twenty-three he became a 'volunteer teacher', practising this activity from 1995 to 2000, still in Khartoum. He requested and obtained admission to a college in Romania, as well as a visa, but did not have the money for the journey. He got to Syria, where he hoped to earn enough money to be able to continue to Romania. He worked hard as a cleaner in a restaurant, but earned too little. There were many Sudanese in Syria at this time, and some were returned to Sudan. 'No way out, I gave up', he says, but in fact he did not give up completely. Ready to go anywhere, the easiest country was neighbouring Lebanon. He entered illegally, as all Sudanese coming from Syria do. Many Sudanese workers, from both South and North, then settle in Beirut for short periods (six months or a year), often living in extremely precarious conditions (ten or twelve single men in a two-room apartment) and working as caretakers, rubbish collectors or watchmen. Some end up remaining there, without really having planned this.

Without documents, and thus at the mercy of his employers, Peter has worked since his arrival in Beirut first in a petrol station, then as a hotel cleaner and, for the last five years, as a cleaner in a nightclub (he is paid $350 per month). Like him, several hundred other Sudanese from Beirut (mostly from the South) have relatively stabilized themselves, with one eye on their home country, sometimes even visited by a relative. But the prospect of return becomes more remote. Just like Peter's plan to go to Romania. And for Hashani, the prospect of returning to Sri Lanka also dwindles, even if return home is stipulated or at least presupposed in the contracts that bring to Beirut workers from Sri Lanka, the Philippines, Madagascar, Bangladesh or Ethiopia. To acquire residence papers is very costly, they explain, taking into account both official and 'unofficial' expenses of regularization which amount for each person to $3,500 plus an initial $1,000 guarantee, and a further $1,000 each year for renewal. These are not sums that are spoken of in government administrations or NGOs. But this is what they know, and what dissuades them from trying to 'become legal'.

Peter and Hashani are among those persons referred to in Beirut as *bidoon* ('without'), a term of foreignness that denotes lack of papers but also of rights in general, despite their ties of work which make possible a stable existence. Peter is often insulted in the street because of the colour of his skin: 'Black people are called *Shaytan* ("Satan"),' he explains, 'and some people make the sign of the cross when they see us.' He helps to run a Christian association of South Sudanese in Beirut, which plays an important part in assistance to new arrivals, as well as establishing relations with at least a section of the Beirut population (such as nuns and monks, or Lebanese husbands of foreign workers), and so a minimum place for peaceable sociability.

This position of exclusion/inclusion explains the qualified image that Peter and Hashani's family left me with: inclusion through work, exclusion by almost everything else, strong individualization of everyday life, occasional 'communitarian' gatherings on Sunday morning. This ambiguity corresponds to another old figure of relative foreignness, that of the *metoikos* in ancient Greece: the term for 'residents without city rights'. They lived *in* the city, for which their subaltern labour-power was indispensable – Greek democracy needed the excluded in order to exist. But they were outside all its rights – social, political and property. In contrast with pariahs, their presence was not forbidden, and they enjoyed relative liberty, in contrast with slaves. But they were also, like Peter and Hashani (and their two children) in Beirut, settled for the duration in an in-between that they 'occupied' and 'inhabited' with relative success.

The squat is the characteristic form of urban residence of this illegal presence in the city, of the condition of 'residents without civic rights'. The so-called 'Gaza Hospital' squat in the Sabra district of Beirut allows us to approach this reality via two undocumented migrant workers who have just arrived there. Gaza Hospital is the name of an eleven-storey building in which close to 500 people live in a precarious situation. Built in the 1970s by the Palestine Liberation Organization, when this had its headquarters in that district of Beirut, the hospital was gradually abandoned after the eviction of the PLO in 1982 and its move to Tunis. Partially destroyed that same year by the Israeli army when it invaded Beirut (leading to the massacres at Sabra and Chatila), then burned at the time of the 'war of the camps' and the 'internal war' between 1986 and 1987, it was finally abandoned for medical purposes at the end of that last event.[15] According to stories collected in 2012, the Gaza Hospital squat was founded in 1987 by three Palestinian women who had fled the violence of the neighbouring Chatila camp and were wandering the streets of Sabra with their children in search of shelter. They entered the building, which had been completely deserted after a fire that damaged several floors. The Syrian army which then occupied the Sabra zone allowed them to enter and settle in the partly ruined building. 'Then in three days, people arrived and it was full', one of the place's three founders explains. Other Palestinian refugees from Chatila joined them, then others again from other Beirut camps or other parts of the city.

Controlled today by two Palestinian families who have invested a great deal in transforming the building, Gaza Hospital is the home of Palestinian and Lebanese-Palestinian families, of Syrian families who have long been settled there, as well as Syrian migrant workers and many Syrian refugees, but also of Egyptian and Sudanese migrants, and finally of Bangladeshi migrants who have arrived in the squat more recently. These last rent rooms in the basement, which were built by a son of one of the two leading families there. At the end of 2012 there were a total of 127 dwellings of various size (most often one or two rooms, with a very few apartments of three or four rooms), and some 500 inhabitants.

Eight storeys when it was opened, the squat now counts ten, and an eleventh is under construction. No one has a property title, but a distinction is made without too much conflict between who is an owner, who is housed for free, and who is a tenant. For a few, at least, the squat has become an object of investment (construction) and profit (renting), even if the overall impression is that of a 'vertical favela', extremely precarious in terms of hygiene, water and electricity supply, refuse collection and waste water. An NGO, the Norwegian Refugee Council (NRC), supported by the Humanitarian Aid and Civil Protection department of the European Commission, intervened in 2008 to improve health conditions in the building.

The people who have remained in the Gaza Hospital squat are the least legitimate and most fragile inhabitants from Chatila, since they did not have to justify their right to resettlement in the camp when it was reconstructed under the aegis of UNRWA, the UN relief and works agency for Palestine refugees in the Near East, after the end of the 'war of the camps'. Illegitimate, either because they lived in unofficial zones of Chatila outside the camp boundary, or because they were housed or sublet without an occupancy title in the camp itself. In many respects, therefore, Gaza Hospital is an extension of the Chatila camp. It is under this rubric that the NRC intervened, from its office situated in the Chatila camp. Family and friendship ties with Chatila inhabitants remain strong. The few hundred metres between one place and the other are regularly crossed on a daily basis. But the squat does not enjoy the exceptional legal and political status of the camp, being in a space that is entirely Lebanese and Beiruti. On top of their illegitimate status vis-a-vis Chatila, the Gaza Hospital inhabitants face the illegality of their settlement in the Sabra district. (There is in fact a legal void about the status and future of the property of the Palestinian Authority after its departure from Beirut.) Added to this is a bad reputation bound up with the insalubrious nature of the place and rumours of arms traffickers – as if a Palestinian 'contagion' spread from the camps to the city by way of Gaza Hospital . . .

How were the establishment and survival of this place possible? How was it transformed and stabilized, to the point of becoming, twenty-six years after its opening, a place of enduring urban presence for several generations of refugees and migrants in a precarious situation, with a possible insertion (even if marginal) in the city? Gaza Hospital is in fact the culmination of several histories. A Palestinian history, of course, as we have briefly mentioned. But also a history of conflicts and displacements in the region, the latest – Syrian – episode of which has had substantial effects on the life of the squat, in both economic and social terms. Many Syrian refugees (potential new tenants), in fact, are adding to the Syrian families and workers who have long been present. It is also a history of migrant workers coming from a wider geographical area – in the main, building workers and domestics – whose mobility and precarious living conditions in Beirut (sometimes very temporary) lead them to the squat as a possibility of access to the city: workers from Syria, Egypt, North and South Sudan, migrants from Sri Lanka, Bangladesh and Ethiopia. Finally, an urban history, that of the city of Beirut, which has made Sabra a moral region different today from the 'Palestinian grouping' that it was in the 1960s and 1970s. Beirut commentators now describe Sabra as a 'zone of cosmopolitan misery', and Gaza Hospital in its way embodies this most completely. Grouping together several generations and several waves of migrants and refugees, the squat is the site of a renewed alterity in the city at the same time as a site of mobility.

The foreigner in his labyrinth, or the tiers-instruit

Finally, let us take the case of an Austrian Jewish emigrant, who left in 1939 at the age of forty for the United States, where he settled with his wife and children, and where he died twenty years later. He was a sociologist and would soon be employed at the New School of Social Research in New York, which in the war years became a refuge for researchers and teachers in the social sciences and philosophy, Europeans who were persecuted and threatened on account of their Jewish origin.

Alfred Schütz, this émigré sociologist, drew on his own experience to reflect on the experience of adjustment, interpretation and apprenticeship that is the lot of the foreigner everywhere. He was interested in the way that cultural models intersect and superimpose themselves, generating a new 'habitual way of thinking' that is singular and syncretic. The stranger, in fact, arrives in the new situation with a way of thinking that he sees as self-evident and natural, and he has to orient himself in a 'new cultural world' (language, customs, laws, folklore, fashions, etc.), understand it and use it. 'In other words, the cultural pattern of the approached group is to the stranger not a shelter but a field of adventure.'[16] It is even, he added somewhat later, a 'labyrinth in which he has lost all sense of his bearings'.[17] From this test the foreigner draws two fundamental characteristics, on the one hand objectivity and 'intelligence of the world' (he has discovered that

70

'the normal way of living is far from being as assured as it seemed'), on the other hand an 'ambiguous loyalty': reluctant or unable to replace one cultural model entirely with another, the foreigner is 'a cultural hybrid on the verge of two different patterns of group life, not knowing to which of them he belongs'.[18]

A number of more recent publications have sought to describe and understand this ambivalent 'border' position in which the emigrant/immigrant finds himself.[19] There are three basic reasons why I find it important to mention this particular foreigner – a European immigrant in the United States in the mid-twentieth century, and his 'cultural labyrinth'. First of all, he prefigures an increasingly 'ordinary' condition in the cosmopolitan world that we are currently entering. Each test of alterity with which we find ourselves confronted makes the ways of life and thinking of the place of arrival a singular 'labyrinth' in which we lose the sense of orientation. If this test reinforces the objectivity and ambivalence of the migrant's border position, we should note that the places and situations of this test today are both globalized and multiplied in comparison with Schütz's American experience in the 1940s. The capacities of displacement, and the circulation of images and information on a world scale, make these tests increasingly numerous and everyday. As a result, in a context that is increasingly often cosmopolitan and in which each person is involved, the division between foreignness and familiarity represents as commonplace a test as that of the 'labyrinth'. Placed in a position of relative foreignness in a given social situation, each person thus has to verify both their own place and the relative character of their own alterity and that of others. Finally, beyond geostrategy and so-called 'protectionist' policies, it is this anthropological experience that tends to reduce or make more difficult the profusion of new walls since the 1990s. Without ever managing to suppress it totally, since, as we have seen, the border places in which foreigners today spend an increasingly long time, whether they are wanderers, pariahs or *métèques*, themselves become places of a new cosmopolitism.

Being-in-the-world on the border: a new cosmopolitan condition

Little by little, the wandering of the 'vagabond' traces a path without return, as distinct from the original Odyssey in which the migrant's native town of Ithaca seemed to be both first and final staging-post. The distancing of the 'pariah' makes the confined place

71

of the undesirable a border between societies and nation-states, an in-between rendered liveable, but from which it is hard to escape. And finally, the marginality of the *métèque* defines a foreigner open to unlimited exploitation, present in the urban space but without access to the 'city'; in other words, without rights, socially undesirable yet economically useful. They squat, they camp, they live in the interstices of urban life. They all experience, with greater or lesser social and economic comfort, a cultural 'labyrinth' in which their consciousness of belonging to the world is formed, while their distance from inherited identities grows.

The brief portraits of persons and places that we have just presented make it possible to sketch a picture of these social 'figures', modelled or conceptualized in the sense that we have sought to give them a character of generality. But if these persons help us in this way to understand the condition of the foreigner today, the theoretical 'figures' are not exhaustive: individual 'portraits' keep their singular character. This is not just a formal remark. The experience of anthropologists, in fact, is always marked by such singular encounters, often well hidden behind the 'informant', and through which the researcher has found a real friend and often a fine connoisseur of the society that he has come to study. Very often too, however, this relationship remains marked by the tie of affection alone (which we try rather clumsily to distinguish from 'objective' information), without drawing all the theoretical advantage from the encounter with a *subject* of speech and action that would have been possible. This basic question will remain central to the rest of the present inquiry (particularly in the foundation of an anthropology of the 'other-subject' in chapter 6). Right away, however, it invites us not to draw too many conclusions of an 'identitarian' character from these portraits. What the figures proposed here suggest are social possibilities of relative foreignness in which the dimensions of work, residence, personal and family itinerary are essential, as well as the contexts in which each person lives their foreignness and is culturally transformed in the process. And the names I have chosen to give an account of these experiences – the wanderer, the pariah, the *métèque* – clearly seek to be historical and relational, thus universal in their foundation and their process, rather than ethnic and particularist. Besides, these figures do not embody social categories, but rather ways of being foreign or conditions of foreignness; they are present to a greater or lesser extent in every person in the process of living a border situation, representing a moment of uncertainty and relative foreignness.

Each of these portraits contains a part of each of the figures. The

African 'vagabond' at the Emmaus centre in Paris has the desire to learn and work which propels him both into the life of a contemporary *métèque* and into the test of the labyrinth and of rapid cultural change. And the two 'outsiders' (*bidoons*) in Beirut embody in their very union a cultural symbiosis and re-creation at the same time as this couple and their children constantly risk finding themselves in the wandering of the 'vagabond'. The migrants' 'adventure' on the Mediterranean border probably provided a subjective motive for escaping from the cultural labyrinth in which they find themselves, for understanding where they are and learning to act, even if they have also felt the same anxieties and psychopathologies that Bobo N'K does in his camp. For the pariah is not the opposite of the undocumented worker – the two are interchangeable, depending on context and biographical moment. The opposite of them both is the citizen. In France today, the status of *sans-papier* relates to this old form of the *métèque* on the margin of the political city, and all the more exploitable given this lack of citizenship. Having become useful, he can find himself a 'pariah', an experience that many immigrant workers in France have had in recent years, finding themselves in 'camps' (administrative holding centres, the antechamber of expulsion) after ten years in the country and several years of work (in construction or catering), on account of being in an 'irregular' situation. And the young Afghans of Patras – as well as, elsewhere in the town and at the same time, the Sudanese, Palestinian or Somali migrants, and more generally all those who fail to arrive somewhere – waver according to the individual concerned and the moment of their trajectory between the three figures of the vagabond, most often represented among the migrants in transit (those whose displacement was extended in time and space, to the point of becoming a wandering), the pariah (set apart, in a camp), and the *métèque* (foreigner in the city, casual worker, without rights).

The task of linking together research on the management of populations and territories, on the one hand, and on the management and over-exploitation of foreign labour, on the other, still lies ahead.[20] The relationship between these two research orientations coincides with a philosophical dilemma between a Kantian, political orientation that describes itself as the 'cosmopolitical idea', and a Marxian and social orientation described as 'proletarian internationalism', two models that constantly intersect and both aim at 'overcoming the limitations of a citizenship purely coextensive with the institution of the nation-state', as Étienne Balibar puts it.[21] Sandro Mezzadra and Brett Nelson, for their part, show how the links between migration, work and precariousness in the context of globalization have 'dis-articulated the dyad worker–citizen' and formed new distinctions within manual labour.[22]

Finally, the figures of 'border dwellers' presented here lead us to extend the investigation and reconsider the cosmopolitan condition today as a whole. This presupposes 'denationalizing' as much as 'de-ethnicizing' the way of thinking the foreigner.[23] This must be included in an anthropological thought of alterity in general, and analysed in various degrees of relative foreignness according to context, or *in situation*. How do we become foreigners, and how do we cease to be so? By multiplying borders while the means of mobility have spread across the planet, is globalization making the condition of foreigner disappear? Or is it not, on the contrary, making it the most widely shared condition in the world, no matter what the inherited identities? It is this research that needs deepening on the basis of the borderlands to which the border dwellers have led us – places where an experience of cosmopolitan life is constituted, both specific and universal, ordinary and anticipatory.

An ordinary cosmopolitism

The word 'cosmopolitan' is generally associated with a 'globalized' way of life – the world of international experts, technocrats, business leaders and image creators who speak of the world and globaliza-tion, moving rapidly and fluidly between one place on the planet and another. From airports to planes and congress halls, from identical shopping malls to hotel chains, they actually live in a global bubble from which they scarcely emerge, if at all, and they need not move themselves much in order to travel, as they don't really change their dwelling. The world itself, with all its borders, its contours, its detri-tus, its smells or its barriers, rather makes up the blurred backdrop to their free and comfortable journey. To define this ensemble collec-tively, we can speak of a global class as a social and cultural minority without ethnicity, defined in opposition to the 'locals'. This is sug-gested by the sociologist Zygmunt Bauman, who sees the globalized elite as both excessively visible and at the same time inaccessible, 'floating above the local world', whereas the locals, for their part, form a global but anonymous majority whose movements are slower, more difficult, and sometimes risky . . .[24]

There are others, often grouped into movements and voluntary associations, who seek to be 'citizens of the world' or even 'alter-mondialists', differentiating themselves from this global class and thus rather less cosmopolitan. Though they may also call themselves 'cosmopolitan', what we observe in their case, to be precise, is that this means setting out a political position about the world and its governance that is more or less representative, democratic or universalistic. This is 'cosmo*political*', or at least a precursory sign of what may one day be a cosmopolitical mobilization. The philosophy of this world politics echoes this, and we could say that there already exists a philosophy of the cosmopolitical, which has every chance of winning a greater place in political philosophy as a whole. Discussions bear on the meaning and comparative advantages of multiculturalism, and on conflicts of universalisms – or, as Judith Butler has recently proposed, on the idea of cohabitation, a kind of zero degree of the cosmopolitical.[25]

Finally, in the same order of ideas, but moving from world politics to a certain conception of the 'global society', the sociologist Ulrich Beck has opined that to be truly cosmopolitan means having a cosmopolitan 'consciousness'.[26] He refers to the common conception of risks, for example in terms of health, that are shared simultaneously right across the planet. There would thus be, to be quite precise in terms, an *identification* with the world as totality in relation to something that is happening somewhere, 'elsewhere', but of which we see images and hear commentaries all around: this is the 'risk' of the 'risk society'.[27] Bird flu, tsunami, 9/11 . . . both our consciousness and our commitment are then solicited. And yet we also participate globally in the Olympics, in the World Cup – something particular suddenly becomes a symbol and a link and for a moment gives us the feeling of being in society in one and the same world, but this happens by way of images, commentaries, flows of information, without the experience of each particular subject of this 'consciousness' being really affected by it. Its context, therefore, is indeed Ulrich Beck's 'risk society', but equally a (global) 'performance society', a 'society of the spectacle', etc. The common point of these forms of global society is their virtual aspect. The society seems to rest on nothing more than the perception of a mediatized event, or even just a media one, which unites 'us' on a planetary scale, but just for a moment, and without this 'consciousness' corresponding to any real shared experience.[28]

These three most common usages of the 'cosmopolitan' word and idea (global class, cosmopolitical, cosmopolitan consciousness) do not describe the cosmopolitan *condition* in the sense of a lived experience, everyday and ordinary, an experience of sharing the world, no matter how inegalitarian and violent this may be. My different conception of cosmopolism is drawn rather from the experience of border situations, in the broad sense in which I have used the term. I have given possible illustrations on the basis of my field studies in different parts of the world. Other situations of this kind might very well complete this set of portraits and figures of border dwellers and borderlands, and render it more complex. But I can, I believe, argue coherently that cosmopolitism is the experience of those women and men who experience the concreteness and roughness of the world. This ordinary experience of the world is the experience of crossing borders, a situation that can extend in both time and space. And it is in border situations that the relationship with the other is put to the test, with an unknown who is also the embodiment of what the world is for those who find themselves there, arriving at the border.

Who better than the 'uprooted' to give us the concrete and empirical trace of this new cosmopolitan condition, and to reflect on the political perspective that it establishes on a common world scale? Migrants moving from one country to another, one region to another, descendants of migrants or of more distant deportees who have kept with them the identity image of the foreigner . . .[29] All these people in displacement anticipate a reflection that holds good also for their contemporaries more or less temporarily settled in a place on the 'surface of the Earth' (Kant), and for whom it may be useful one day to consider themselves as cosmopolitan if they themselves have to change their anchorage.

Many works of social science in the last twenty years have shown what we might call the centrality of migration in understanding the development of the world in general. Nina Glick Schiller (with Linda Basch and Cristina Szanton Blanc)[30] introduced reflection on the cosmopolitism of the migrant in the mid-1990s, stressing that the latter was anchored 'in more than one society' and that transnational life pervaded the everyday experience of both individual migrants and their families. In France, the sociologist and ethnographer Alain Tarrius also saw 'transmigrants' and the poorest among the migrants as the bearers of a specific cosmopolitanism, forming its own networks and territories. In Brazil, Gustavo Lins Ribeiro observed a 'popular cosmopolitanism' in his studies on migrant workers involved in street trading and the informal economy more generally. And more recently, Nina Glick Schiller extended her reflections on transnational migrants by posing the question: 'Whose cosmopolitanism?' What contemporary social process does this correspond to, what aspirations and desires?[31]

For Hein de Haas, author of a synthesis on the theme of international migration and its importance in understanding contemporary social life in general, the theoretical effects of attention to migration have only recently emerged: these are part of a wider current of studies and the coining of new concepts associated with migration ('transnational', 'multicultural', 'diasporic', 'creolization', etc.) or concerning the life, identities and experiences of the migrants themselves. In certain contexts, he notes, when the 'aspirations' to migration and the 'capacities' to leave evolve in the same direction in favour of mobility (which is not automatic), a 'culture of migration' then forms, developing an 'increasing antipathy towards traditional, agrarian lifestyles' while contributing to a rapid change in the conception of the 'good life'.[32]

As we shall see, despite the feelings of foreignness that those people settled in a place may have towards migrants, the latter are already detached from the territorial, familial and cultural anchorage of the place that they come from. The 'outsiders' no longer correspond to the identity that the 'settled' attribute to them with the national, ethnic or racial labels that they have available. It is starting from this situation of double 'de-identification' of the migrant (who no longer corresponds to the identity of his society of origin, but equally not to that which the society of arrival assigns him) that we shall go on to tackle the question of the cosmopolitan subject. This is an 'other-subject', detached from the identity assignment that the receiving society attributes and even acting against it. This detachment, and the symbolic void it provokes, may lead the migrant to try and portray migration as more attractive than it really is, and to construct an image and narrative of themselves as 'adventurer'.[33]

These different approaches and observations have contributed to decentre the gaze on societies, and they often meet up with my own studies and analyses. For, if I were to summarize, the persons in displacement whom I speak about here are remote from the global class who circulate in a sealed aseptic bubble, different from the champions of world citizenship whose path they sometimes cross, neither more nor less conscious of the risks and spectacles globalized by the media than the other inhabitants of the planet. Their cosmopolitism derives from the fact that they necessarily have the world in their head, even if this is not sought or projected, even if they did not construct a personal theory of it in advance. We find here the basic principle of the cosmopolitan realism of the Enlightenment philosopher Immanuel Kant: that we have to understand one another 'because the Earth is round . . .', a principle whose effect is to keep one aloof not just from any utopia or romanticism, but also from any ingenuity: it is globalization itself that has 'exploded the postulate of unity itself'. In a *negative* sense, as Étienne Balibar notes, we probably do live in 'a single world, in the sense that it is no longer in anyone's power to escape the effects of the actions of others, and in particular from their destructive effects'.[34] The case of refugees, of those forcibly displaced, of migrants in an irregular situation, is just as exemplary from this point of view. In this case, in fact, the discovery of being in a world wider than local or even national boundaries is an experience strongly felt, a painful and a dangerous one, but it is also full of expectations and hopes, projections into a distant future 'home', built in a de facto multilocality.[35] To elaborate strategies, to imagine oneself an 'adventurer', to understand that one is entering the test of a cultural 'labyrinth' by crossing borders – these are all so many clear expressions of a cosmopolitan consciousness, but one very different from discourse on the joy of being 'global' or on the cosmopolitan aesthetic. There can very well also be, on the contrary, a cosmopolitan consciousness of who is undesirable in the world, or at least less desirable, a consciousness of the *métèque*, the wanderer or the pariah, who certainly knows and sees himself as being in the world, because the world (in the sense of displacement, the border, other people) manifests itself and forces him to view himself in relation to others. It is a pragmatic cosmopolitan thought, a thought *in situation*, without any globalist discourse being needed to prove the reality of this experience of the world. It is a de facto state, the fact of being in the world at the border, and of having to deal here with the organization of everyday life and the definition of one's place in society. We can say, therefore, that this cosmopolitism is one of the ordinary expressions of the decentring of the world, that is, the fact that the world as it is acquires its meaning and construction at the borders.

That is why I would like to take these reflections further, using the starting-point of migration to link more closely the cosmopolitan condition to the test of the border. I will argue that ordinary cosmopolitism, as this has arisen from the concrete everyday experience of the border, denotes a condition that is not *substantially* bound up with particular social categories or impoverished classes of migrants, even if it is largely on these that the present reflections are based. It seems to me that we can draw from this migrant experience a decentred point of view on the world; as has been done by the philosopher Seloua Luste Boulbina, who, in a brilliant essay that draws on the work of Edward Said (in particular his *Reflections on Exile*), situates the most clearly 'decolonized' thought, that emancipated from any assignment of identity, in what she calls 'between-worlds', those worlds 'between' that are formed by experience and the 'science of the concrete' – the experience of migrants on their travels.[36]

The image that I believe I can detach and in a certain sense 'universalize' on the basis of my research is that of the in-between space.[37] We can observe on all sides a contemporary tendency to the proliferation and diversification of these border spaces or situations, within which a decentred experience develops among those who live and meet there. Moreover, the reflexivity that necessarily accompanies this knowing-how-to-be in the world is strengthened by the duration and repetition of the border position for those women and men who move around and thus live more than others the encounter between different local worlds. With the spatial and temporal widening of borders, this condition is potentially generalizable, and anticipates a culture of borders as a global culture in the process of becoming. This is a cosmopolitism both wider and more universal, more genuine and authentic, than that which people today have in mind when they talk of cosmopolitism, in the current conceptions already mentioned. The monopolization of the cosmopolitan idea by the media global class, by the cosmopolitism of world citizens, or by the consciousness of media globalized events shows that cosmopolitism, just like global mobility, is marked by multiple inequalities, and that its definition is an object of conflict. If it is important first of all to say from where and of whom one is speaking of cosmopolitism ('whose cosmopolitism?'), it is also important to conclude with the best possible description of cosmopolitism ('which cosmopolitism?').

This everyday and commonplace cosmopolitan condition, therefore, cannot simply be reduced to its sociological component (the circulation of the poor, a 'popular', 'transnational' or 'migratory' cosmopolitism). In anthropological terms, it is formed by the experience of the border, which globalization is generalizing, and with which we have to learn to live. (The proof *a contrario* of the truth of this statement can be found in the development of identity-based enclosures – nationalist, urban, neo-local or neo-tribal – which everywhere show the difficulty of understanding and living these border situations.)

Broadening the study to all border situations, that is, all situations in which a test of relative foreignness is shared, we can reduce this foreignness to what is common, and relativize the distance from the other, whatever the language of this alterity: ethnic, racial or humanitarian. This facilitates recognition of the 'other-subject' who exists through these manifestations of alterity of which the border is the site. By decentring the focus of investigation to the border, it is possible to apply an alternative to the repetition of identity thinking and the trap this constantly holds out for calls to 'live together'. This will be the object of the second part of this essay.

Part II

The Decentred Subject

— 4 —

QUESTIONS OF METHOD: DECENTRING RECONSIDERED TODAY

The moment of uncertainty and the political importance that the question of borders has assumed in the world today have given rise in the social sciences to various 'crises', debates, and more generally a period of conceptual, methodological and thematic revision. The 'contemporary turn' that has marked anthropology during this period enables us to envisage an indispensable *aggiornamento*. The issue at stake is a simple one – involving not only anthropologists, but also the uses of social sciences by those who question their utility today and seek a dialogue with them. Can we still understand the world around us when its boundary and characteristics have been profoundly transformed in recent decades? Can we understand, from the anthropological point of view, the place and involvement of each person in the world, when this has acquired the (planetary) dimensions that we see today, and when at the same time distances have been reduced, so that each place on the planet has become technically accessible in a few days at most, generally in a few hours, or with a few clicks, thus creating new temporalities and spatialities of social and cultural life? Concerned as it has always been with the study of people in society, can anthropology still help us to live our 'presence in the world' (the experience that each day makes up our human condition in society) in this global context? These are the questions that we now have to tackle, before pursuing the investigation of the emergence of a cosmopolitan subject.

A critical moment: the contemporary turn in anthropology

It is unnecessary to go very far back in time in order to see that the last few decades have been marked by a general crisis of major social and cultural paradigms, a crisis whose onset may be dated between the end of the Second World War (1940s and 1950s), the wave of decolonization (1960s and 1970s) and the end of the Cold War (1980s and 1990s). Three changes in this context have particularly concerned the foundations of anthropology: transformations in representations of the individual, the formation and gradual imposition of the world scale, and the multiple troubles and conflicts associated with the question of borders, whether they bear on the very existence of these, their delimitation or their role. There is a connection between these three changes from the anthropological point of view. My reason for bringing them together here is to present the context in which anthropology, in some thirty or so years, has had to revise its concepts completely and invent new ones, renew its fields and the manner of approaching these.

First of all, the accelerated individualization of destinies and the rise of individualism as social model, or the rising glory of the 'I' throughout the world, have challenged the foundations and mediations that connect us one to another – 'anthropological places', 'intermediate bodies', the role and structures of kinship relations, communitarian forms of access to land and resources, etc. Should we believe that anthropology has to retreat back to what remains of 'traditional' systems, at the cost of an ever greater reduction in its space of exploration, description and understanding of the world? Should it not rather shift its gaze, or more exactly duplicate or even multiply this, while transforming its ways of investigation, so as to match the transformations and displacements of the actors and practices studied, and starting from networks rather than from normative structures, individuals rather than the groups or collective identities studied and named previously in other contexts?

Secondly, the image of a finite world (planet Earth) as enveloping and homogenizing framework, beyond local or national contexts, has challenged the boundary of what is common to 'us', from the classic 'village' or 'ethnic' communities to the 'European community', even the 'international community' – the latter proving less obvious than the former, above all for reasons of scale and thus intensity of 'internal' communication. The word 'community' is then the object of a new focus and questioning. In public debate it has become practically equivalent to that of identity. 'Identity' imposes itself on 'community' and overdetermines its meaning in the generally national contexts of complex societies. These latter are marked by social inequalities and public polemics (for example between identity policies, communitarianism and universalism). Doing anthropology of these necessitates the re-problematizing of the relationship between a social organization, a cultural dynamic, and the assertion (generally oppositional in national and global contexts) of a 'we' that demands recognition. This relationship, taken as structurally harmonic and stable in the so-called 'simple' societies studied by ethnologists in the most remote corners of the planet, becomes disharmonic in so-called 'complex' societies marked by cultural heterogeneity and a great diversity of social ties and adherences. The question of knowing what 'makes for community' in all these places today thus refers the anthropologist to the study of contemporary situations in which individuals re-create the common, without the essentialist hypothesis being necessary to this situational study and without one part of the world being from this point of view more 'non-subject' than another.

Thirdly, and as if to continue and summarize these two crises of the 'I' and the 'we', the question of borders is posed – borders of spaces, of cultures and, more confusedly, of identities in and of globalization. The global grand narrative of 'without borders' developed in the 1970s and 1980s was an expression of this crisis as much as the building of thousands of kilometres of walls has been since that time, to protect residential districts or nation-states. The accelerated transformations of locality, culture and identity, like the seeming consensus around the cultural homogenization of the globalized world, have equally led certain commentators to evoke the threat of a disappearance of the 'other'. And yet, the differences proclaimed are rendered more visible than ever in the global context: whether more aesthetic, parodied or fictional, they circulate further and faster. The question of borders thus reintroduces a problematic of relationship in which discourses of identity dominate, by expressing in a political and violent fashion the oxymoron of globalization that is also a double negation of the border: ever more walls in a world without alterity . . .

The world, I and we – this is the new social and cultural configuration, briefly summarized here, on which the 'contemporary' critique of anthropology is founded, at a reflexive moment in the course of which its problematics (ethnic and civilizational), its approaches (monographic and structural functionalist), its descriptions (totalizing and monological) and its fields have simultaneously become the 'territories' of ethnologists (villages, tribes, communities). In France, it is Marc Augé and his 'anthropology of contemporary worlds' that have offered the most advanced formulations of this critique and actualization of anthropology.[1] This has in a way sanctioned a broader movement in the exercise of the anthropologist's craft, a movement marked by the superseding of the ethnological objects that had previously been privileged, ethnic and monographic, in favour of a wider reach, open but a priori undetermined, towards 'contemporary worlds', a process still in the making, in situation, sometimes unpredictable, in changing contexts and scales of magnitude.

Studying these 'worlds' in formation or transformation has implied an opening to themes of research that are new to anthropology, adapted to the evolutions of the global context whose effects cannot be overlooked if we seek to grasp the situations observed in their entirety: development, health, migration, work, urbanization, poverty, politico-religious movements. These objects of research have led ethnologists to global societal questions, thus breaking with the North–South cultural separation and empirically leading towards globalization. Conversely, students and researchers in other disciplines have taken up tools and concepts from ethnology to aid them in thinking all the worlds in transformation. This movement, even if it has promoted the present multitude of thematic subdivisions on the basis of which it has become hard to see a common anthropological horizon, has also offered arguments to the project of a general and multidisciplinary anthropology.

During this watershed period from the 1970s to the 1990s, a series of convergent critiques and theories were developed in Europe and the United States. All of these, if with certain important differences, formed part of the contemporary turn in anthropology that is presented here, and that I believe is a possible basis for progress in updating the tools of anthropology. In a few years, in fact, new explorations of 'coevalness' have appeared from a combination of research, information and writing,[2] critiques of the monograph form as writing and as fiction,[3] theoretical and methodological considerations on the delocalization of lived and observed situations, and thus the necessity of a 'multi-situated' ethnography.[4]

More generally, North American anthropology has also experienced a 'philological turn', in the expression of Tobias Rees,[5] taking literally Clifford Geertz's famous formulation that the anthropologist must 'read cultures as texts, over the shoulder of the informants'. What has been going on in the course of this period is thus a broad and radical critical reversal. Classical ethnology, ethnic and monographic, has been criticized as a fiction emanating from an 'author', and as a relationship of domination that denies the 'dialogism' inherent in research. But what to put in its place? If it was simply fiction, literature, idiosyncrasy, the genius or caprice of the author, then anthropological knowledge would be impossible: this is the critique generally made in France of the analyses of so-called 'textualist' anthropology, which in its extreme form proclaims the 'end of fields' – this critical moment, moreover, has been subsequently revisited by its main authors as one of an 'opening or demolition, depending on how you see it, without anything being put in its place'.[6]

The political context and the moral crisis of the 'First World' in the 1960s were the determinant period, in both the United States and France. The North American 'demolition' was more a moral and political revolution than an epistemological one, if we believe the contextualization of it that the protagonists of that era make today.[7] A situation marked by the Vietnam War, which was in a way for American anthropologists what decolonization was for the Europeans, and for French anthropology in particular. It was a time of crisis and rapid change in the fields and contexts of anthropology. In France, critique of the role played by ethnology in colonial or imperialist domination was intended, according to its most radical opponents, to lead to the disappearance of the discipline.[8] And African researchers who went on to construct the object of a 'postcolony' confirmed this radicality,[9] not knowing what to do with a European ethnological knowledge marked by an 'ethnographic authority' that was very political in its very principle.

To take up George Marcus's question that I have already cited: what to put in its place? How to do anthropology today in a context of the decentring of the world and the 'decolonization of knowledge'? It is important in my view to take up and deepen the critique of the 'great divide', to rethink anthropological decentring and adapt the method of observation and analysis to the contemporary world. These are the three questions of method that I want to tackle in the rest of this chapter, before returning to our investigation of borders.

The end of the 'great divide'

Starting from the critical moment whose main lines I have just described, the idea developed that an 'anthropology of the contemporary' would define an alternative anthropology of an other that had, by contrast, remained 'classic' and thus a point of reference for some (those attached to it as a 'Golden Age'),[10] while immutable and superseded for others (those who criticized it). In this way of thinking and classifying, the anthropology of the contemporary has either been qualified by additions (which may be called 'sociological': the city, conflict, mobility, development, etc.) or, on the contrary, by subtractions (supposedly 'ethnological': structures of kinship, local languages, the cult of ancestors, etc.).

It is true that both sides indicate, by the greater or lesser place that they occupy in the description and interpretation of fields, a substantial change in the contexts of inquiry (individualization, delo-calization, globalization, present-ism, etc.). I shall take one example of this general contemporizing of the facts that the anthropologist deals with. If we take the 100 or so inhabitants of a forest village in West Africa, the 450 passengers on a Paris–New York flight, the 500 inhabitants of a tower block in the Paris region or even the 3,500 tourists at a resort complex on the north coast of Bahia in Brazil, the human scale makes these configurations equally observable and comparable for anthropological investigation, yet the differences in meaning are considerable, and we may think first of all that neither the same concepts nor the same methodological procedures can be used in one or the other case. However, these four places today all involve mobility on a greater or lesser scale and with greater or lesser intensity, and their occupants may well be just as much at home as anywhere in the world. Finally, it is no longer really incongruous today to imagine that the persons occupying each of these four spaces are connected with some others living in the other social and cultural configurations mentioned here (African village, aeroplane, tower block, tourist complex) by various kinds of network, economic activity or kinship.

The problem, therefore, with this superficial partition between the 'anthropology of the contemporary' and 'classic ethnology' is that change and mobility are increasingly present everywhere, and so are no longer really divisive from the point of view of fields. To defend this partition of knowledge (and thus maintain the 'great divide' of the world between modern and exotic societies), anthropology would have to be confined to the old form of human groupings (those that were characterized as 'ethnic groups' at the time of their discovery), excluding from its field the contemporary forms of groupings, assemblies, unions or communities in the process of being made, born or transformed.[11]

From ethnic group to ethnic identities

This territorial partition between a 'classical' anthropology and a different contemporary one is unsatisfactory from the theoretical point of view, and equally so for conceiving research on the ground, where it takes place. It reproduces within anthropology itself the principle of the 'great divide', dualist and culturalist (even 'civilizational'), between tradition and modernity, ethnic group and class, 'them' and 'us', particularisms ('with the so-and-sos') and universalism ('with us'), and so on. We should remember that this dualism, generally rejected in synthetic and reflexive presentations of anthropology today,[12] was the first conceptual framework for ethnology at its birth, when it was the business of explorers. It founded the 'exotic' representation of others, considered literally external to the Western world. Then it was confirmed by the great culturalist presentations of the first half of the twentieth century, using formulas that became canonical and caricatured, often since criticized ('the Trobianders ...', 'for the Dogon ...', etc.), no matter the wealth of the information gathered or the interpretations proposed by its authors.[13] This long episode made the ethnic group the model of alterity – the ethnic is always the other – and the obligatory pathway to anthropological knowledge.

Forgetting the historicity of these discoveries of the distant other (in contexts of colonization and colonial administration of populations to be controlled, separated, classified) anchored the ethnic group in the very essence of the craft for a long time. The idea of the ethnic group was initially an external and all-encompassing framework of identification to characterize peoples (*ethnos*) about whom a certain unity could be observed in terms of social and economic organization, language, farming or cultural practices. Explorers and colonizers gave all-encompassing names to these organizations of remote zones and the 'others' they discovered, conquered and administered. Ethnonyms were then the commonly used names, those most convenient for the government of indigenous populations. Much has been written about the coining and uses of ethnonyms. Among the most remarkable critical analyses, we should mention that of Jean Bazin, if I may quote him at length here, given that his argument deserves to be presented as a whole:

> As distinct from a people or nation, who are the product of a history, the ethnic group is in fact the result of a preliminary operation of classification. In this respect, all ethnology begins as a zoology, having only the appearance of a rational and scholarly taxonomy. We could

certainly imagine a kind of ideal ethnologist, scrupulously deaf to any preliminary naming and concerned only with the best classification of the manners and customs observed, in the manner of an entomologist or mineralogist, with the aim of obtaining a rigorous nomenclature making possible a table of genera and species: an attempt impossible to achieve, since, as distinct from butterflies or stones, humans classify themselves, so that the names by which observers know their groups are never unconnected from those they attribute to one another. In this way, ethnonyms were in each case actually uttered by certain of the actors involved – if only as an insult or jibe by hostile neighbours or ignorant conquerors – before becoming a scholarly label. The ethnologist does not invent fictitious entities or arbitrary names ex nihilo, for the needs of his cause, but perhaps it would be better if he were to do so.[14]

The notion of the ethnic group has been criticized in many studies from a historical point of view, and as a political or imaginary 'construction' in which the imprint of the colonial power was determinant in freezing and separating societies.[15] It has been shown several times that the noun phrase 'ethnic group' did not really correspond to these isolates, that it could well be conjunctural, and that the old societies, particularly in Africa, were linked by trade, politics, language, matrimonial exchange or conflicts over land; in short, that it was more a question of 'chains of societies'[16] than of homogeneous entities, with continuous transformations of their boundaries. The names of ethnic groups, however, have continued in use as an approximate term, without a claim to precision.

At the same time, but on the basis of research in other places, a new problematic appeared, that of 'ethnic identity', in contexts of social contacts and changes bound up with migration, urbanization and industrialization, as also with the development of 'marginal' contexts (poverty, social exclusion, etc.) and on every continent. Ethnonyms, whether old, transformed or new, could be used as labels in these contexts of contact, competition or conflict. It is thus clearly and systematically vis-à-vis 'others' that the question of 'ethnic groups' arises. And it is on the borders of groups, in a confrontation with others that is as much cultural as social and political, that the differences are constructed and manifested.[17] Finally, the diversity of modes of identification in heterogeneous societies has led to broader study and reflection on contemporary identities, diluting 'ethnic identity' among a wide spectrum of identity options in the context of changing situational commitments.[18] Other questions then arise, in particular that of the new identity-based 'essentialisms', which we return to now.

Identity-based essentialisms and ontologies

Rogers Brubaker and Frederick Cooper, in a brilliant and scathing essay,[19] have emphasized the distinction between identity as a 'category of practice' (meaning its now widespread use in different aspects of social and political life and in personal, media, political, etc. commentary about these aspects), and identity as a 'category of analysis' (a concept used in causal explanations). In this latter aspect, they question any use of the concept (which, depending on the particular case, means either too much, or not enough, or nothing at all) and ask: what is being spoken of under the name of identity? Their focus of attention is the critique of analytical uses of identity and the possible substitutes for this: 'identification', 'categorization', 'self-understanding', 'social place', 'group', etc. But they leave unexplored a question which is inseparable from the first since it lies at the root of this conceptual malaise, that of the everyday or political uses of the notion.

Moreover, Brubaker and Cooper stress the possible coexistence in the same research, or the same discourses, of two postures that they respectively call 'constructivist' (which views identity as a social and historical 'construction', for analysis to 'deconstruct') and 'essentialist' (which assumes the primacy of an identity in itself over all its relational or contextual 'alterations', a primacy based on the idea of a purity and original homogeneity). But they relate this ambiguity to the opposed couple of knowledge and commitment, in my view rather too simply and rapidly: the former of these would fall on the side of deconstruction (and the 'object') while the second inclines to essentialism and assumes a 'belief' in the identity itself. We can say in response to this that commitment is not in principle incompatible with criticism and freedom of thought (something not relevant only to researchers). And that freedom to think, and to produce a knowledge free from personal compromise, should in no way be subject to the necessary involvement of the researcher in his 'field'. The two positions have to be kept together. In my view, the theoretical essentialism of one wing of anthropology is not an effect of ethnographic involvement, but more deeply a 'trace' of the early ethnic specialization of the discipline. Which implies a self-criticism of the foundations of the discipline and not just a conceptual adjustment.

Thus, faced with the proliferation of border situations as described in the previous chapters, as well as what Étienne Balibar has called 'conflicts of universality without an advance solution', and Judith Butler 'conflicts of universalisms', certain anthropologists in the last few years have set out to explain the new cultural state of the world by way of a so-called 'ontological' orientation. By recourse to the paradigm of a world divided into great cultural systems, they seek to offer responses to the misunderstandings and disagreements that are so common in today's world, which is certainly much to their merit. Based on earlier monographs whose quality is not in question here, these approaches take up the culturalist creed, whether deliberately or not: frozen and decontextualized cultural portraits are compared or confronted with one another. This operation of contextual reduction and atemporality is particularly clear in the argument of an 'Amerindian ontology' championed by Eduardo Viveiros de Castro, with whom the 'ontological' stance is most directly marked by ethnic reference, even if the author claims to reject any kind of ethnicism, particularly contemporary ethnopolitics, and appeals to a structuralist legacy that claims universal relevance.[20] Other analyses of the division of the world that derive from this so-called 'ontological' stance have been offered by Philippe Descola, Bruno Latour and others.[21] Though there are major differences between these approaches, all three take the same name borrowed from philosophy. This is in fact their unifying characteristic: a project that combines the metaphysical quest for an (ontological) *being-in-itself* with anthropological places, cultures and identities, at the price of having to decontextualize the ethnographic reality of *being-in-the-world*. At the end of the day, philosophers are not happy with these efforts, which for them pertain to a sociological 'verification' or 'veridiction' that they do not know how to use, while anthropologists are equally unhappy with the decontextualized abstractions in which societies, or even the human itself, end up by disappearing. Anthropological ontologies, for their authors, are virtual constructions on different scales, from the most micro, local and ethnological (Viveiros de Castro) to the most global, planet-wide and eco-sociological (Bruno Latour). These constructions, with their universalist intention (which certainly is not something to criticize), do indeed supply the keys for their own intellectual construction, but not those for their use 'in situation' and in context. This lack would be understandable on the part of a philosophical argument; it is less so for an anthropological one whose truth is always relative to study on the ground, with its particular place, context and relationships – it is this relativity of anthropological knowledge that makes it possible to keep at bay any kind of 'cultural relativism' in the sense of a culture frozen and intrinsically associated with a single identity and place.[22] Without in any way wanting to put these attempts in the dock – as I repeat, they have the merit of attempting a global thought and seeking generalization – we can say that what we find here is the radical expression of extensions of the intellectual opposition between structure and context, meaning and function, that marked in the 1950s the bifurcation between structuralism and situational and processual anthropology, represented on the one hand by the work of Claude Lévi-Strauss, inspired by the models of linguistics, and on the other hand by Georges Balandier, close to the anthropological studies of the Manchester School.

Ontologies are thus, according to an abstract globalization of the local, structural constructions which, on this basis, assume the perspective of the 'whole'. This is a double totality. On the one hand, it is the 'indigenous intellectual structure'[23] that assumes, as in the older and original holistic tradition of ethnology, an identification of the part with the whole (embodied in practice by the 'privileged informant' and in theory by the notion of the 'persona'). The identification of the subject, seen as a 'persona', with the 'structure' leaves no remainder.[24] This conception relates to the philosophical figures of the 'object-subject' or subjected subject, and gives no possibility of conceiving the subject of disorder or dissidence.[25] On the other hand, the ideal of totality is also found already in the definition of 'perspectivism'. This notion – which cannot be equated with the assertion of a necessary decentring of the anthropologist endlessly moving between multiple points of view (thus well beyond cultural relativism), a position I shall argue for later[26] – represents in fact an identity-based version of decentring, as with the case of the 'Amerindian perspectivism'. Whereas the new decentring that I support here is an epistemology of anthropology in general, perspectivism is, as Oscar Calavia Saez emphasizes, 'an epistemology *with* ontology'.[27]

On the basis of this ontological 'perspective', totality (and its incarnation in the old reactivated notion of 'persona') is reintroduced into the abolition of the border between human and non-human, nature and culture, ecology and sociology.[28] When, to return to the Amerindian case, the ethnologist ends up speaking in the name of the jaguar, we can rightly maintain that this ontological perspectivism has lost the meaning of decentring and taken instead the path of reification of the ethnologist's own abstraction, trapped in the narcissism of his own thought despite his protestations to the contrary. For the reality reconstructed in this way actually caricatures the constructivist approach: from the symbolic function of the jaguar for the shamans who invent its myth, mask and meaning, we have moved to belief in an inherent reality of the being of the jaguar, of whom the shaman is simply the ambassador among humans.[29] This quite logically ends up with the oxymoron of an anthropology that is both post-human and non-human.[30] Hence the necessity of regaining a hold by ethnographic study of the situations, contexts, stakes and contexts of cultural dynamics. Of a return to ethnography, situational and contextual, and to contemporary analysis.

The context of this 'Amerindian ontology' is provided by an artificially closed world, a cosmology (or representation of the world) in which none of the Yanomami, Araweté or Tupi identified with it actually participates, since none of them lives in a structural isolate. The world of globalization, moreover, deserves no more attention on the part of the anthropologist than a brief negative verdict, moral and aesthetic, given in a few lines.[31] This is another aspect of the effects of the decontextualization of the ontological perspective, the global world and its concrete influences finding no place in ethnography, or, logically enough, in the analysis of cultural facts observed locally. In the same way, no human being actually corresponds to the model of the Amerindian, Amazonian or Yanomami 'sociocultural system'. Of course, the author accepts and champions the 'fiction' produced as a necessary abstraction; perspectivism actually aims to deploy indigenous thought beyond itself.[32] The problem is that the evidence of the fields, the American ones in particular, is that those persons and groups who are the identity-based references of this construction actually circulate, and with them circulate ideas, knowledge, relationships, ways of doing things, etc. They are not out of the world, neither outside the reach of finance capitalism nor outside that of Brazilian or international agro-industrialism, which is particularly destructive in Amazonia; they are not outside globalization in general, not far from UN agencies and international NGOs. All these actors interpellate them, and by this constant interpellation they arouse in return individual and collective responses, including various identity-based or even 'essentialist' constructions, as forms of revolt, dialogue or strategy.[33] From this point of view, the ontological procedure is close to the so-called 'essentialist' strategies that anthropologists of the contemporary encounter today in their fields.

This brings us to Brubaker and Cooper's critique of identity as a category of practice or analysis, to which I shall now add the following question: is it actually necessary to believe in the truth of essentialism? As we shall see, in studying the construction of identity-based cultures by actors in contexts of conflict, so-called 'essentialist' language is in large part an effect of the politicization of identity assignment. It is in this context that it begins to exist, expresses itself, and is most interesting for the anthropologist to tackle: as a contemporary form and an object of reflection whose strategic reason relates to nothing other than contemporary politics. If identity is an endless quest, if the identity-based essence is not a 'thing' that can be isolated, then essentialism is nothing but a language, unusable analytically but to be investigated 'in situation'. In other words, we need to go beyond identity so as better to understand not only its uses but, still more, what lies beyond. To understand the why and the how of the procedures that lead certain persons or collectives, at a given moment, to use this or that so-called 'identitarian' language, and to make it, depending on the particular case, the language of a withdrawal into oneself, a rejection of the other or, on the contrary, of a ritual, aesthetic or political subjectification. To understand, therefore, how other languages (coming from a geographic 'elsewhere', or from a more or less distant 'before') can be taken up, transformed and used to bring into existence other subjects in a particular contemporary conflict situation (see chapter 6).

Finally, if the culturalist 'great divide' cannot, in my view, be any longer the basis of anthropology, it is above all because the existence of the world as made up of social practices and situations has become observable everywhere, an empirical fact as much as a theoretical one.[34] If the possible fields of anthropology are no longer determined by their place on the map of the world, if they can be geographically either distant or near, then anthropologists can also not be satisfied in their knowledge by the fact of geographical distance and the more or less illuminating effects it was previously able to give them about the societies studied, and about their own societies in return. They must therefore completely reconsider the question that made for the whole theoretical originality of the anthropologist's craft: the question of decentring. This is what I want to develop now, in this second 'question of method', with the aim of improving the means of knowledge of the world and its border.

Decentring reconceived

Decentring, an old founding gesture of the ethnological approach, leading from the self to the other, must today be completely reconceived, since it is directly challenged by the crisis of alterity in the world today. Who is the other? How and where is he or she to be 'recognized'? How does the border marker move between self and other? This is the question I shall tackle here, introducing three dimensions of decentring: cultural, epistemological and political.

Beyond cultural decentring

Cultural decentring lay at the very root of anthropology. It consisted in detaching oneself from the inherited cultural presuppositions of one's own society, and suspending all judgement so as to open oneself to the relativity of every culture and the discovery of others. This was not done in a day. Distant explorations, initiatory journeys and other 'detours'[35] successively embodied this vocation of the anthropologist to effect a cultural decentring, eventually to return grown and informed of the diversity of the world.

This was the basis of the exploratory enthusiasm of the first ethnographers, for example Mungo Park, of whom Adrian Adams could say, commenting on his account of his explorations in the 'heart of Africa' in the late eighteenth century, that he was a 'traveller without history', meaning that for this Scottish doctor, whose first journey this was, his availability to others was the effect of a forgetting and abandonment of self.[36] Cultural decentring, in the words of Maurice Godelier, gives the possibility of a free thought transformable not just into a stance of scholarship, but also into a political and moral one: 'Understanding the beliefs of others without being obliged to share them, respecting them without prohibiting oneself from criticizing them, and recognizing that it is among others and thanks to them that one can better know oneself: such is the scientific heart of anthropology both today and tomorrow, and it is also its moral and political heart.'[37] To sum up, what is generally called decentring is this personal, authentic, and even voluntarily candid experience of 'cultural relativism'.

But what and where does one return from today? We need to press further and 'globalize' this stance well beyond cultural relativism. In other words, it is not just a question of decentring the gaze on the world by way of anthropology (in its relativist ethnological tradition), but rather of decentring anthropology (in the sense of the knowledge of anthropologists) by the gaze of the world. The first sense, ethnological and old-established, persists in the name of diversity or an aesthetic curiosity for everything that is different. I do not challenge the qualities and attraction of this aesthetic gaze and intervention on and vis-à-vis the 'other'. But, as shown by cultural tourism, by the arrangement of the exhibition in the Musée du Quai Branly,[38] or again by many cultural creations in the world today, the aestheticizing of the 'other' is a modality of appropriation/integration of images and objects whose meanings change by being moved into a changed social and semantic context. In this process, objects (in the material

96

sense as well as the epistemological one) circulate, take on new life and are otherwise transformed, while the subjects, for their part, have disappeared – a disappearance that the proclaimed 'diversity of cultures' does not avoid, this expression becoming nothing more than a compensation for the dispossession of the subjects involved.[39]

To base anthropological knowledge on the cultural decentring of ethnological tradition is further invalidated by the circulation of knowledge today. The polemics of recent years apropos of so-called 'postcolonial' or 'subalternist' research currents have shown very well a certain 'flattening' and a general relativizing of the theoretical, technical and political models existing on the planet. What the Indian historian Dipesh Chakrabarty has called the 'provincialization of Europe'[40] is today an established fact on the level of economic, cultural and social realities.

To sum up, the decentring that is needed today consists in overcoming the opposition between 'cultural relativism' and absolute universalism, so as to invent a universalism whose social and political context of reference is no longer a particular nation, civilization or culture, but the entire set of exchanges that exist on the world scale, of which persons in displacement, as we have said, have everyday routine experience. This is expressed both in a growing number of border situations (spatial, administrative, social or symbolic) and in a cosmopolitan condition that is increasingly often experienced, thus increasingly commonplace.

If it simply persists on the path of cultural relativism, the space of anthropology and its chances of contributing to the understanding of the contemporary world are considerably reduced for everyone. To be contemporary, therefore, anthropology must be less nostalgic, not to mention less of an apologia for what previously existed and what still exists 'elsewhere', at the price of reducing astonishment and fascination by reducing the distance from the other. It must emerge from the culturalism that is in a sense inherent to the ethnological 'programme', while rethinking this cultural and globalized dimension of decentring in present situations. Decentring, here and now, thus means taking account of globalization, and particularly of the greater circulation of knowledge, imaginaries and models that this has generated. In other words, conceiving a thought of the world based on an assumption of equality between all situations and conditions observed from the point of view of their place in knowledge.

The construction of epistemological decentring

Decentring anthropology is not so much a question of a reversal of gaze between former colonial countries and those formerly colonized, since this would mean that the global context had not changed. The theoretical question that is really posed in a perspective of decolonization of knowledge is, in my view, a double one. On the one hand, as we have just seen, there is the question of the possibility of a cosmopolitical context of knowledge, which implies neither consensus nor homogeneity, but simply the recognition of a common scale of magnitude and exchange. In fact, with increasing clarity it is the multipolarity of knowledges and points of view on the basis of which the world is viewed and represented that constructs the ensemble of anthropological knowledge about the world.[41]

On the other hand, beyond this cosmopolitical aspect of anthropology, there is also the question of envisaging the possibility of a world anthropology in which the ethnographic observation of local situations can be done everywhere with the world in mind, just as the persons observed in different social scenes have the world in mind in their own practices – in particular those persons in displacement, migrants and all women and men who have frequent and routine experience of borders as a relational context, as we have seen in the previous chapters.[42]

From whatever place the anthropological gaze on the world is applied, if it is not to risk enclosing itself in an identity-based essentialism to which its local anchoring orients it (a localism, or an inverted ethnocentrism), this gaze must also extract, from the first – cultural – decentring, the epistemological rather than culturalist dimension that will enable it to decentre itself in all fields. It is this epistemological stance that will make it possible to reconstruct and share a universal dimension of anthropological knowledge. This is why it is interesting for our argument here to return for a moment to the philosophical origin of the idea of decentring, in the age of Enlightenment, and to what ethnologists later made of this.

Decentring was the argument of Jean-Jacques Rousseau's *Discourse on the Origin and Basis of Inequality*. His argument is the non-natural character of human society and the need to conceive the other in order to think and relativize every social and political configuration.[43] This is what led Claude Lévi-Strauss to say that Rousseau had founded ethnology with this work.[44] Contrary to this interpretation, however, and more generally to what has most commonly been concluded from it, another reading is possible. It is not so much the 'savage' or the other in oneself (one's 'identity') that interested Rousseau in this project. The 'pure state of nature' did not have the status of the reality of a part of the world (largely unknown to the European worlds when Rousseau wrote), it was a bold hypothesis, not very secure in empirical terms but necessary, as he himself recognized in presenting his *Discourse*.[45] While forcing himself 'to form conjectures based solely on the nature of man and of the Beings that surround him, about what Mankind might have become if it had remained abandoned to itself',[46] this hypothesis enabled him to describe in counterpoint the non-natural, that is, the social and political path of societies into 'servitude', 'inequalities', 'conflict' and the production of 'supernumeraries' as an effect of the appropriation of the land, which Rousseau chose to take as a starting event: 'The first man who, having enclosed a piece of ground, to whom it occurred to say this is mine, and found people sufficiently simple to believe him, was the true founder of civil society.'[47] This declaration denotes the 'event' whose theoretical import was central for this philosopher.

In other words, it was 'civil man', his contemporary, whose characteristics Rousseau, the self-denoted 'citizen of Geneva', sought to describe, whose critique he sought to make, and vis-à-vis whom the hypothesis of the state of nature was an 'operator of alterity'.[48] On the one hand, it enabled him to show that things 'could have been otherwise' (a formula that could well be that of the 'deconstruction' of the seemingly obvious). On the other hand, to show that things '*can* be otherwise', by making or modifying the *social contract*, thus by intervening in law and politics.

Should we see Rousseau as an eighteenth-century revolutionary, or as 'the most ethnographic of philosophers'?[49] Claude Lévi-Strauss saw Rousseau's *Discourse on Inequality* as promoting a 'primitive identification' that, in his view, made him the first 'ethnographer', 'our master' and 'our brother'.[50] But apart from the fact that Rousseau never conducted ethnographic research, or even made long-distance journeys (unlike some of his contemporaries who were more curious about other worlds), we can think that it was more the method or the 'anthropological asceticism'[51] that interested Rousseau, rather than the discovery of the world. In other words, it was an epistemological stance, the need for a counterpoint to consider how the contemporary world of the author was constructed. This epistemological dimension has been shown very well by the reading that Louis Althusser gave in his three lectures on Rousseau (recorded in 1972 and published by Yves Vargas in 2012). Althusser flushes out the concepts of Rousseau's *Discourse* and its lack of realism,[52] thus restoring it to philosophy (and, we may think, the possibility of a general anthropology), rather than to the ethnology of savage man. Althusser shows how Rousseau needed to create a 'void' or an 'outside' of reason. Emphasizing the 'nothing' or the 'forest', this reified vision of primary disorder and chaos enabled him to go on to evoke in a radical way 'denaturation' as a founding process of the social.[53]

The immediate effect of epistemological decentring, as I have tried to present it in this critical re-reading of anthropological decentring, is the observation that the operator of alterity is the limit itself, the border in its full density, and not the different appearance. We find the chaotic and uncertain world of the limit in the visit that Tocqueville made to the Saginaw forest, the long border depicted earlier. The 'other', precisely the man or woman who embodies alterity, is the subject of the border, being visible and present, and a relationship is established with them, initially uncertain but increasingly less foreign and increasingly familiar. The place of the other, the border, is different from the exotic, fictional, virtual, ideal or dreamed-of elsewhere, as long as there has not been a relational experience of the latter in which a border of lived experience is re-created, which transforms the place and the individuals involved there.

Political decentring: the question of the other-as-subject

A third decentring follows logically from what we have already said. The object of our attention should be *everything that the border is the place of*: whether things that happen in this situation (a limited or even liminal one) or something that comes from 'outside', reaches there and proceeds further, upsetting the established identity-based order. Epistemological decentring is thus at the same time political, in the sense that it privileges action and the watershed moment that introduces a change into a given social order, thus offering the possibility of seeing and understanding the movement and change that is going on, identifying the other-subject who is the bearer of this disturbance or, to use the words of the philosopher Jacques Rancière, who utters and brings into existence a 'share of the shareless'.[54]

This new decentring founds a regime of epistemological equality between all observable situations, and opens the way to an anthropology of the emergence of the subject in each observed situation (as we shall see in more detail in the final chapter). It enables us not to renounce but rather to apply in a fundamental way the decentred gaze inherited from the oldest anthropological gesture.

A contemporary and situational anthropology

If cultural decentring has long been seen as 'the' fundamental anthropological gesture, in a programme or lineage that is essentially *ethno*logical and of culturalist orientation, the decentring that now becomes central for giving meaning to the anthropological gaze on the world is *epistemological* and 'in situation'.

Epistemological decentring is already situational, it involves the anthropologist's investigation. On the ground, it means shifting the place and moment of attention from centre and order towards edges and disorder. It means taking, as observation post and starting-point of reflection, border situations in the very generic and anthropological sense of spaces and situations of the in-between, thresholds and limits, but also moments of uncertainty and indecision. It is necessary constantly to be there and decentre oneself, to seek everywhere the limit of social unity, of the place or practice observed. I have for example considered the space of refugee camps, the 'ghetto' of migrants in the forest or of their descendants in the city (or on its outskirts), the border zone between Guinea and Sierra Leone, that alongside the port of Patras in Greece, the districts where Afro-Colombian migrants congregate on the outskirts of Cali, or again the space-time of the street invaded by the carnival parade in Bahia, as all so many space-times of *border situations*. By shifting the focus onto the in-between of borders – which, as we have seen, can be grasped from the point of view of space, time and relationships – the descriptions and analyses of the anthropologist acquire the means of seeing processes and origins, contacts and transformations. What I shall tackle now is the third point of method, that which involves the updating of anthropology's modes of observation and analysis.

WYSIWYG: *what you see is what there is*

It is clear that the reality of the new ethnographic fields I have just mentioned – though the list can be extended – can no longer be confused with the illusion of timelessness on which the habitual mode of description known as the 'ethnographic present' was based – an absolute present of a supposedly eternal culture apart from history, in which the ethnologist was in a sense the qualified specialist. The 'ethnographic present' has been the form of writing by way of which ahistorical truths were supposedly provided, even though the information on which they were based was collected at a particular place

101

and time. As Johannes Fabian wrote in 1983, 'if we compare the uses of time in anthropological writing with those of ethnographic research, we discover a remarkable divergence. I shall call this the schizogenic use of time.'[55] On the contrary, he goes on to note, it is necessary to recognize the 'coevalness' of the ethnologist and his or her objects, and draw the consequences of this in anthropological description, which is not separable from interpretation.

The ethnologist's process of knowledge, whatever the nature of their field, actually proceeds between two poles that postmodern critics have sucessfully identified. On the one hand, the dialogue of the field, in the sense that it is at a moment of exchange with his hosts that the ethnologist learns things: this dialogue inscribes the contemporaneity between the researcher and their 'object' in the properties of the very materials gathered. On the other hand, the fiction of writing – 'fiction' here meaning not a lie or an invention, but a description that is selective, synthetic or analytic, and responds to a certain convention of writing specific to the anthropological tradition.

One of the risks indicated by the so-called 'textualist' critiques mentioned earlier is the production of a monologue, that is, a single discourse that does not echo the plurality of voices heard on the ground, but also, we should add, a total and unified view of the field observed, from which conflicts, deviant forms and divergent subjects are absent.

Moreover, writing in the so-called 'ethnographic present' transcribes in the mode of an absolute or eternal (in other words, atemporal) present the data gathered in an actuality in which pragmatic issues, arising from the moment at which these data were collected, may well have had a decisive influence. The 'ethnographic present' makes the contemporary contexts of the collection of data disappear.

It is these various biases that make for what Fabian called the 'schizogenic use of time'. How can we avoid this? By re-establishing the contemporaneity of actions, statements and exchanges observed in situation and in their context, starting from the principle that what I see is not an altered version of truths that have arisen from another place or time, inherent ontological identities that are more 'real' than those I observe, but that have been lost or disappeared and need to be rediscovered by eliminating those contemporary elements that would spoil the image (electricity generators with strong diesel smells, Coca-Cola bottles, damage to the soil, the alcoholism and suicide of Amerindians).[56] What I see, hear and note is the reality of what I share, in its true context and true temporality. 'What You See Is What You Get' (WYSIWYG), as advertisements for new software programs said in the 1990s, meaning that what you saw on the screen was the image of the page to be printed. We can take this advert and say apropos of the anthropological field of investigation: what you see is what there is, there is no hidden identity-based or 'cultural' truth that the ethnologist has to reveal, behind the contemporary truth of what is observed. On the contrary, a writing that breaks with this 'schizogenic' tendency will have to be ethnographically reflexive, in empathy with the situations observed, allowing a closer description of the research findings, and therefore more contemporary.

What is the contemporary for anthropology? First of all, it is the trace of what is in the process of happening in the actual moment and situation of the investigation, and therefore its reflexive presence in the anthropologist's text. The trace of movement, of change, of the first breath of what is to come.

To find how this principle is applied in anthropology, we can start from a research 'current' that formed in the 1950s and 1960s, and whose lineage would be determinant for contemporary anthropology. It is found among French and British anthropologists working on colonial fields and those of decolonization in sub-Saharan Africa, such as Georges Balandier or Gérard Althabe in France, and Max Gluckman or Clyde Mitchell in British anthropology.[57] Balandier's analyses of the 'colonial situation' in central Africa, those of Gluckman or Mitchell on the presentation of relationships between whites and blacks in the context of social or ritual situations in southern Africa, contributed in a decisive way to defining this situational approach. It is interesting to note that this was born in the midst of a major political conflict in world history, decolonization, which in a way was echoed in an equally major theoretical conflict, one that saw a situational and contextual conception of anthropology beat a narrow path between the then dominant culturalist and structuralist interpretations.

The contribution of situational anthropology

Situational anthropology made it possible, first of all, to grasp in its totality the complexity of what was happening in the colonial context, instead of keeping only the cultural and ethnic aspects artificially separated from their context. On this framework, ethnographic reflexivity became a real theoretical tool, giving a central place to the relationship between the anthropologist and his or her contemporary. Ethnography is the material of the contemporary in anthropological knowledge. Grasping it thus means constructing anthropology from a reflection on the situation, based on relationships and communication formed between the observer and the subjects of his research.[58]

The situational approach subsequently made it possible to take account of social or political situations marked by the unforeseen or by an extraordinary and uncertain character, even an exceptional one, in which change could be studied. It was not a question of denying the importance of 'social structures', rather of approaching these only from the perspective of the effective constraint that they imposed on observed situations. On this point, the epistemology developed by Jean Barzin for observation and description allows the situational dimension of contemporary anthropology to be spelled out more clearly:

> In reality, society is not something I can observe. No matter how remote or small it is, I can never take a perspective from Sirius. All that I ever observe are *situations*. To observe a situation (as distinct from observing a planet) is to be there. If I observe it, I form part of it, though in the position of an outsider. Out of scholarly interest, therefore, I act so as to find myself (even by provoking them) in situations that present a degree of relative foreignness, but sufficient so that, not knowing what they are doing, I undertake to learn this.[59]

This is a pragmatic posture for anthropology, conceived on the basis of a 'degree of foreignness' that is not ethnic or culturalist, but relative and pragmatic ('for the moment, I don't know what they are doing'), and according to which the ignorance in which I deliberately place myself will disappear when I have been able to understand and describe how they are acting. The hypothesis is humanist because it is anthropological ('the human race begins with my next-door neighbour') and not culturalist ('this is their custom and it is irremediably other').

The situational anthropological procedure thus presented is doubly distinct from structuralist presuppositions. On the sociological side, by avoiding at the same time social prejudices (formed by a blind determinism), intellectual reifications (assuming abstract categories to be real) and a deductive theoretical procedure (going from analytical categories to practices as 'illustrations' of these), the situational approach investigates the weight of contexts in observed situations. On the anthropological side, rather than seeking to isolate facts from their context so as to extract universal laws from them (in this way losing everything that they owe to these contexts, thus to history and geography, and forgetting that things could have been otherwise in other times and places), the situational analysis brings the universalist ambition of anthropology to bear not on a supposedly structural or collective unconscious, but rather on the processes, conditions, forms and effects of the observed dynamics. This leads for example to an investigation spurred by the recurrent creative and dynamic effects of border situations, which runs through all the reflections of the present work.

Finally, there is one last aspect that I see as crucial, but which pertains more to feeling or intuition than to method in the strict sense of the term. It is not very far from the previous question (the relation between structure and situation), but in this case, rather than resolving it by a convergence between ethnographic research and contextual analysis, the question is how to approach a dimension of facts that is vaguely definable a priori by what we could call 'all the remnants' of structural analysis. It is an unthought, an in-between or a counterpoint, corresponding for example to what Victor Turner has called the '*anti*-structure'[60] and, in a fairly comparable epistemological positioning, what Marc Augé has called 'non-place' (a concept whose success has led people to forget that it is constructed in relation and in opposition to the 'anthropological place'). In the same way, this instance corresponds to what Georges Balandier has analysed as the necessity and dynamic of 'disorder'.[61] And this same in-between corresponds again to the border situations described earlier, marked by a social or ritual liminality. We can see in a general way that all these 'instances' are pervaded by practices of a transgressive, individual, informal or unforeseen type, description of which allows us to deploy decentred analyses of the emergence of subjects. In this decentring of the gaze, finally, the place of social order is relativized, becoming no longer the norm, but a moment and a part of a process in which order and disorder alternate and confront one another.

The situational approach thus makes possible an empirical foundation for a true anthropology of the subject, as the decentring it permits is above all epistemological. It consists in 'seeing coming' everything whose place is a border situation. By taking up a position in the place of separation from an 'outside', a void or a supposed 'state of nature', in fact an unknown (individual, fact or world), I place myself where an encounter takes place with an 'external real that forcefully imposes itself on us, questioning our habitual ways of thinking'.[62] And after this long methodological detour, this takes us back to the border. A border of identities, place and cultures, within which the capacity to act will have the name of 'subject'.

— 5 —

CIVILIZATION, CULTURE, RACE: THREE EXPLORATIONS IN IDENTITY

The decades of the decolonization/post-Cold War/global governance sequence, from the 1950s to today, have seen a revision of the models and concepts needed to understand the world. The contemporary turn in anthropology, which we have just discussed, developed in this context. Thinking in this change of contexts requires a constant questioning. While the change has given rise to critical analyses of 'identitarian constructions', bringing to light the key place of border situations for understanding identity-based discourses, the latter have continued to spread as a political form. Political in the sense of the exercise of power and of divisions between the recognition of some and the relegation of others, or political in the sense of languages of rejection and collective action for recognition.

Three notions have more particularly marked the conflicts of the late twentieth and early twenty-first centuries across the world: that of civilization – which we shall study here by investigating the meaning and uses of the notion of civilization in the ways of seeing Africa and on converse strategies coming from Africa; that of culture, which we shall examine in relation to the mobility and identity of migrants in the Pacific region of Colombia; and that of race, its meanings and its uses, more particularly in France and in Brazil. The three cases studied here all have something to do with displacements, borders and globalization. And they show the complexity of the identity question as a social question.

Civilization as hyper-border: mirrors of Africa

Samuel Huntington's book *The Clash of Civilizations* has clearly shown that the language of civilizations is above all a language of international relations – at best diplomatic, at worst warlike.[1] This political language dominates and traps an entire other dimension, cultural, historical or geographical, which we would prefer to use 'peacefully' to say all the good that we think of others.

Everything indicates that in a world in recomposition, the hyper-border could well be, as Huntington claims, 'civilizational', with civilizations corresponding to vague 'collective identities' based on the author's understanding of religious secularization. Huntington combines the violence of the identity-based 'clash' with a weakness of cultural argument. His language is warlike, for without ever saying exactly what he is speaking of when he refers to 'cultural' or 'civilizational' borders, or what there is to understand in the societies at which he points his finger, he conjugates culture and civilization using a military metaphor: 'the platoons are tribes and ethnic groups, the regiments are nations, and the armies are civilizations'.[2] In his critical reading of Huntington's 'civilizations', Étienne Balibar observes that 'the existence of borders at which the conflict of civilizations is played out has as its correlate, in this perspective, the constant possibility of war as an expression of its political logic'.[3]

But if it is exacerbated today in global public debate, this political and identity-based – even warlike – dimension of the idea of civilization is not new; it has been present from the start of its uses as a way of thinking and classifying the 'other' in a context of domination and violence. Civilizational language is warlike. It is mechanically external (conversely, as soon as one enters and immerses oneself in an unfamiliar world, the idea of civilization becomes obsolete and inoperative). It pertains to a culturalist caricature, at best hermeneutic (interpreting the culture of others as a homogeneous and isolated block), at worst classificatory and naturalist, even racialist (compiling inventories and tables of 'other' cultural traits). The inventory of irreducible differences labelled 'other' creates a barrier that assumes the impossibility of communication and mutual understanding. This obscurantism is where the trap lies.

Why should the word 'civilization' be the first step on the scale of values of integration into the world? Why believe in the reality of the categories and hierarchies of values that it produces? How can its warlike language make a claim to universalism? We shall try here to answer these questions, by surveying a few decades of the changing use and meaning of 'African civilization'.

The 1950s: 'One civilization accused by another!'

African 'civilization' only appeared on the world cultural stage when it was brought into crisis: it was an updating at the same time as an entry onto the stage, between the end of the nineteenth century and the first half of the twentieth. Indissociable from the racialism forged as a 'theory' of unequal races throughout the nineteenth century, the European gaze on Africa bore the imprint of representations of the 'slave-other' and the racialization of the violent domination that had marked the centuries of the Atlantic slave trade and slave societies.[4]

Having arrived to 'commercialize, Christianize and civilize', colonialism would discover African civilizations at the same time as it found itself in the process of damaging them. Ethnology would be responsible for revealing this alterity, as an objectifiable whole, by way of conceptualizations that were varied but mutually associated, and converging on the idea of an African culture or philosophy: ethnic and tribal entities, primitive societies and arts, beliefs, cosmologies and unwritten knowledge, the worlds of magic and ritual. By naturalist procedures of summary and inventory, the material of an 'other' ensemble was found, but one whose qualification as 'civilization' was not automatic, given the unequal relationship of the colonial and imperial context in which these civilizational characteristics were constructed. The revealed discovery of a 'civilizational' difference was made in a confrontation, contrast and conflict of representations of Africa, in which anthropology was involved well beyond its initial mission, which aimed to produce colonial knowledge.

Just as ethnology was, at its origins, at the same time a science of alterity and a child of colonialism, so the recognition of an African civilization (or of many) was ambiguous from the start. Proceeding from the most distant perspective to the closest, this gaze sought to reach the 'heart' of a civilization at a single stroke, its penetration achieved in the name of an a priori holism attributed to the 'other' and built around the central idea (indispensable in this reasoning) of the 'persona': in the supposed holism of the other, the whole and the part are superimposed, each individual embodies the whole of a society, a culture, whereas the individualism opposed to it supposedly comes from a 'self' – and European 'civilization' is the supposed place of this valorization of the individual, the sign of modernity. Besides, everything that is brought to light in this context to characterize the persona in black Africa pertains to such very particular themes as funerary cults, the worship of ancestors, sacrifice, cosmology, which define a set of practices perceived, rightly or wrongly, as foreign to Western civilization.

'Civilization' in sub-Saharan Africa thus became the name of a synthesis of regional diversity legible from outside, achieved by way of a number of dualist distinctions: forest/savannah, farmers/herders, stateless ('acepehalic') societies/state societies (possibly with classes of merchants and warriors), polytheism/monotheism, patrilineal/matrilineal, etc. These distinctions were still too simple, but provided a few swift keys for deciphering an alterity that was in actual fact quite reduced: the division into moieties that certain ethnologists made their golden rule, and particularly the forest/savannah opposition, which, as Georges Balandier notes, 'represents no more than the most convenient of attempts made to arrange the discouraging African diversity'.[5]

If we proceed in the opposite direction through successive circles, from the 'heart' of societies out to the most remote surrounding 'world', we see the totalizing civilizational gaze break down into a multitude of parts, transitions and secant spaces. But the dominating figure itself thickens the border between outside and inside. A first border of alterity is located on the boundary of the lineage, and then by successive degrees on that of the 'great lineage', the clan, tribe and finally ethnic group: lineage (itself or its extensions) is a 'communitarian' heart of identity and society that is always referred to in connection with black Africa, but whose singleness is in fact fragile. Lineage appears as a sphere of social constraints, and its breakdown leads to an emancipation in which the other spheres of constraint are not immediately visible. The urbanization and decolonization of the 1950s and 1960s thus marked an increasing fragilization of lineage throughout sub-Saharan Africa, and a 'seizure of initiative' by individuals as workers, migrants or town dwellers.[6]

Between the slowness of histories in the family world and the rapid change in political, economic and postcolonial contexts, the possibility of a completely lineage-based society was put forward. At the very least, the African presence was expressed in the postcolonial formation of 'supra-ethnic' powers by the symbolic instrumentalization of lineage: supreme power on the national scale was legitimized as a symbolic articulation of lineage powers and their vertical extension up to encounter and proximity with the white world, supposedly all-powerful. This form of government marked a good number of nation-states in the first phase of independence. The articulation between

109

African and European 'worlds' was the major political and theoretical question in this period of decolonization and 'development': an articulation between domestic and capitalist 'modes of production' in the economic field,[7] between white states and African states,[8] or between (postcolonial) oppression and (imaginary) liberation in the field of religion.[9]

We therefore need to go back a bit further in time in order to see the question of alterity problematized quite differently, along with that of conflict and/or contemporaneity apropos of and starting from lineage, in a different political and interpretative context. Georges Balandier recognized the existence of an 'undeniable "primitive dirigisme"' while warning against an 'illusory liberation of individuals'.[10] If Balandier certainly highlighted the perspective of a loss (a 'weakening of traditional frameworks'), this was because he was led in the context of the 1950s (only a few years after the great UNESCO studies of racism and cultural difference in the world) to investigate the hold of 'Western civilization' on an Africa still under the colonial yoke. His approach was distinct from that of ethnologies of ethnic and tribal culture studied outside of context, a procedure against which Balandier stood as a champion of decolonization, seeing this as also having a cultural dimension.

This was the committed and political stance that guided and motivated the writing of *Afrique ambiguë*, a book published in the 'Terre humaine' series two years after Claude Lévi-Strauss's *Tristes tropiques*. Chapter after chapter, Balandier spells out the empirical reasons for the necessity of recognizing civilization in black Africa, in both the west and the centre of the continent. He introduces an exchange with one of his 'informants' in the following terms: 'To hear him, everything has been lost that could give existence a full and exalting sense. After having summed up all the present "miseries" [. . .], he concludes our series of interviews with an ambiguous morale: "That's civilization!" This is one civilization being accused by another. We are judged by a modest peasant from a very humble village.'[11]

Since the start of the colonial enterprise, 'civilization' was in fact perceived as the possession of the West (as indicated, moreover, by the use of the term 'civilized' to refer to those Africans who had attended European schools and learned French or English). At the same time, the new anthropologists of this generation broke with the Africanist ethnology known as *griaulienne* – after Marcel Griaule, who undertook in the 1930s the most systematic research into Dogon cosmogony and 'African thought' (this intellectual legacy continued

110

through to the 1980s). Breaking therefore with 'Africanist ethnology', the new generation of anthropologists, seeing the close but uncertain perspective of African independence, waged a real struggle against the steamroller of 'Western civilization' and were thus led to write their own contribution to the elaboration of the concept of civilization for black Africa.

Michel Leiris, who was a contemporary of Balandier, had taken part in the Dakar–Djibouti mission under the direction of Marcel Griaule (before breaking with the latter a few years later) – an ethnographic expedition carried out in 1931–3, which Leiris's diary relates in largely initiatory and poetic terms.[12] Leiris then expressed his position in a text written for UNESCO in 1951, entitled 'Race and Civilization'. His conclusion was pessimistic, noting the violent advances of Western industrial civilization and the risks that this violence involved for the world. His polemical reflection at this time went hand in hand with an egalitarian humanism:

> Who could maintain that the Pygmy hunter, in the depths of the Congolese forest, leads a life less adapted than that of our European factory worker? The fact is that still today, in the vast crossroads that the world has become and the means of communication that he has at his disposal, the man of white race and Western culture holds the upper hand, no matter the threats of collapse that he feels rising from within and outside against a civilization that he regards as the only one deserving that name.[13]

This political version of a struggle for the equality of civilizations went together with an aesthetic analysis and revelation of the artefacts of civilization, particularly in areas where formal comparison was possible, such as architecture, masks and sculpture. It is interesting to follow here the way in which a major European sociologist, Norbert Elias, was able to discover, love and interpret the work of traditional artistic creation on the occasion of a two-year spell at the University of Accra in Ghana, where he arrived in 1962 (Ghana under Nkrumah had then been independent for five years).[14] Elias did this by investigating the place of the artist and/or artisan in society, and vis-à-vis his work, as he would do for art in Western societies. Spurning a curatorial enthusiasm for conservation in the face of the disappearance of artworks and the impossibility of reproducing them since they were born in a social or sacred context that was tending to disappear, and keeping an equal distance from any ethnicization or 'civilizational' praise, Elias emphasized two aspects that very directly echo the debates and commitments mentioned here.

111

On the one hand, the masks and statuettes he collected were works whose original intent was not aesthetic but rather sacred and communitarian: 'In the course of rituals, these masks *are* spirits or gods, who appear in person to their people. Outside of these occasions, the sentiments that they arouse sometimes disappear completely and, no longer having any power over people, they may be thrown away and abandoned to weather and termites.'[15] In parallel with this, he notes, the creators of these artefacts perceived themselves as artisans rather than as artists.

On the other hand, Elias takes up in his own way the struggle for equality that his contemporaries were waging: 'the artistic significance [of these 'sculptures and other works of art'] goes beyond these closed communities (even if it is hard for their members to be aware of this). Perceived in its totality, it must be considered a major stage in the development of artistic creation and its productions as an important part of the artistic heritage of humanity.'[16] This point of view is quite classically dualist ('closed communities' versus 'humanity'), as if the political or aesthetic struggle for civilizational equality was trapped from the start by the obligation to characterize and thus maintain the very idea of civilization.

1980s and 1990s: deconstructions, reinventions

What became of the idea of African civilization after the wave of independence in sub-Saharan Africa? As shown by the conflicting commitments already discussed, the idea of civilization, like that of identity, intervenes when the question of borders is raised. It is interesting therefore to see what happens to it at a moment when we find ourselves 'on' the border.

The relationship to the other produces the need to think one's identity detached from the context of birth and in a way that can found a thought of exile. It is the triple displacement – at the same time the exile of the subject, the gaze of the other, and the decontextualization of cultural practices – that provokes the attempt to objectify certain practices and their convergence in a new context of interpretation: this was how the dance of ritual possession became a major feature of African civilizations, as Georges Balandier notes, but we see that it is in exile that this objectification takes place, as well as a transformation: 'The dance of possession belongs to one of the deepest layers that African civilizations reveal to us today. It is a phenomenon of extraordinary vigour, a constant while so many other cultural traits have disappeared', he could still write in *Afrique ambiguë* (1957), continuing: 'The transplanted and dispossessed blacks introduced it into the New World, where it became the conservatory of their lost civilizations: voodoo in Haiti, *macumba* and *candomblé* in Brazil, *santería* in Cuba, whose echoes still reach us, sometimes desacralized but still powerful.'[17] Roger Bastide, a contemporary and friend of Balandier, mentioned in the same period before African independence the 'preserved African cultures' and the 'principle of rift' that in Brazil separates the 'African' from Western culture.

Cultural shifts have continued their constant advance, to the point of being analysable today no longer in terms of conservation and rift, but only according to cultural dynamics related to the social contexts of their creation, processes and contexts that are in constant transformation at both local and global levels. However, if the spirit of a 'conservatory of lost civilizations' is today making a return on the planetary scale, and particularly focuses on African civilizations, this is practically no longer the case in the debates and writings of researchers who have largely 'deconstructed' it, but is rather under the aspect of 'heritage'. On the one hand, an institutional heritage project led by states and UN agencies: from this point of view, Senegal and Benin are in the lead among West African countries in a global movement of African culture, largely deterritorialized, whose wide area, complexity, and cultural and political potentialities have been shown by Paul Gilroy's work,[18] itself located on the watershed between deconstruction and reinvention. On the other hand, in a contemporary sense, the heritage approach has been taken up by social and urban movements whose ethnopolitical strategies involve the quest (in the form of return) for a cultural identity, reinventing for the occasion what it would be better to call an identity-based culture (see later in this chapter). The 'African diaspora' across the world, a network that is in part heritage-based, is the conceptual angle that gives meaning and a multilocalized territory to strategies of emancipation that are anchored and sometimes even bogged down in a *postcolonial* history.

As we have mentioned, a change of paradigm set in at the watershed of the 1980s and 1990s. This reanimated, while modifying, a counter-civilizational discourse whose conflictual content had already become clearly apparent at the time of the independence struggles of the 1950s and 1960s. This gave way to a critique that was already embryonic, and to a more radical theoretical 'deconstruction' in the 1960s and 1970s, a period marked in the Western world by emancipation struggles, cultural insurrection, and support for independentist, anticolonialist and national liberation movements.

Finally, in the post-Cold War period, the resurgence of identity on the ruins of deconstruction replays case by case the map of African civilization in the struggles over heritage that enable certain African countries to achieve both a political and an economic place in a globalized world under construction. Thus, the cosmogonies and masks of the Dogon as presented by the ethnologist Marcel Griaule are today in Mali a local and national resource; they are brought out and polished to promote development by way of cultural tourism:[19] for young people in the Dogon lands, the game now consists in 'playing Dogon', and the object is to be identifiable and carve out a place on the global scale.

A global and diffuse African presence

Can we still speak of 'African civilization', and if so, how? The term is still used in a very generic way, taking advantage of its simplicity and its false obviousness, in order to interest a wide public, both scholarly and touristic, in Africa. The contents of books explicitly devoted to it (as proclaimed by their titles) today restore the complexity and 'discouraging African diversity' (Balandier), for example in the form of a dictionary which has very varied entries (regions, states, leaders, themes, etc.) yet gives no definition of 'civilization': this simply serves as a geo-cultural marker.[20] In greater detail, from an empirical point of view, the term covers a set of cultural practices united in supra-ethnic and supra-local contexts, but which leave or have left an identifiable imprint in space, even if the boundaries of this are vague. Thus, the political form of empire or kingdom is associated with the idea of civilization, which makes it possible to link together culture, space and power in terms of simple ideas: the Gao or Songhai empire, Mandingo civilization, Bornu empire and Hausa civilization, the Kongo kingdom and civilization, etc.

Finally, works on the civilizations of black Africa may include a critical reflection on the place of the question of civilization in history, thus showing the ambivalence of the theme, both criticized and used as an 'entry' into other problematics. This is the case with the work of the historian Élikia M'Bokolo, *Afrique noire: Histoire et civilisations*.[21] On the one hand, the unity 'black Africa' is decomposed into questions and periods with a great deal of overlapping. The questions of borders and boundaries, imbalances and confrontations, guide studies of political and ecological spaces or historical periods. The critical approach, that of deconstruction (discussed earlier), is also found in the uses of the term 'civilization'. Out of twenty-eight

114

occurrences indexed, the notion is used twenty-three times in a critical sense or as critique of a usage cited: critique of the 'humanitarian and civilizing principles' invoked to justify colonization, the colonists' 'civilizing duty' based on forced labour, or again the presentation and questioning of the 'ideology of the three "C"s' (the 'civilizing' of Africa by Christianity and commerce).[22] Four times, with the same authorial distance, the term is used in the opposite sense, that of African emancipation, or of pan-Africanism and contemporary movements that assert the superiority of 'African civilization' over European. And finally, just once, 'civilization' denotes in a more conventional sense the material and intellectual culture left by a long and brilliant history, that of the Bamum in Cameroon, their kingdom and their writing. It is not hard to imagine that this relates to the major place that material culture and masks hold in the history and actuality of royalty in this region of western Cameroon.[23]

It is obvious enough that Africa's presence-in-the-world does involve objects and practices recognized as cultural (pertaining to art and thought, where the world of reference is that of UNESCO), leading both to contemporary artistic inventions and bricolage, and to heritage strategies that are apparently conservatory. On the global scale, what seems to be taking shape today is a 'concert of civilizations' that has become an unavoidable stake in global multipolarity, whereas the fragility of nation-states makes the idea of a 'concert of nations' or a 'league of nations' rather bankrupt. This global 'reality' is built around the fiction of civilization while being the very opposite of a 'war of civilizations'; and it is a discursive instrument of recognition that can be used by Africans dispersed in a multiple, heterogeneous, deterritorialized Africa-space. Is this a renewal of the struggle for recognition of one civilization against or vis-à-vis another dominant one? Not exactly, since the colonial context is over and the scale of relationships has changed.

The political presence, and the (privatizable) economic presence of Africa in the world, are certainly in the sights of this critical reflection on the very idea of civilization as applied to Africa. The three conflictual temporalities we have discussed here are now gathered in a single hand: colonial conflict, anticolonial deconstruction and postcolonial reinvention. To emerge from these three unsettled conflicts is to 'emerge from the dark night' and decolonize thinking of Africa as championed by the historian Achille Mbembe, himself inspired by the work of Frantz Fanon.[24] It also means escaping from the identity trap that the very idea of civilization illustrates, whatever the polemical response that is brought to this.

115

Some people seek to defend an African presence in the global 'concert' by seeing this sphere as a place for the (re)construction, by elites, of an 'African identity'. 'This reconstruction', notes Mbembe, 'is conducted in two directions. One of these consists in an effort of re-enchantment for tradition and custom. The other proceeds by abstraction from tradition, its main concern being the emergence of a modern and deterritorialized self.'[25] It is noticeable, however, that the search for African recognition *in* the globalized, cosmopolitan world transforms and muddies the conditions of production of locality. The reunification of local and global strategies still lies ahead.

I shall make a few comments on the basis of an observation conducted in postwar Sierra Leone (in the north-east region of the country, around the town of Kailahun) in late 2003, as a contribution to this debate. In this region, pacification depends on 'customary chiefs' who, though native to the region, have in fact returned from Harvard University to participate in postwar reconstruction. On the occasion of the renewal of the long ceremonies of male Mende initiation (the *poro*), which had been interrupted for more than ten years because of war, the new 'paramount chief' challenged and saw off the disrespectful intrusion of international humanitarian organizations, which were numerous in this savannah region. In the time of disorder and renegotiation that marked the immediate postwar period, the savannah was thus reappropriated and reoccupied by its inhabitants. The alliance between chiefs who had returned from a distant and formative journey to the United States, and peasant families of initiates who had 'returned' from their refuge in neighbouring countries, was the necessary condition for the symbolic effect of a 'tradition' that was completely replayed on a new stage, at the same time local and global. It was in the interstices of three worlds united in this one place (the international humanitarian and security community, the returned African elites, the 'returned' peasant families) that this effect was possible; it was here that it acquired its double constraining and transforming duplication; and it is the traffickers, negotiators and translators who hold the keys of this change.

The migration of spirits: mobilities and identity-based cultures

The contemporary period, starting from the watershed of the 1980s and 1990s, has been a time of manufacture (generally urban) of identity-based cultures, rather than one of simple manifestation of 'cultural identities'. Asserted as self-evident, ancestral and inherited,

116

these are superimposed on the most varied foundations of exhibition and mediatization (carnivals, websites, art and cinema festivals). In this way they gain access to the 'global' world and, especially in Africa and Latin America, to the subsidies that this visibility may bring. At the same time, and under the effect of this work of positioning on a global scale, they have experienced a period of profound transformation in their symbolic corpus.

To develop this argument, and to understand better the cultural changes associated with mobilities and the crossing of local, regional or national borders, we can 'follow' the migration of spirits from the Pacific forest in Colombia – a region of forest, rivers and mangroves, bordering the equator – to the small town of Tumaco, the primary urban reference for inhabitants of the region, then to the city of Cali (the third largest in the country after Bogotá and Medellín) and Charco Azul, one of the most deprived districts in the vast working-class sector of Agua Blanca on the periphery of this city. These sprits (imaginary characters from the world of the forest) accompany the trajectories of migrants and are transformed along with them.[26]

The Devil, the priest and black culture (Colombian Pacific)

I can say that I 'discovered' black Colombian culture in the small town of Tumaco on the occasion of a carnival held there in 1998, shortly before the arrival of the paramilitaries who banned all such festivals for several years. In the rain and mud of a very poor equatorial region and town, which regularly experienced the caprices of the ocean (high tides, floods) and the rapid and destructive spread of fires (in a town very largely built of wood), this little carnival was bound to be disordered and 'dirty', very much in the popular carnival tradition. In 1998, then, a procession (*comparsa*) known as the 'return of the marimba' marked for the first time the official opening of the carnival. The little show was composed of a selection of various mythical elements, largely drawn from regional memory and assembled in an unusual presentation which I shall briefly describe. We have first of all to explain that the marimba is a kind of suspended wooden xylophone based on the Mandingo balafon. It consists of eighty tablets made of hard palm wood (*chonta*), set above sounding tubes of bamboo (*guadua*). The marimba is generally played by two performers, each using two sticks with raw rubber ends to strike one half of the keyboard, either the bass (*bajos*) or the treble (*tiple*). The existence of the marimba is attested beyond Colombia on the Pacific shores of Ecuador and Peru. It is the main instrument of the old

117

'marimba balls', 'Negro dances' or *currulao*: festivals that were formerly held in the riverside villages of the region as well as in the small town of Tumaco. They have now disappeared in this form, and since the 1960s have sometimes been depicted on stage, with a few choreographic modifications, in shows of traditional music and dance.

In the procession in its honour, the marimba is held two metres above the ground by four men on stilts, preceded by a priest, Father Jesus Maria Mera, walking in front of the stage. He represents a legendary priest active throughout the region in the early twentieth century, who it is said forced the blacks, on pain of excommunication, to throw the marimbas into the sea because they were the 'instrument of the Devil'. Two other characters, likewise on stilts, play side by side on the same marimba: one represents the Devil, dressed in red and with a horned headpiece; the other represents a famous marimba player (*marimbero*), Francisco Saya, who died in 1983 and who, according to local legend, dared to 'defy the Devil' and defeated him by his playing. Throughout the procession the burlesque fight between the Devil and the *marimbero* is played out behind the priest's back. They are surrounded by three characters whose costumes represent some of the best-known *visiones* (apparitions, spirits) of the Colombian Pacific region: the Duende (mischievous sprite, musician and seducer of young virgins), the Tunda (female *visión* of the mangroves and forest) and the Viuda (the widow, who generally appears in cemeteries). There is also the green and white flag of the town of Tumaco, stretched above the marimba.

When I asked for explanations as to the meaning of this inaugural procession, its organizers spoke to me at length of the legends of Father Mera, the marimba and the *marimbero* Francisco Saya. According to these commentaries, the Catholic church, dominant and white, repressed pagan displays: in the opening procession, the character of Father Mera embodies the power of the church. He is the only character for whom the (black) actor has his face painted white. Behind him, the formerly banned marimba ball (or 'Negro ball') is represented, along with the *marimbero*'s defiance of the Devil. The *marimbero*, 'black with smooth hair' or 'black with Indian hair', represents, I was told, a figure of resistance, clandestine and ethnic.

For its promoters, the 'return' in force of the marimba embodied by this *comparsa* (which, we should recall, officially opened the town carnival this and the following year) is metaphorically the 'return' of the black culture of the Pacific that was repressed both in history and in the present. These 'returns' make fun of Father Mera, and make the 'greatest of *marimberos*', Francisco Saya, an ethnic hero. The *visiones*, for their part, are neutralized; they seem to have lost their magic power that was formerly diabolized as a force for evil, but today is effaced from the scene.

The local legends summoned up by the authors to promote a culture labelled 'black' (subsequently called 'Afro-Colombian', and later 'Afro-descendent') have thus been reinterpreted and thereby transformed. This is particularly the case with the figure of Father Mera, now far more white than he was previously! Several accounts, both written and oral, as well as legends gathered in the more remote riverside villages, speak in fact of the priest as a *padrecito negro* ('little black priest'); 'his hair was rather curly, he was dark brown verging on black', and his grandfather had been a slave.[27] Father Mera believed in the Devil and the *visiones*, which is why he 'defied' them, so much so that people still say today that he might well have been the Devil himself.

The legends of Father Mera, the marimba and the Devil circulated from the rivers to the town and, like other urban legends,[28] can still be further elaborated with personal touches (someone saw someone who saw someone who saw the *visión*) and so spread further. All along the parades, soon covered with the flour and mud of the carnival, a number of *visiones*, alone and skipping along like the habitual figures of carnivalesque devilry, thus parade alongside Donald Duck, Macho Man or a drunk and lustful priest: these are the Duende, the Viuda, the Tunda and the Madremontes. One of these characters, the Tunda, is also found in the city of Cali, where it has undergone major transformations.

The Tunda as urban monster (Charco Azul, Cali)

In Cali, a city with over two million inhabitants, the vast working-class *distrito* of Agua Blanca occupies the entire east side. At least half of its 600,000 or more inhabitants are Afro-Colombian migrants and their descendants who have come from the country's Pacific coast. One part of the district, built on a marshy zone, has long been marked by a number of ponds, which started to be filled in towards the end of the 1980s. One of these, Charco Azul (the 'blue pond' that gave its name to the surrounding district, which is one of the poorest in the city), has been the place of a legend, some elements of which I shall now summarize.

In the stories of the district's inhabitants, there are several possible apparitions of a character who lives at the bottom of the marsh and became famous under the name of the 'monster of the blue lagoon'.

From the 1970s through to the mid-1980s, dead bodies were frequently found at the bottom of the pond, always of young men. The 'monster' supposedly drew its victims to the water and drowned them; people speak of up to a hundred corpses. The bodies were shrunken and completely dried out, it was said, instead of being swollen with water. The woman whose features the monster is most frequently said to assume is also known for 'seizing men and taking their sex' – she attacks young men, but neither children nor women.

Tunda is the name most often invoked for the woman of the marsh. As we have just seen, this character is one of the several *visiones* of the coastal forest of the Pacific region, from where the greater part of the black population of Agua Blanca migrated a generation or two ago. In fact, this urban image represents a synthesis of different *visiones*. First of all, it recalls the character of the Tunda, who appears at night in the forest, 'kidnapping' children whom she attracts by passing for their mother, grandmother, sister or aunt, then making them disappear, though she does not do them harm; or else she attracts young men whom she calls by appearing indistinctly in the distance, squatting and smelling (odours of ground coffee or fried shrimps), with the aim of taking their sex. Some of these men wander after her into the forest and become *entundados*, possessed. Only the godfathers of the victims are able to find them (since the victims, children or young men, 'resist returning'). To do so, they frighten the Tunda by banging drums (*bombo* and *cununo*, two traditional percussion instruments of the region) or firing rifles, brandishing a cross or burning a candle. When the victims are discovered, their godfathers exorcise them by saying prayers (the Credo), bathing them in holy water, praying and burning herbs. In fact, the godfathers simply act as substitutes for Catholic priests, who are generally responsible for exorcisms. This belief gave rise among other things to the legend of Father Mera who circulated in the region to combat the *visiones* that were seen as incarnations of the Devil.

To sum up, this *visión*, like the several others that accompany it, seems to refer to three contextual elements. For one, it warns against the risks of the forest by symbolizing the fears that are born there: the *visiones* are then protective agents, a form of control that indicates the path of prudence in access to the hills, rivers and uncultivated zones of dense vegetation. According to certain leaders of the ethnic and ecological movements in the region, by this threat to the imprudent it protects the forest itself against outside projects, agro-industrial ones in particular. For another, it is a means of taking charge of burgeoning desires and a form of sexual education: the unassuaged Tunda seduces male youths as the Duende seduces young girls by playing the guitar or marimba. Finally, all repelled in the same way (cross, candles, prayers) and exorcised, the *visiones* refer to the paradoxical history of the presence of a missionary church that systematically diabolized and persecuted any form of popular belief, pagan and animist, but used the *visiones* to attract adherents by showing itself more 'powerful' than them. Thus, several interpretations have been 'sandwiched' together to give a meaning to this *visión* that blends different registers (sexual, religious, environmental) with a new register, urban and political, recently added.

How is the Tunda integrated into the new urban world of Charco Azul? It is found 'in the air', people say, though it does have its favoured zones. It only frequents the forest and is not found on water, though some people say it can be encountered in the mangrove zone or on the edge of a small river. Other *visiones*, for their part, live in the water, like the Riviel, a little light that appears at night in a pirogue and leads travellers astray, and the Madre d'agua, who can draw people into the water and drown them (like the marsh woman of Charco Azul). However, neither the Tunda nor the Madre d'agua frequents the towns, or even cultivated areas. Only virgin forest and water are their preference. Another *visión*, however, a 'companion' of the Tunda, can be found in the city; this is the Viuda, the widow who frequents streets and cemeteries. In Tumaco, an old man told me that the Viuda was 'a beautiful woman who falls in love with a man and leads him to a place where she can put an end to him, that is, kill him. When the man realizes that she is a spirit, he runs away but remains ill.' He must then be exorcised, just as after an encounter with the Tunda.

We see then that the Tunda 'monster' of Charco Azul is a synthesis of several *visiones*. She focuses the only trace of nature within this urban space that lacks a forest: the marsh. This is all that remains of a culture that disappears with the traces of nature as identity reference of the origin of this district's inhabitants. This interpretation coincides with what is said some hundreds of kilometres away by certain inhabitants of the Pacific region and the forest, according to whom the *visiones* disappear with the advance of large plantations, the felling of trees, the blazing of paths by the bulldozer, and urbanization. In reality, however, they do not disappear but migrate, moving and transforming for as long as the migrants have need of them to give meaning to their existence in migration.

In fact, one of the explanations provided by other inhabitants of the Charco Azul district who comment on the episode of the dead bodies found in the marsh, now past, is that it corresponds to a period of violence in the city bound up with narco-traffic conflicts (the Cali cartel). A hundred or so corpses were thrown into the marsh. The *visiones* thus form a way of reading the urban actuality, but they are no longer the same. In the transition from the Pacific coast to Cali, they have fused in two ways. On the one hand, between themselves: the spirit of the marsh takes over and synthesizes features taken from the Tunda, the Madre d'agua and the Viuda, while taking the generic name of Tunda. This last has a greater value than the others, particularly because it is the only name that is indigenous (*embera*) and not colonial. In cultural activities bound up with the black movement in both Tumaco and Cali, representations of the Tunda are actually created, mingling indigenous, African and sometimes European features. On the other hand, vampire stories from TV horror programmes are not far away, as shown among other things by the new term 'monster of the lagoon', used more recently by young rappers to tell in their own way the story of this episode, the character and the place.

The Ashanti rap group from Charco Azul, formed in 1992, some years later composed a song entitled 'El monstro de la laguna azul', which recounts this episode. In this song, according to explanations given me by the authors, the 'monster' is a metaphor for the district's exclusion, itself treated as a 'monster' in the gaze of the rest of the city. They wanted their song to become a hit that would 'show the origin of Agua Blanca'. Now largely filled in, the marsh bordered the route of a new main road, and part of the district was under threat of destruction. The current issue was popular mobilization against the expulsion of inhabitants and the defence of a district that was formerly considered as an urban 'invasion'.

Borders and temporalities of identity-based cultures

Several borders have been created and more or less crossed in recent decades, in the course of the mobilities and cultural inventions of migrants across the world. In the case of the Pacific coast and the cities of Tumaco and Cali, the border between the visible and the invisible is occupied and often crossed in the city as well as in the forest, even if the spirits have changed their shape and function with migration; the border between nature and improved space thus still serves as interpretation, and makes the marsh the identity reference for the home territory in the city of Cali; the border (which has a wall along part of its course) between the Charco Azul district and the rest of the city strengthens the feeling of its inhabitants that they have been violently rejected and threatened by the urban authorities; but the most striking border is that connecting what is local and what comes from the so-called 'global' world, a border whose frequenting and crossing represents a determining change. We shall dwell for a moment on this latter aspect.

The political and cultural ambitions of black Colombian leaders logically aspire towards – and are inspired by – strategies emanating from political and economic networks that diffuse on a global scale the point of view of the cultural identity of the African diaspora. UNESCO's 'Slave Route' project, conducted since 1994, is one aspect of this global network that is present locally. But the diaspora also functions as an interest group at the level of major international institutions. In the late 1990s, for example the Inter-American Development Bank, an international NGO and the Canadian Council for International Cooperation brought together black organizations from Bolivia, Brazil, Colombia, Costa Rica, Ecuador, Honduras, Mexico, Nicaragua, Peru, the Dominican Republic, Uruguay and Venezuela to launch a project, AfroAmerica XXI, that aimed to promote the emergence of an Afro-American economic network. The search for supranational partners (Organization of American States, UNICEF, UNDP, International Labour Organization) and the formation of associations of black entrepreneurs and 'Afro-American banks' were encouraged as privileged instruments for economic and social development outside of national structures, which in this case were decried en bloc as clientelistic.[29] In their turn, these strategies aroused the local emergence of social claims in a so-called 'Afro-descendent' language that favoured a reflexive and strategic revisiting of local culture and ancestrality.[30]

What is really new in this case, however, as in other comparable ones on other continents, is that these local strategies 'jump' the stage of municipal and even national borders to reach an international sphere of recognition by way of transnational networks (in this case, those of so-called 'diasporic' networks). Here they sometimes find reparation for wrongs experienced and felt locally, and support inter-vention, for example, in the legislative process at the national level.[31] These two-way movements between 'here' and 'over there' are at the same time relational, intellectual and political; they form subjects less rooted than global, despite the emphatically localist language that they are led to use.

In other words, it is quite unlikely that the urban ritual of the 'return of the marimba', which has become a symbol of the black culture of the Pacific coast, could have existed without the social,

123

cultural and pedagogic action developed in Tumaco and its region by various international organizations, public and private, during the preceding twenty years, that is, throughout the 1980s and 1990s, the importance of which in cultural and political reconfiguration on a world scale we have already noted several times. Likewise, the cultural work on the legend of the Tunda that in Cali has become the 'monster of the marsh' was conducted by a local group of rappers who called themselves by a famous African ethnonym (Ashanti). In this context, appeals to external legibility lead to translations, comparisons, a certain mimetism and a desire for harmonization between local symbols and their global meaning. Symbolic corpuses are transformed, and the cultures thus produced can no longer be referred just to a single 'identity' (whether local, ethnic, racial or other), despite having been never so much proclaimed as identity cultures.

It is no longer possible to speak of 'syncretism', since the cultural contexts themselves have been transformed, integrated and mingled. In the early 1970s, Sydney Mintz and Richard Price championed the thesis that Afro-American culture was a 'creation' whose 'basis and precondition' had been the new social institutions of slavery, rather than the result of an 'encounter' out of context between two cultures, African and Western, white and black, more or less preserved or readapted. The creation of Afro-American cultures was situated in the social context of the newly forming colonies of the New World, an unprecedented world that did not exist elsewhere, marked by slavery and the domination, military and political, of white colonists. The slaves who arrived there were not constituted into groups, but were masses of individuals; they formed 'crowds', Mintz and Price held, even 'very heterogeneous' ones, and not communities. All that they genuinely shared was their enslaved condition, 'all – or almost all – the rest had to be created by them'.[32] Certain regroupings formed in the slave context, whether colonial or independent, subsequently became sites of identification for slaves and black people: Catholic confraternities reserved for blacks in Brazil, Maroon communities (in Colombia, Brazil and the Caribbean), festival and carnival societies, etc.

Far from corresponding to a superficial syncretism behind which were hidden supposedly pure identities, or to a rift between African and American worlds, all these practices, institutions and beliefs were born and developed within social and spiritual contexts in the New World that were shared, composite phenomena: worlds that were racially mingled and mixed, violent and chaotic.[33] It is in a continuation of this historicity that the contextual and situational production of identities and cultural change takes place today. Of course, the context has changed. The local/global relationship is now the social framework within which the circulation and mixture of information takes place. Today's cultural hybridizations do not bring into contact worlds that are absolutely foreign to one another, still less 'civilizations' to be discovered, naturalized and classified. The local/global relationship is the 'basis and precondition' for the cultural dynamic observed at a given place. It creates an in-between situation, embodied in places and moments of encounter, exchange of ideas, misunderstandings and new political conflicts, giving rise to new symbolic corpuses and new political subjects, increasingly informed of – and formed by – their cosmopolitan condition.

Race and racism: how can one be black?

Along with civilization and cultural identity, race came to dominate as a language of human relationships and international relations in the twentieth century. Its false air of a basic truth, supported by the biological allusion of its origin, made it the most violent trap for identity-based thought.

It is not enough, however, to say that races do not exist. Certainly, humanity is a single species whose variants, continuous in both time and space, are the fruit of long histories of migrations and peoplings since time immemorial; and these variations are not just phenotypic, but also linguistic, sociological and cultural in general. This truth, the most simple and universal, has not prevented many radical forms of rejection of the other in the name of race, the extreme of which is rejection of the idea of a common humanity. Social science does not choose the society that it studies. It has to make do with what exists. And if races do not exist, racism (discrimination, segregation, hatred or even racial extermination) certainly does so, and prior to it racialism, in the sense of a racial idea of identities and the world. To deconstruct and supersede racialism as the most radical of traps for thought requires here again an examination of its uses.

Racial thought and the racial language of alterity were forged at the heart of slavery and colonization. In the world that arose on the basis of the Atlantic slave trade (sixteenth to nineteenth centuries), particularly in the abolitionist period of the second half of the nineteenth century, a naturalist and classificatory thought was developed to form a substitute for the slave relations that were coming to an end, placing the 'white race' on a higher level of moral, intellectual or

125

aesthetic values and the 'black race' on a lower level. To examine in detail the truths proclaimed by the authors of racialist doctrine only confirms their lack of any scientific character (no matter the sophisticated classifications in terms of craniology, biology or anthropometry in which the nineteenth century was so prolix), as it also confirms the screen of prejudices by way of which their distant discoveries were transcribed.[34] Moreover, this desire to give meaning, at that particular time, to the discovery of the other was inscribed from the start in a relation of domination that was to be given a rational basis. In this power thinking, the first person to think in terms of race is the one that dominates.

This is what made racialism the most radical and violent way of thinking the other, providing in a sense the 'model' of biopolitical alterity that can only conceive the 'pariah' as outside of social space; in racial thought, the power of life and death may be exercised to its limits, with genetic selection on the one hand and the suppression of life on the other, by 'letting die' or exterminating the undesirable. This racial thought of the inferior other is always a discourse in a particular situation, whether that of established biopower or that of the conquest of power in struggle, conflict or war: this is what founds the problematic according to which, given that races do not exist, the only real question for social science is what Michel Foucault referred to as 'race war', although he did not pursue this line of reflection as far as that of the biopower that is concomitant with it.[35] The genealogy of this race war is possible only in specific contexts, which thus systematically qualify its meaning.

The relativity and uses of racial language lead us to revisit the question of *relative foreignness* that, along with the expanded conception of the border, has provided the basis of our reflection up to now. The countries that in one way or another inherited the history of the Atlantic world (with the slave trade and slave society, colonial conquest and colonial society) share a problematic of the black condition within their national space.[36] This contemporary black condition takes various forms right around the circumference of the black Atlantic. To stick to the two countries under discussion here, Brazil and France, it is bound up in the one case with descent from the deported slave, the 'piece of ebony' sold in the Americas, and in the other case with the intergenerational transformation of the 'indigenous' or colonial 'subject' into a clandestine migrant, refugee, inhabitant of urban peripheries, or indeed someone suspected of being all these things. The histories that followed from colonialism and those that followed from slavery led to relative positions that are different today. As Pap Ndiaye shows in his study of the black condition in France, the 'suspicion of foreignness' is not everywhere the same: 'Unlike in the United States, where being black does not place someone in a position of "foreignness" vis-à-vis the nation (despite certainly arousing other forms of suspicion), black people in France and Britain are often perceived as outside the imagined national community.'[37] This foreignness, embodied as it were, creates a 'visible' border, or what in Brazil is called a 'colour line', which in many social circumstances it is better not to cross so as not to find oneself in a world that is foreign and possibly hostile. This relative manufacture of a foreigner 'within' is built onto the racial ideas that were formed in the history of these nation-states, and are reactivated in their respective presents. In France, 'immigrant', 'issuing from immigration' or 'second-generation immigrant' are now labels that 'perpetually identify those persons concerned with a foreign origin, duplicated, as far as black people are concerned, by a skin colour that assigns them an ineffaceable foreignness'.[38]

How, under all these constraints, can one be black today? I shall answer this question by placing it first of all in the French context, which, however, I shall examine in the mirror of a different experience, that of an anthropologist who has worked for many years in Brazil, Colombia and black Africa.[39]

Republic and racial thought in France

Since the early 2000s, the political context in France has integrated the presence of 'visible minorities', immigrants and descendants of immigrants from black Africa and the Maghreb. To keep just to the most significant events, I shall mention: the presence since 2002 of so-called 'ethnic' candidates (mainly West Indian and French North African) in national elections (a number of whom joined François Hollande's socialist government in 2012); the riots of November 2005 in the working-class suburbs of the big French cities; the formation of the Representative Council of France's Black Associations (CRAN) in November 2005, that is, in the middle of the period of the riots. Gradually, the more or less euphemizing notions of 'visible minorities', 'persons issuing from immigration' or even 'persons issuing from diversity' (*sic*) appeared, along with public debate on 'positive discrimination' or 'ethnic statistics'.

We shall start by revisiting the 'banlieue riots' of 2005. These marked the presence of an 'African-French' or 'Franco-African' and 'Franco-Maghrebin' contestation, to use terms that are generally

127

shocking in France, but can be translated word for word into English, Portuguese or Spanish without provoking the least upset. This does not mean that these other countries have resolved any better what France has difficulty in recognizing. It simply signifies that there is no absolute value of race, that it is a language that was certainly globally diffused in the course of the twentieth century, but also undergoes strong national variations. Each country (or each group of countries that share a common history) has its history of racial thinking and racism, and it would be in vain to seek the 'proper' model to follow.

The French 'model' is profoundly marked by two seemingly contradictory experiences, republican and colonial. Proud of a 'non-racial' social model (which movements such as the African National Congress in South Africa also championed in the 1980s), the Republic has remained stuck in its colonial history without having really come to terms with a racial action and thinking marked by the context of colonization: a colonization that was at the same time repressive and 'civilizing', thus of a double violence, physical and symbolic, sociopolitical and cultural, with a view to integrating into imperial France the peoples of West and North Africa, taken and frozen into the categories of the colonial situation. This double violence remains the reference point for the French way of viewing the other peoples it has had dealings with in its history, these 'other' neighbours being the very people who migrated to the 'metropolis' in the 1960s, attracted by the calls for immigration of that time, or else their descendants today who are both French and African, or 'Africans of France'.

The expression 'Africans of France' is not as scandalous as imagined by those who uphold an African identity as fixed reality, immutable and localized. The necessary stocktaking of the postcolonial situation would be incomplete if we did not take into account, in the same theoretical framework, the integrating scope of the French egalitarian idea. This had effects in terms of African political culture in the period between the Second World War and independence. Such was the case in the intellectual world of African studies and among African political elites in France. In the 1940s and 1950s, accordingly, solidarities were formed actually within the project of civilization/integration '*à la française*'. This integrationist policy created, on the one hand, a lasting connection with a student, bureaucratic and political elite, which the following decades were to damage.[40] Sometimes strong personal ties (even if marked by differences of status), social solidarities and political networks were formed in this period. A French left that was militant and close to the 'ground', that of the Communist and Socialist parties and the CGT trade-union

128

federation, fostered connections supported by social mobilizations.[41] This led to the emergence of, or at least influenced, African political leaders such as Senghor, Houphouët-Boigny, etc., who became deputies or government ministers in 1950s France.[42] At the same time, social scientists (sociologists, economists, anthropologists) embarked on descriptions and analyses of African colonial realities and their dynamics (the 'colonial situation'), and translated their commitment into the training of critical and politicized intellectuals and, in some cases, participation in the independence movements.

It is this relationship, certainly ambiguous but at the same time one of solidarity, that has been lost in the recent period with the transformation of the ties between Africa and France and the loss of this relative social and cultural proximity that existed alongside colonial violence. A certain nostalgia is present on both sides in the crisis of Franco-African relations. Today there is a transition from the postcolonial paths of the human adventure towards other, global, routes which tend to 'decolonize' it.[43] Those who no longer succeed in crossing the borders that were previously those of the colonial 'metropolis' all end up turning away from it. The 'sub-Saharan' migrants who knock on the walls, fences and detention centres of Ceuta and Melilla, of Lampedusa in Italy, Le Mesnil-Amelot in France, in part reorient their migration in other directions – the Middle East, Asia, North and South America.[44]

In just a few years, France has discovered, by way of the sporadic, violent or minority expression of unaccustomed voices, almost inaudible in the past, a racial question that other major countries – the United States, South Africa or Brazil – had already experienced and made explicit as a national problem, and that at various times they have tried to resolve. The riots and demonstrations for civil rights of the blacks in the United States in the 1960s, the Soweto riots and the gradual building of a multiracial opposition to apartheid laws between the mid-1970s and the 1990s in South Africa, were great moments in the history of these countries. In a more gradual form in Brazil, from the black political and cultural movements under the military dictatorship of the 1970s through to the 'affirmative action' that became official in the early 2000s despite being much contested in society, the racial or 'colour' question has also marked social relations and political milieus.

Brazil: from 'racial democracy' to 'multicultural nation'

Brazil is trying once again to escape from a hierarchical and racial thinking formed in the mould of slavery, which was abolished only in 1888. Since the 2000s there has been much discussion of 'reparations' and 'affirmative action'. The racial quotas (or quotas of 'appearance', as we would say in French) that were established then have not radically changed the conditions of young black people in the universities or on the job market. Moreover, they create confusion over modes of identification, with 'colour identity' becoming more strategic than ever at the same time as it is publicly proclaimed as an essentialism, even an identity of origin. Race, origin, genetics: if it is cause for concern that the political world and in part that of scholarship are rediscovering naturalist themes, we can see here a logical continuity (even under the appearance of a reversal) with the profoundly racialized ideas of social difference that arose from slave society.

In the second half of the nineteenth century, European racialism spread among the country's elite, particularly due to the presence of Gobineau, thinker of the 'inequality of races' in the French embassy at Rio in 1869–70.[45] The notorious 'fable of the three races' – white, Indian and black – that the anthropologist Roberto Da Matta[46] has discussed dates from this epoch, and produced the main prejudices that prevailed after the abolition of slavery in 1888: the marginality and non-nationality of the Indian, the social inferiority of the black, and the social, moral and aesthetic superiority of the white. Contemporary with these theories, a romantic representation of racial purity developed an aversion towards miscegenation. Then, from the abolition of slavery through to the 1930s, a policy aiming to 'whiten' the population was developed: public campaigns promoted European immigration, with the aim of 'Aryanizing' the country. These gave a particular connotation to interracial unions: among the intelligentsia there was talk of having the black race disappear in a few decades; in black milieus, union with lighter-skinned partners would permit what was called 'race washing', 'improving the race' or 'purifying its blood'.[47]

The praise of miscegenation that developed in the 1930s in the context of Gilberto Freyre's quest for a theory of the Brazilian nation shows this very clearly; the idea of miscegenation did not exclude racial thinking, but was actually born from this.[48] Then a linguistic slippage was gradually effected from the 1930s to the 1950s, leading from a presentation of the virtues of 'mixing genes' – as Freyre's strange concept of *miscigenação* can be translated – to the Brazilian myth of 'racial democracy' that others took on the task of systematizing in his place.[49]

In the wake of the Second World War, several French and American intellectuals showed in the context of a wide UNESCO programme the very original 'Brazilian contribution to humanity'. At a time when the world had just experienced a war in which an ideology of racial purity had led to terror and extermination, Brazil offered what seemed a quite particular example of a country where, if political democracy was certainly far from being satisfactory, at least racial conflict was absent despite a great human diversity and endless mixtures, which (no one was mistaken on this) did not exclude differences of treatment and prejudices.

Since this time, for both internal and external use, the model of 'racial democracy' has been used to conceptualize a certain tolerance, alongside the status quo of discrimination against those Brazilians with black skin. This nationally specific model was based on the major work of Gilberto Freyre: according to him, Brazilian society enjoys a social and ethnic 'democracy' more powerful and authentic than political democracy. These ideas have since marked Brazilian racial thinking. Later, in the 1960s, the governing elite made this the basis of a 'racial peace', deceptive since founded not on equality between all, but rather on the 'prejudice of not having prejudices'.

In the course of the 1970s, in a national context of rapid urban and industrial growth, black movements against racial discrimination developed, reacting against the illusions of justice associated with miscegenation and against the 'cordial' ways of imposing immobilism and white domination. Racial mobilizations appeared, as in many parts of the world at this time, particularly the United States and South Africa. Black organizations were founded in this decade in São Paulo and in Salvador de Bahia. Ambiguous as it was, the myth of racial democracy was at least sufficiently widespread in society to make the demand for equality between whites and blacks irrefutable, once these movements brought it onto the political stage. The political focuses of these revolts were quite particular: rejection of the whites' cordiality, campaigns against religious syncretism, the valorization and publicizing of love between black men and women, etc. In other words, a series of slogans that are hard to comprehend outside a reversal of the praise of domination and a demand for equality, a paradox that the myth of racial democracy had itself maintained without showing a way out of it.

The new Brazilian constitution of 1988 marked an important development compared with the official image of itself that the country had previously given. Racism was recognized as an irrevocable 'crime', which represented both an acknowledgement of the existence of racism in Brazil and the creation of legal instruments to combat it. The 'pluri-ethnic' and 'multicultural' character of the nation was also cited, and the foundations laid for the distribution of land to persons recognized as 'remainders of *quilombo* communities [of escaped slaves]'.

In the wake of the Durban conference of 2001,[50] the decade was marked by intensive polemics. On the one hand, these related to a basic issue: the post-slavery character of the Brazilian nation. On the other hand, they concerned the practical effects of public policies of a 'racial' character: the distribution of 'black lands' to 'remaining' peasants from the old *quilombos* of escaped black slaves; the advantage officially granted to self-declared 'blacks' in access to university and government service. In both cases, the demands for expertise, and more generally legitimation, from Brazilian anthropologists aroused heated discussion.[51] Whether they represented a return to the praise of miscegenation as an immutable social foundation of Brazilian society, or relayed the popular demand for equality at the risk of hitching this to the self-fulfilling prophecy of an ethnic narrative, Brazilian social scientists and other 'Brazilianists' (French and American in particular) have been caught in the snare of the identity trap, and it is hard to see how they can escape from it.

The challenge is certainly complex, and the researcher, no matter how committed, has scarcely any other contribution to propose to this *political* debate than to explain his or her own aporias. For example: how to be a non-racial society while at the same time struggling against racial discrimination, which implies using a racial language? However, without claiming to resolve the current political problems that the racial question raises, we shall argue here, in a more general and less immediately topical manner, that the beginnings of a response can be found in a clearer distinction between the domains of identity and politics, which makes possible a more dynamic understanding of their relationship and their tension, in France as well as in Brazil, despite their major historical differences.

Citizenship without identity

Brazilian politics and debate have had the advantage of bringing into the public realm a subject considered unhelpful by some, embarrassing by others, that of 'Brazilian-style' racism. This political advance is even the main result from the point of view of recognition of the black condition in Brazil. Open discussion about positive discrimination or ethnic statistics in France in the early 2000s had a comparable polemical effect, despite the debate being 'muzzled' in advance by a belief in the naturally egalitarian virtue of the Republic. This belief assumes that the ethno-nationalist effects of such a principle are forgotten when it is applied to the colonial context despite its boundary of equality remaining unchanged. In this context, it excludes and leaves 'behind' the Republic a section of the members of the nation, indigenous and subjects. Which tends to demonstrate that in reality there is no naturally 'pure' model of the Republic in the sense that citizenship actually refers in practice simply to the state and not to nationality. For just one year, in 1793, the most radical moment of the French Revolution, a statute on foreign citizens was promulgated, separating citizenship from nationality. The model of a 'citizenship card' (rather than an identity card), drawn from this period, was taken up by the participants in the 'march for equality' of 1983, who saw themselves as 'sociologically French (being mostly born and socialized in France) and in the main legally French, but still constructed and treated as foreigners'.[52] In other words, the model of citizenship without identity exists in reality insofar as it makes it possible to detect the hiatus and excluding effects of a confusion between the political people (*demos*) and the ethnological people (*ethnos*), and to note the inequality that results from this.

Conversely, we cannot be sure that assertion of the universal and untouchable value of the *res publica* plays in France or elsewhere today the egalitarian role that it was able to have in other historical circumstances. In the name of a struggle against 'race' or 'ethnicity' that confuses concept and reality, 'object' and 'thing', the universalist assertion covers over in an authoritarian way dissonant voices that complain about an unjust Republic. This violence can only be answered by de-essentializing reflection on racial essentialism, as on identity essentialism in general. This makes it possible to see racism as having two present components, observable in the concrete situation and not in some remote and disembodied spheres of pure thought. These are found in the basic minimum statement of racism as the pure negation of the other: of 'negating, silencing' this 'other'. Silencing the other (their speech or simply their presence expressing a rejection of what is) presupposes radicalizing their alterity. It is in this sense that race is the extreme of biopolitical alterity, the last border, as biological justification of invisibility or of the disappearance of the undesirable. Rejection of the other does not exist in an abstract form;

133

it is the rejection of the other who lives – that is, who expresses by their speech, by the presence of their body and by their visibility – a disharmony, a disorder or a disturbance in a given context. It is when this *dissensus* is expressed that it is answered by the absolute rejection of the 'other', to 'silence' them, racial hatred being the ultimate extreme because at the limits of the human.[53]

In the context of France today, recalling the values of the Republic sounds like the cultural censorship of a political expression – of body or speech. This is all the more obvious when the speech that is dissonant in content is different also in form – something that is not absolutely new in the history of popular mobilizations, the place of immigrants in working-class categories and popular social movements being a constant of history.[54] This paradoxical injunction ('submit so as to be equal!') is therefore not initially a social or cultural question that awaits a response which we should help to bring out; it is in itself a political question that is raised, the question of democracy. According to this conception, access to politics would be reserved for citizens who are more authentic than others because endowed with the correct ancestry or knowledge, or again the correct social integration. An increasingly conditional citizenship whose effect is to leave outside the 'border' of recognition an increasing mass of undesirables. The rejection that is then expressed against their 'difference', devalued in the name of origin or foreign ways of life, replays the identity trap on the national political stage.

Escaping the identity trap

In the three areas of investigation we have presented here, in which the object of conflict is civilization, culture and race, we have seen attempts at, conditions for, and sometimes the successful emergence of subjects where most commonly what is seen is only identity determinations, present or inherited. I do not argue here that these identity determinations and inertias do not exist – on the contrary. But the gaze that we bring to bear on these movements, when this is itself decentred and freed from explanations in terms of identity, can relate identity assignment to the multiple imaginations and strategies that subjects deploy in order to free themselves from this.

That leads me to revisit and sharpen my critique of the use of identity as an analytical category. This use makes identity the ultimate truth of an individual's or a collective's expression or action; that is the identity trap. It rests on at least three basic mistakes. The first consists in believing that the identities of other people can be defined and frozen once and for all in an absolute form, outside the context of relationships in which they are uttered at a given moment. This denial of actuality has the effect of 'essentializing' them in a language either racial ('blacks'), ethnic ('Roma'), religious ('Muslims'), urban ('ghetto'), or some other still to be invented. The second mistake consists in assuming the passive submission of individuals to collective identities created by these languages, while recognizing for oneself a constant process of change, an autonomy of the subject, and above all the singularity of a signature, which disappear in the collective identity assignment of the other.

The third mistake, finally, consists in a myopia that prevents people from seeing that contexts have changed. A certain ethnic 'passé-ism' on the part of anthropology is still an issue here: it is just as if an eternal ethnology of ethnic groups could survive the transformation of the world! One of the palpable effects of this passé-ist belief is to maintain the idea that an identity truth lies hidden behind any people who express it. This is an idea formed on the basis of a confusion between the *ethnos*, the 'ethnological people' (and the mechanical association, an old and outdated one, between people, place and culture that it assumes) and the *demos*, the political people. This alone is the contemporary of the anthropologist, and the languages of subjectification that the latter observes here and now must be understood in their contemporary context. They may borrow available words and signs in the (dominant) language of dominations without being the expression of hidden identity 'truths'.

Emerging from the identity trap makes it possible to focus a contemporary attention on contexts and processes – possibly metaphorical, mimetic, ludic, parodic or aesthetic – of today's languages of emancipation. These languages may alternate very quickly for the same individuals and groups. Thus, in the north of Brazil, on the poor periphery of Manaus, the same inhabitants will call themselves 'Indians', 'Métis' or 'Afro-Americans', depending on the institutional support, the interlocutor, or the chances of access to certain resources that they can 'negotiate' with these different ethnonyms.[55] And in the Pacific region of Colombia, as studied in this chapter, we observe that depending on the context of conflict and their interlocutors, the same persons or movements will rather call themselves 'blacks', 'Afro-descendants', 'peasants' or 'ecologists', each time rehearsing a different version of an alternative 'strategic essentialism'. What counts for them, as I see it, is to create each time the possibility of a subject of speech who seeks to win a place, an acknowledgement, certain rights, against the historical abandonment of the lowlands of the Colombian Pacific or the north of Brazil.

To understand contemporary movements, to understand the new political form that they are experimenting with, is to understand how other languages (which arose elsewhere or in the past) serve to bring subjects into existence, in a particular conflict situation, against the identity assignment of which they are the object. It is this exploration to which I shall devote the following chapter. After examining the conditions of possibility of an anthropology of the subject, I shall describe the forms of presence of the subject *in situation*, depending on whether its expression is ritual, aesthetic or political.

— 6 —

LOGICS AND POLITICS OF THE SUBJECT

So far in this book I have emphasized a relational conception of the border, expanded, uncertain and open, along with the central place that the border assumes in a generalized context of decentring the world, and the need for a renewal of theoretical and methodological tools. The final stage in these reflections will bear on the meaning that can be attributed to the man or woman who is called a 'subject' when this is in tension with their identity assignments and frees itself from these. For, in the context of a globalization that is experienced and 'in crisis' – its economic and financial crisis being only one aspect of a wider crisis of solidarities and politics – simple binary oppositions – 'we' and 'others' – must yield to an understanding of the complexity of the world in which the experiential test of the other and of the border is both more frequent and more commonplace.

I shall argue here, continuing the attention I have paid to migration and to the cosmopolitism that is born in border situations, that the question of the formation and expression of the subject is central to contemporary anthropology. Because of this relative novelty, we need first of all to make a detour into the domain of concepts that have arisen in a number of neighbouring disciplines, and then place them 'in situation', in the investigation, to furnish better tools for the contemporary gaze on the world.

An anthropology of the subject

Anthropology is not really equipped to tackle by itself the question of the subject. What we need for this is to expand the spectrum of its means of knowledge and thus, while revising the concepts it has

137

forged in its own history, look beyond its limits and create other concepts.

How does the subject arise? And how can we grasp him or her, that is, see, describe and understand them? We first need to revisit the different ways of tackling individuation – by which we mean the forms in which individuals are conceived and 'constructed' by the contexts (societies, groups, spaces) in which their life unfolds.

From person to individual: ethnology and sociology

Anthropology has long been interested in different theories of the *persona*, a notion whose meaning can range from that of a mask, tragic or ritual, to social or sacred status. Africanism in particular has made the notion of persona the key concept that connects each individual to a culture, a place, a social structure.[1] In the lineage context, each is defined by a position they occupy in the genealogy of the lineage, each individual exists through the relationship that unites them with others, living or dead, real or imagined. The individual as persona is made up of mediations right from birth to the ancestors, to the gods, then to others. This is attested to by ancestral 'traces', divine manifestations or the scarification inscribed on bodies.

For Marcel Mauss, the *persona* defines the notion of individual by the incorporation of moral and social norms and values: it is the individual in their moral and thus societal dimension.[2] The persona thus ultimately refers to anthropological totalities that the ethnologist grasps according to an assumed transparency between an informant, a space, a society and a culture. In this operation, individuation takes the form of an identity between the part that I observe (ethnographic observation) and the whole that I never see, but to which we generally give the names of 'society' and 'culture', or 'ethnic group'. The whole of a culture and a society is incarnated, incorporated, in a persona that acquires meaning for the ethnologist only insofar as it is transparent as a whole. In this use of the notion of persona, therefore, there is a question of method that is also a question of representation of the individual in the world: in this so-called 'holistic' procedure, anthropology is founded on a dualistic vision – that of the 'great divide' discussed earlier, or that of Louis Dumont, who contrasted holism and individualism.[3] What we call the 'privileged informant' then has no other rationale than to speak and embody the 'whole' of the society, culture or ethnic group whose reproduction the ethnologist will then present elsewhere – bearing an external gaze and addressing himself to a still more external public. The image or fiction is thus born of a coherent 'other' totality, ignoring or smoothing over conflicts, gaps and heterogeneous forms for the purpose of analytical coherence.

What is lost in this ethnological fiction associated with the conception of the transparent persona as part of an ideal and invisible whole is the relational dimension of individual identity, the intrinsic necessity of an alterity in order to construct any representation of self; it is also its contextual dimension and the transformations it has undergone with the change of contexts.[4] This is what legitimizes criticism of the individualized and totalizing representation of the notion of persona, in short the 'identitarian' notion.

It remains nonetheless – and this would already be enough not to neglect this notion's heuristic contribution – that historically a massive response to the grip of lineage was escape from lineage when an 'outside' opened up, and in particular with decolonization. Thus, in black Africa from the 1950s to the 1970s, departure for the towns and urban peripheries was synonymous with emancipation – which gave migration itself, already in this period but in a different sense from that of today, a political significance beyond the mere line of flight that it embodied in each individual trajectory. It was literally the quest for an 'air of freedom' in the cities . . . before being for many the discovery of a place of abandonment. The African cities described by anthropologists in this period were marked by an ambivalence of social status, symbolic position and political involvement that affected these new city dwellers, urbanized rurals, villagers in the city, etc.[5] The question of individualization and its effects thus forced itself on those involved, in a pragmatic perspective accompanied by a certain objectification and distancing from the places, identities and cultures of 'origin'.

In quantitative studies, the individual 'atom' is isolated and utilized to correspond to criteria of sociological classification (by age, sex, income, occupational category, place of residence, etc.), which never manages to account for 'everything' in the notion of persona (as it loses the social, symbolic or historical complexity offered by methodological holism), or for the sum of all individualities (since these resist dissolution in the mass, in categories or classes).

As for the individual 'produced' by the process of individualization (arriving alone somewhere outside his context of lineage, family, village or community), they should not be confused with the normative individual, that which individualism establishes in terms of the opposition already mentioned between, on the one hand, the caste-assigned person in India or the lineage-assigned person in Africa

139

and, on the other, the 'Western' individual. They are not reducible to this, yet this is the model of 'governance' that they must deal with. A model that is seemingly duplicated: on the side of the individual, Robert Castel distinguished first of all between positive and negative individualism.[6] If the international expert, the traveller or even the city dweller are typical figures of the positive discourse of freedom of the 'individual' against the oppression of the 'persona', at the opposite extreme the negative version of individualism is realized in graduated modalities of social depreciation: these are the figures of dispossession, of the 'precariat', the marginal and the vulnerable.

But the 'positive' version has itself developed to excess (what is now known as 'hyper-individualism'), to the point of its own valorization being questioned. The sense of individual autonomy, with projects, successes and failures, the intimate joys and sufferings of a full life – in work, love and friendship, always lived and experienced as unique, specific, and in this sense very 'rich' or 'enriching' – this sense of a full individual freedom and responsibility may become an inverted caricature of itself, in fact its nightmare. The 'construction of self', alone in the face of the generalized commodification of the world, scarcely leaves any other outcome in the face of the laws of the market than to know how to sell oneself, not 'living to tell the tale', in the fine expression of the Colombian novelist Gabriel García Márquez,[7] but rather how to produce a CV in real time, to oneself be a product rather than a consumer. When the hyper-individual or the 'individual by excess' ends up suffering a hypertrophy of the self, the 'individual by default'[8] is then exposed to the same social and symbolic constraint, with the small difference that he is not – or no longer – successful. Thus, the corollary of the valorization of the individual is his *exhibition*, and the acute perception if not the actual experience of the risks that accompany this seemingly 'positive' form of being stripped bare.

The individual condition can never be grasped outside the orders of discourse that represent it, whether in the anthropological languages of persona and lineage, or in that of the society of individuals. Elementary and ancient as they may be, on the present political stages these figures are the basis for a caricature distinction between 'liberalism' (individualist) and 'communitarianism' ('identitarian'). However, as I have tried to show, these two figures of reference are both as constrained and constraining as each other. We come back then to the truth illusion of identity, all the more serious as it plays a driving role in politics and sometimes in political violence. Transformed into a stereotype of political analysis, the caricature opposition between liberalism and communitarianism gives a frozen, almost statue-like, image of the relationship between individual and collective logics.[9] More generally, this identity-based reading leads to a deadlock, in terms of the multiplicity of signposts for individual action and in terms of the question of movement, change and logics of action – which are not reducible either to a 'politics of difference', more or less 'communitarian' and 'identitarian', or to a society of individuals and its exaggerated ideological form in the politics of indifference. It is between the two that the whole question of the subject lies, with its multiple facets and conditions of emergence.

From subjectification to subjects: anthropology and philosophy

The individual constructed by contemporary individualism risks no longer being anything but this extreme expression of subjectification represented by the hyper-individual, as much as if not more so than by the destitute individual.[10] What comes after individualism may seem initially beyond the grasp of an anthropology which is interested above all in the ways of producing the 'persona' and his or her identities in a particular society, as well as, later, in its critique and the search for new explanatory models in a globalized context. Hence the simultaneously melancholic, enigmatic and paradoxical character of a research topic such as the 'ethnology of solitude' that Marc Augé ends up with.[11] This is certainly the major aporia in the anthropology of contemporary worlds founded as a critical anthropology. It is the point of reference and the theoretical moment when we have to make room for a third concept, the *subject*, decentred in relation to the social and ambiguous figures of the 'persona' and the 'individual', but connected to these. How can we work with this concept and transform it from an anthropological perspective? Let us see first of all where it is already very much present, in a dialogue with political philosophy.

We first need to understand a divergence that has occupied philosophers for several decades, as indicated by Étienne Balibar: 'The antithesis subjection/subjectification [that] has characterized all French philosophy since the second half of the twentieth century, one guiding thread of it being what could be called the problematic of "modes of subject-formation".'[12] What concerns us here is the figure of the subject in relation to power and action. Two modalities – the subjugated or the acting subject – are regularly opposed, without it being possible or in my view desirable to decide which would be more 'true' than the other. Both may be present in each individual, in

141

contradictory and alternative ways, or else combined and conflictual. But reflection can be enriched and made more precise by recourse to situational investigation and with the aid of its attention to places, others and powers.

We thus have a 'subjectification' in the sense of the subjection of bodies and identity places to a sovereign power, in a perspective that remains broadly structuralist. The 'object-subject' lies in relief in these analyses, which Michel Foucault made a start on.[13] Two procedures participate in this subjection, well exhibited by Mathieu Potte-Bonneville: the panoptic one of course, the model of a control society that mechanically subjugates, but also and above all reflexive control 'of oneself by oneself'.[14] Due to this wonderful mechanism, Foucault's *Discipline and Punish* could as well be called 'Discipline and Punish Oneself'.[15] In his study of 'French-style subjectivity', Étienne Balibar insists on Foucault's unity of object and subject: 'The question of the subject and that of the object, combined in a double process of subjectification and objectification, of subjection of the individual to rules and construction of the "relation to self" according to different practical modalities, are thus not opposites but rather two faces of one and the same reality.'[16]

This hold that total and unitary power has over the individual is thus not exactly a 'subjectification without subject'; it is literally the subjectified and incorporated object. Foucault did not abandon any idea of the subject in the face of this, but he summoned it to an intimate resistance in the name of a freedom that is always possible – since this freedom must indeed exist, in his view, for the subject to be considered co-author of his subjection. This resistance is embodied in 'subjectivity', 'care of the self', which is why the private world appears as a withdrawal, and a subject is literally reduced to his or her being (as indicated by the suffix *-ity* which only appears at this moment). In a commentary on 'care of the self', Frédéric Gros argues that Foucault's figure of the subject 'is the very opposite of what has been either denounced or exalted as contemporary individualism';[17] the subject is thus not a hyper-subject, and it is in the Foucauldian 'care of oneself' that we should seek for expressions of this other-subject that disconnects and detaches itself from its constraints.

This may well be the case, but in this way we leave the relational public sphere. And 'intimate resistance' is largely secret, if not illusory; it is a hidden niche, even a withdrawal into oneself, rather than an expression of oneself vis-à-vis others. It lacks the test of alterity: what goes on here is only realized, effective and observable in a transition to the public space. Frédéric Gros certainly demonstrates that 'techniques of self' and the learning of them presuppose a relationship 'which tears us away from the inertia of a received identity, fixed and frozen by parental education or society'.[18] But the situations in which something of the self becomes an actual part of the subject vis-à-vis others still have to be made clear, and this test of alterity is not made explicit in Foucault's analyses. The question remains unresolved, both for philosophical investigation, which seeks a response, for example, in the materiality and the traces of public forms of complaint and protest by way of which 'monstrous lives' confront the reading of their judges and governors,[19] and in everyday writing, as we shall see later apropos of the subject as author. But it is also a workshop for what we may generally call an anthropology of subjectivities. For the research of situational anthropology, the relational dimension of self – in a particular place, vis-à-vis others and in the confrontation with authority – is the indispensable angle for all research into the subject.

The subject in situation: an ethnographic proposal

To take up these questions from the anthropological point of view, and translate them into fieldwork, I shall consider three more or less discernible figures of the subject. These figures do not denote types of individuals, but rather operatory modes of relationship to oneself, to others and to the world. They are expressed in each person with greater or lesser intensity, according to situations and relational contexts, and are in fact closely linked together. In this respect, their description makes it possible to 'situate' the possibilities and contributions of anthropological research better towards understanding the contexts of emancipation in the world today.

The first figure we shall examine is that of the *subjugated*, in the original Foucauldian definition of the subject as incorporated and 'subjectified' subject. This refers to the idea of a constraining totality, a set of incorporated norms that leads each person to play – or even 'overplay' – their role. This modality was already present in the notion of *persona* familiar to anthropologists in other contexts (and ideally in the 'privileged informant'). Once extracted from its culturalist and 'identitarian' contents, the concept of 'persona' thus coincides in part with the definition of subject – but only in part. This part, which we shall refer to as being that of the 'object-subject', refers, in the anthropological programme, to everything that can be known about the identity (or identities) of subjects according to their history and their memory, their biography, the places where they live or have lived, the collectives to which they belong.

143

Two other conceptions of the subject can likewise be tested from the point of view of anthropological research, as well as connected or confronted with one another. One of these, the intimate subject, refers to Foucault's second definition of the subject, engaged in the 'care of the self'. The other is the subject in situation, vis-à-vis others in a public space. These two figures aim at an emancipation and a certain freedom for the subject, but they maintain a different relationship to politics and identity.

The meaning of the *intimate subject*, engaged in the care of the self, is close to what is generally called 'subjectivity' or 'subjectivities'. One wing of anthropology has in recent years been interested in subjectivities, in the sense of the set of states and emotions by way of which the social is manifested in each individual. These approaches have expanded the field of anthropology and the spread of its own interdisciplinary character towards psychoanalysis, psychiatry and philosophy.[20] By integrating emotions into the very heart of the perception of social constraints and action, they propose a way of thinking differently the question of the 'hyper-individual' – who, whether 'loser' or 'winner', is perceived in individualist theory as atomized, lacking mediation. In this sense, these anthropologies of subjectivity are probably one possible response to the paradoxical programme of an 'ethnology of solitude' as proclaimed by Marc Augé and already mentioned. We still need to make clear what connection there is between this subjective dimension of engagement and care of the self, centred on the figure of the concrete individual (at the risk of losing the social dimension borne by the ethnological – and more broadly, contextual – definition of the persona) and what I shall now introduce into these reflections: the subject in situation.

In tackling the subject in situation, anthropology investigates mediations rather than an identity-based 'truth' of the subject. The programme I propose here is to keep identity at an analytical distance, by accepting that subjects can 'work' it, oppose it or free themselves from it. This also involves a distance from a subjectivity posed a priori by reference to the cultural, social or psychological, specificities given in advance of individuals involved in observed situations. Thus, it is unnecessary for a subject to be inherently angry for an 'angry' subject to be expressed in forms that can range from individual rejection to collective blockage or boycott, as we shall see. Nor is it any more necessary for an individual to be at all perverse for a rejection of this or that constraint by authority to find expression in his circumventing it or diverting it, in a more or less collectively organized way. And similarly, but on the ground of cultural identity, it is not necessary for a black Brazilian to be 'really' African in order to claim himself 'African' in an ethnic language and a ritual context in Salvador de Bahia – a point I shall return to.

The connections between the different figures and different moments of expression of the subject are complex. Observed in situation, the 'subjugated' subject (or object-subject, as I have described him) may, for his part, overplay or even anticipate his role and thus give the impression of 'co-producing' it, willing and fully desiring it. Qualifications such as 'positive' or 'negative' no longer have any meaning here. For we can equally observe this 'individual by excess' in connection, for example, with the self-victimization generally noticed in the way refugees assume their victim image in the presentation of their bodies or in their testimonies: presentation of a suffering self is the condition for their being taken charge of by humanitarian organizations, and confirms these in their symbolic domination of the humanitarian stage. But the obviousness of this rather too simple analysis of the co-production of the status of victim is overturned and superseded by two 'scandals', related but different, that are closely associated with it: that of the 'lying refugee' (or 'false refugee') and that of the refugee *confronting* the humanitarian. The first of these is not understood by the theory of the object-subject (the *subjugated*), as the essential point here is a moment of reversal and regain of initiative by the man or woman who decides, in a given situation, to construct a narrative that traps power (of assistance or security) on its own ground, expressing itself towards it. As I have had the occasion to show in a study on the confrontation between refugees – whether 'false refugees' or 'clandestine' migrants – and representatives of the UNHCR in Guinea who were preparing to organize a collective return to Sierra Leone, this kind of 'disagreement' [*mésentente*][21] can end with stone-throwing and the refugees' refusal to submit to UNHCR head counts.[22] This reversal (accompanied by a violent gesture, one form or other of rupture, etc.) is certainly not systematic, but we observe here a change that takes place between what the refugee is supposed to do or say as conceived by the defining order, and what he actually does say and do. It is in this action that an other-subject can actually be observed and described.

Anthropology has to free itself from any identity model that might lead it to impute, seek and possibly proclaim a more or less 'hidden' truth behind observable processes and situations, and refer this to an identity 'core' or a primary definition of a self or a 'we'. Decentring will enable it to observe and understand the dynamic opposition between identity assignment and the emergence of a decentred subject that frees itself from assignment of this kind. In this context, the subject can be understood in social science as a hybrid concept for a hybrid actor who finds himself on the border (of place, of the familiar, of habits, of the everyday). And subjectification can then be understood as the 'process by which a subject becomes capable of shifting himself without, however, tearing himself completely away from his condition'.[23] This relative tearing away or provisional shift are what an ethnography of the situation can exhibit, to the extent that a dynamic of the situation is observed. In other words, it becomes possible to describe an action or a *politics of the subject* that exists for the time and space that coincide with the situation. This is then defined as a moment in a social process, and the place of an encounter between a plurality of personal processes and this common moment. Everything that makes for a border in this situation – uncertain and in-between identity, distinction and relationship, negotiation and conflict – is propitious to the emergence of the subject.

The decentred subject: three situational analyses

If we focus on the socialized and relational sphere, and the conditions that make this a field for the anthropologist, we come across several cases of this figure of the subject 'who imposes himself' and, by this irruption, 'challenges our habitual ways of thinking', forcing on us a decentring:[24] this is the subject who speaks out, seizing speech, initiative or space, directing us to the analysis of a situation and a moment, rather than that of a social structure or a biopolitical apparatus that produce and freeze identity assignments. This is what I have learned from the situations that I want to mention now, with the sole aim of identifying some possible figures of the subject, which may be completed by other figures, thus opening a space of research and reflection that are free from identity analysis while still seeking to understand how subjects themselves treat their relationships to identity assignment.

The ritual subject, or the subject as duplication of self and world

The first case I shall present here is inscribed in a context of ritual liminality, when a situation occurs that breaks with the ordinary identity assignment: it is in this liminal situation that those subjects exist who take the name 'African' or 'black'.

Each year, in Salvador de Bahia in Brazil, in the black and mestizo

146

district of Liberdade, the first carnival appearance of the black group Ilê Aiyê takes place in the course of the Saturday night before Mardi Gras. 'Here are the Bahian Africans', the group declared at its first carnival in 1975. Its provocative attitude and the official and media condemnation this aroused also led to a real enthusiasm among the city's black youth, who saw this as a space of expression, leisure and self-valorization. By proclaiming its refusal to see whites parade in its group, Ilê Aiyê became the expression in the Bahian carnival of the movements of black racial revolt and political organization that had developed at the same time in the United States, Europe and South Africa. Then, in a few years, a whole panoply of ceremonies, rituals and heroes was born and formed the image of African reference in Bahia: figures of the black Mother, of the Ebony goddess, of Zumbi, hero of the resistance of the Maroon communities in the seventeenth century (*quilombos*), as well as hundreds of samba compositions and a ritual of 'opening of paths' inspired by Afro-Brazilian cults, peopled this duplicated world that was known as the Black World, *Mundo negro*.[25]

The Ilê Aiyê parade is still a remarkable event, in the sense that it is distinguished from the surrounding carnival confusion by mobilizing a large group (at least 2,000 participants) who are very calm, very respected and very respectable. A strong and shared sentiment is created with the parade, despite its being confined for everyone to the carnival time. The tie to a symbolic Africa acts as a communitarian mediation between all those present. A momentary community is formed, and the samba words composed by the amateur authors of Ilê Aiyê are sung: 'I am an exotic black', 'We are the Bahaian Africans', 'By the colour of my cloth [the carnival costume] you can see I'm African', etc.

We may ask what the meaning is of this festive and ritual creation of a subject called 'Bahian African', a political subject wearing a seemingly 'identitarian' mask. It is first of all the conversion, during the interval time of carnival, of a subaltern social and political position, despised or stigmatized, generating a 'contrary' reaction. To be this 'Bahian African', in the presentation of a self *duplicated* in and by way of the Bahia carnival, means first of all not being the 'black' of racism and Brazilian society in everyday life. A gap is created between an assigned identity and a subject that asserts itself by refusing this. Far more than an assertion of identity, this is in fact a space of subjectification: subjects emerge, at a given moment and in a place propitious to this expression, by imposing their speech against the identity inscribed in the language that subordinates, inferiorizes or

147

diminishes them. But this clearly has nothing to do with a 'return' to the African continent, or with any desire for a 'black party' (which besides does not exist). It is in fact a subject against identity, not a subject defined by this.

The meaning of this creation is then the potentiality or emancipatory 'becoming' contained in these moments of a political action outside its predictable context – an emancipation that is in fact unpredictable, since the carnival street is only accidentally seditious for those who put on the festival as a cathartic popular entertainment. These are movements of emancipation whose political meaning is elaborated against and/or at a distance from the order that institutes their identity: being thus at the limit, they position themselves as an 'anti-structure'.[26] It is in no way surprising that this anti-structure should sometime take for the duration of this action the imperfect, 'makeshift' and provisional language of the *community against society*. This is even a fairly recurrent figure in anthropology, that of initiatives of revolt and refusal, of a voluntary marginality either political or artistic.

Moreover, the ritual context of the masquerade and the presence of the mask are a major piece of information. We learn by this that the subjectification operates what we might call a *double* duplication: it is a liminal space-time outside the everyday (the parade), in which a moment of duplication of self is lived (the mask, and disguise in general) which is the result of a work on the self, as we shall see in more detail in the next case. This is what enables it to exist under a mask other than the social one that makes for the person's existence in his everyday life. For this context of ritual duplication, this interval-time, is renewable and extendable, which makes it potentially seditious. It may last a few hours (the time of a parade), a few days (the 'carnival week' in Brazil), even a few weeks (certain Caribbean carnivals run from 6 January to Mardi Gras). And it can always 'overflow' as well as 'tumble' and 'empty'.[27]

The aesthetic subject, or the care of self and the subject as author

If we have seen in the first example a seizure of space (the carnival street) and a necessary duplication of self by way of the tension imposed on identity by the ritual subject, we shall see in the following cases how, in order to produce an account of oneself, a certain number of conditions have to be met. First of all, a place in which to speak out, where speech can be socialized and understood, first by a nearby interlocutor and possibly then by a larger and more anonymous audience. This is relational speech. Several contexts are possible, as we were able to observe apropos of spaces of testimony and speaking out among refugee or displaced groups. There is for example the interaction with the ethnologist who finds himself there, in a Guinean refugee camp, collecting 'life stories'. As in my own experience, the research could be 'diverted' and transformed by Sierra Leonean refugees into a moment of generalized testimony, in order, as they thought, to respond indirectly to the representatives from the UNHCR headquarters who were visiting the region at that very time and offered certain possibilities of 'resettlement' in a third country instead of collective repatriation to Sierra Leone. Beyond the two immediate reasons (the ethnologist's research, the refugees' demand for 'resettlement' by the UNHCR), a third meaning imposes itself on the situation: that of a moment of speaking out, establishing a subject of speech that imposes itself for a moment in the space of the camp.

Speaking out may also be 'writing out'. This was the case with the notes on scraps of paper, the beginnings of a history, conveyed by the refugees to the Médécins Sans Frontières desk in the Guinean episode recounted earlier. It is more generally the case in every research relationship that creates a face-to-face meeting between knowledge and speech, and thus between object and subject, transformed into an encounter in which speech becomes knowledge and a subject emerges in writing viewed as a medium of the relationship. Philippe Artières discusses this transformation in relation to the undertaking of a medical criminologist in the nineteenth century, Dr Alexandre Lacassagne (1843–1924), who sought to write a 'living encyclopaedia of crime'.[28] To this end, he solicited writings from criminals in prison. 'He entrusted his gaze to the same people who had previously been its object', constituting the observed subject into a producer of the discourse concerning him. In the same period, doctors tried to make the 'alienated' in their charge speak the truth about their pathologies. Their object was to constitute 'living archives of sickness'.

As Philippe Artières notes, 'We thus see personal writing make its entry into medicine' (p. 32). Autobiographies and self-portraits became 'scientific documents'. The texts written by the prisoners selected by Dr Lacassagne, on school exercise books that were regularly passed on to the doctor and commented on by him, responded to an 'autobiographical injunction' (p. 34). The exercise required a work of writing which the doctor promised would have two direct effects on the prisoners: a symbolic effect (they would be read by at least one person, himself) and a material effect (their conditions of detention would be improved a bit for the sake of writing). At the end of the day, however, the exercise produced a 'graphic existence': the prisoner's cell became a 'writing workshop', and the detainees' texts were 'discourses of resistance': 'Far from being discourses of submission and subjection, the detainees' words were disturbing: they muddied what was seemingly clear' (p. 381). Even if they did not think that their writing would change their legal situation, it was a response to a long period in which 'the detainee had been the object of all gazes and discourse'. Dr Lacassagne's request broke a logic, reversed roles from object to subject. For Philippe Artières, 'this was probably the main reason for their writing' (p. 382). Thus, the benefits of writing can be assessed differently. As well as the two direct benefits already mentioned, there was another induced effect: their lives were suddenly transformed, they became authors. One of them wrote: 'My table weighed down with books and notebooks looks to me more like the table of a writer than that of a prisoner' (p. 381).[29]

Another 'book' was written by four Rwandan Hutu teachers in 2000, in the refugee camp of Maheba in Zambia.[30] They took elements from testimonies collected from Hutus who had, like them, arrived in the camp two years before (the camp also took in refugees of other nationalities), to make a single narrative. When I met one of them in 2002, the project was still referred to in the camp as the 'book of the Hutu refugees', a collective text entitled *L'Itinéraire le plus long et le plus pénible: Les réfugiés hutus à la recherche de l'asile*. These teachers presented themselves as its authors.[31] The 'publication' of the account was also done in the camp, where the work then circulated. On this occasion the camp became the stage on which the 'Hutu refugees'' account of themselves as a 'people in exodus' was played. The question for them was then to shed a stigmatized identity which had kept them apart since their arrival, to write against the 'policy of diabolization of the Hutu refugee' and the extreme suspicion of being '*génocidaires*'. The book was dedicated to 'all the world's refugees'. The account set out to construct a universal image (or one that purported to be such) of the refugees by detailing their sufferings – fatigue, hunger, ill-treatment, fear, flight – and their staging-posts through several countries between July 1994 (their departure from Rwanda) and November 1998 (their arrival in the Maheba camp). They wanted to show that a 'twentieth-century exodus [that of the Hutu people] had taken place similar to that of the people of Moses'. The explicit reference to the Bible and the wandering Jewish people also meant that this was an exile with no return. This reference and the term 'refugee' became for the Hutus of the Maheba camp words that acted as symbols vis-à-vis the camp's other inhabitants, designed to identify them with 'victims of war' and 'all the world's refugees'.

These examples show that an account of oneself oriented to others involves an aesthetic concern: linguistic or writing skills, skills of role-playing and presentation of self, are necessary for speaking out. Finally, work is needed in order to create and perfect as far as possible the account as a presentation of self; this is what, beyond the intentions assigned to any particular story, book or theatre play, transforms the 'self' into an author, so that they present themselves at the end of a successful aesthetic work as the 'pure' and 'true' witness, transparent to their 'self'.

The political subject, or the subject as a demand for citizenship

I have defined the refugee camp as an 'out-place':[32] it is not – or not only – a space of atomized and/or abandoned individuals, it is a space on the margin, at the outer limit, an in-between space, where one story among many of the 'foreigner' is rewritten today, a foreigner who remains confined and without a place of arrival. The camp, especially when it endures, represents a border situation; it is a space always under control yet always liminal.

Refugees and displaced persons may be forced to enter camps, whereas others are forced to leave them. The 'geo-logistics'[33] of refugees involves both a control of spaces and a control of mobilities. In everyday humanitarian government they are generally sorted into categories of greater or lesser 'vulnerability', with a greater or lesser right to a particular kind of protection, a particular kind of taking in charge. The UNHCR, for example, uses some fifteen categories of 'vulnerables' who are in a certain sense more 'categorized' and taken greater charge of than others. What is going on here is the implementation of the principles of biopower already mentioned as a means of sorting, classification and division of populations to be handled, which means keeping some of them and excluding others from access to certain types of care or benefit. In this context, protests have taken place, very brief and sometimes very violent, on the part of those refugees who are often the least badly off, as it is these who play the role of leaders – who can speak English, who have a little money set aside and are recognized by the others as able to speak 'in their name'. As I could myself observe in a Sierra Leonean camp, they come and tell the white officials of the humanitarian organizations that 'all refugees are vulnerable', rejecting the categories produced by the operators of humanitarian government. Strikes of refugees

151

employed by international NGOs who demand salaries equivalent to those of the 'nationals', boycotts of the World Food Programme rations, sequestration of relief workers, demonstrations outside the NGO compounds, etc. There are certainly material stakes at issue in these actions (the quality of shelters and food rations, the right to move around and work, etc.), but also and more generally a demand for rights that uses the name of refugee while changing the meaning of humanitarian language. In a certain way, these people are saying: 'We are not the refugees that you think we are. We are other subjects.'

The subject in this case is not a citizen, since no state recognizes this condition; no citizenship law corresponds to their condition as a 'victim' with a suffering and silent body. The individual refugee, detached from his context of socialization and identification (left behind where they were a 'persona'), is kept at a distance, stopped in a place assigned outside any space of political recognition. In this biopolitical context, their action is that of a 'becoming-citizen':[34] they act in politics (declare, question, express disagreement and demand) *as if it was a question of citizenship*, but in a space and a language which are humanitarian and know only the object-subject, the sub-jugated, the silent image and body of the vulnerable/undesirable. They must therefore create the political moment (by a gesture, an act of violence, a brusque imposition, an interruption of the normal course of things) that can transform the dominant humanitarian stage into a 'democratic stage', marginal and liminal, occasional and unexpected.[35] But if the subject is stateless, what they express then demands a space of political legitimacy beyond or outside the sphere of the nation-state that is globally recognized as the space of political right. What is expressed both exists and does not exist: this is a supra-national or non-national citizen, who effects a reversal (for the time of this subjectification and this scene) of the relationship between the rights of the citizen and human rights. The latter are brought into play as a political language, which makes the subject exist as a demand for citizenship.

We observe in this context what can be called a short time of the subject: this is the here and now of these refugee camps which are the scene of these political stages, which do not find a 'natural' legitimacy but render the humanitarian apparatus, or elsewhere the security apparatus, less unchallengeable. And there is also, in a wider and more encompassing context, a long time of the subject: this is the political meaning, in the historical context of control of mobili-ties and national borders on a global scale, of the displacements of migrants, refugees and the 'clandestine' who reject their confinement or encampment, and move *against* any kind of distancing. Their presence and their 'disobedience' exhibit a very political confrontation between the flow of migration from South to North and the flow of humanitarian charity from North to South.

Moments and politics of the other-subject

In the situations we have discussed, subjects come into existence by detaching themselves from their social condition, from an assigned identity (racial, ethnic, humanitarian) and possibly a suffering self. This is how the question of the subject interpellates the empirical social sciences and how we can begin to speak of an anthropology of the subject. If there must necessarily be spaces and conditions, stages or situations, in order for subjectification to exist, whether ritual, aesthetic or political, there are also 'people' who bring themselves into existence as subjects under certain conditions and in a given situation. This is what we now have to think about: there are not only subjectifications, there is also the formation of a subject in a given space and at a given moment, and this is where things become more complex and more interesting. For this moment of subjectification is added (without suppressing them) to the two other figures we are accustomed to, in anthropology and in sociology: that of the persona and that of the individual. Something other is also sometimes happening: the concept of subject then denotes a decentred arrival, it is an intermediate concept closer to speaking out – the seizure of speech, politics, aesthetics or action in general. It is 'in situation', and in a tension with and against assigned identity and place, that the subject arises. A new conception of alterity is thus manifested, that of the *other-subject*; this is essentially situational and 'border-like', it is what happens, and it enables us to advance towards a non-culturalist conception of alterity.

The cases briefly discussed here have enabled us to demonstrate three dimensions of the formation of the subject, which are not mutually exclusive and very likely do not exhaust the question. First of all, a ritual dimension teaches us that a duplication of context makes possible the duplication of self, as exemplified by rituals of reversal or possession, but also the more or less seditious demonstration of carnival, or the more or less carnivalesque character of the political parade. This ritual subject is familiar to anthropology. In it we shall possibly find certain marks, local or ancestral, of the persona and his or her identities: these marks of identity can be mobilized as resources

153

for the seizure of speech and the assertion of a difference. It would be mistaken, however, to see this as no more than an 'identitarian manifestation' that justifies keeping at a distance the place from where it seeks to emerge. This would be an incomplete analysis that lost sight of the essential point, which is the very contemporary desire that subjects have to create a place in the very context where the scene is played out.

We can expand this reflection and investigate the ritual dimension of all subjectification. The ritual moment brings into existence momentary communities, freeing the analysis of these political actions from any identity assignment. The point is to become an other-subject in a momentarily other context. This moment does not produce a transcendental subject or a more 'subjective' or 'truer' identity than others: it creates the conditions for the irruption of a speaking, acting subject, recognized in a localized situation that is shared and observable.

Secondly, the aesthetic part of the seizure of speech (or of writing, or of role) participates, beyond the 'product' of the performance, in the advent of the author as expression of the subject. As soon as an individual or a collective are concerned to present themselves as interlocutor by their seizure of speech, to make a performance of their account, to write a 'book' (as did the Hutu refugees from Rwanda in the Maheba camp in Zambia), or to put on a skit in the street that can then become a theatre stage,[36] they become authors in an aesthetic dimension. They emerge from their 'self', and this aesthetic work of telling oneself makes it possible to work the bodily and biographical material of this 'self' by becoming an author-subject. The 'persona' is thus duplicated in a performance, without disappearing.

Thirdly, the political dimension is both the most evident and that which depends on other means, ritual and aesthetic, of formation (to be 'outside of oneself') and of staging (to create the space of the subject, its stage). The political subject exists in movement, aggressiveness and anger, even in violence. The refugee who wages political action in the camp where they are established for the duration, like the migrant or 'clandestine' on the move, is the very opposite of the 'victim' who is the initial form imposed by their subjection, the caricature figure of the 'negative' individual, desocialized, surviving. They all have to detach themselves in order to irrupt as subject of a 'regaining of initiative'.[37] Their action will directly influence the definition of the places of each in the world, as also, asserting their singularity, their own lives and those of the persons surrounding them.

CONCLUSION: TOWARDS AN ANTHROPOLOGY OF THE COSMOPOLITAN CONDITION

Globalization has put the question of cosmopolitism back on the agenda. This connects us with the century of the Enlightenment and particularly Immanuel Kant's project of 'perpetual peace'.[1] Far from being idealistic, this philosophical and political essay was highly pragmatic. It contains three major ideas and is surprisingly topical. First of all, the Earth is round and we are condemned to get on with one another because we are all constantly meeting up on the 'surface of the Earth'. Then, freedom is the precondition for 'world citizenship', since one has to be able to cross borders in order to experience the world and others, to emerge from oneself, from the assigned boundary of identity. And finally, Kant says, exchange, in particular commercial exchange, will be all the more fruitful if this world scale is effectively put into practice. What is verifiable on the economic level, that is, the power of nomadism, is so also on the social and political level.[2]

The question today is therefore to conceive the possibility of a 'common world', in a context in which our planet is becoming the reality most shared by all humans. A new object needs to be conceived, political and societal, at a time when moving and sharing the same world have become technically feasible. It is as if technical inventions have been more rapid than social and political ones. As if there has been a 'delay' between one globalization and the other. And this gap does indeed denote the difference and, still more, the conflict between globalization and the common world. It is what the philosopher Étienne Tassin calls the 'globalization of *a-cosmism*, a systematic destruction of the world under cover of its economic and techno-scientific domination'.[3] If Kant's vision suffers from *angélisme* ('an abnormal desire to escape from the conditions of

155

bodily existence'), Tassin maintains that this is because it is a pacified thought of the world, which needs to eliminate conflicts to become actuality. A confusion has thus been created between cosmopolitics and cosmopolitism. In my view, however, if cosmopolitics is the quest for a common world (a condition for politics in Hannah Arendt's sense)[4] on a global scale, then cosmopolitism must be the anthropological and sociological framework of this world politics.

It is at this moment that the experience, evidence and analysis of anthropologists may be very useful. Not to reintroduce a fictional exoticism or an absolute difference between other peoples – 'stateless' or 'ontologized'. Dialogue between philosophers and anthropologists should be able to be resumed under the auspices of the contemporary, and particularly on the basis of what we learn from human mobility and along with it the status of the foreigner and the future of borders. These political and contemporary questions also presage the possibility of a common world, since they raise on a global scale the central question of equality in mobility and the crossing of borders, preconditions for the exercise of this world.

The contribution of anthropology to this reflection comes from its anchoring in places where the cosmopolitan condition is being formed today as a commonplace reality. This is all the more obvious a state of affairs inasmuch as it is lived by persons in movement, crossing borders – and increasingly frequently blocked there for a long time.

All persons in movement are central from the point of view of this everyday cosmopolitism, just as are border situations. These are thresholds, dead and transitional times, places of encounter, crossing and conflict, relationships that require unprecedented translations and exchanges. Positioned in this way in the most 'central' place of a decentred world, borders can thus rediscover their fundamental role as a space, time and ritual of relationship.

This allows me to recall an obvious but essential point, effectively dismissed by the obsessive champions of the 'clash of civilizations' that is the foundation of the new world 'governance': relationship to the other is indispensable to the functioning of a common world. There is no common world without alterity. The question then is to transform the global foreigner, invisible and phantom-like, whom identity politics leaves nameless and voiceless behind material or invisible walls, bureaucratic or ideological, into a person whose alterity becomes again relative and potentially closer. On this basis it will be possible to reconsider each border as a new test of alterity where an other-subject emerges, the cosmopolitan subject, come to disturb the existing identity-based order. This subject only comes into existence in an exchange, of which the border is the place. In short, the other-subject is not a being frozen in a distant elsewhere, closed, inaccessible or incomprehensible; he or she is on the border, actually here, in a contemporaneity and spatial continuity of the world that makes it possible to establish a relationship with them.

This is why I saw it as important to redefine decentring in wider terms than cultural relativism, which proves insufficient for thinking universalism in a common world. For the Ghanaian philosopher Kwame Anthony Appiah, the word 'cosmopolitism' is the equivalent of neither 'globalization' nor 'multiculturalism', but literally means 'world-city'.[5] I would happily add that this 'world-city' is made up of the sum of all the border situations experienced today, and that form the common social context where singularities and inequalities, projects of life and representations of the other, are born and confront one another. The cosmopolitan context of cosmopolitics. For the relationships that are formed at border situations can no longer be explained by the ethnic or national contexts in which the discovery of other peoples has been conceived in the past. The circulation of persons, information and knowledge has already transformed the context of individual and collective lives.

The challenge posed to us all now is thus not only to 'de-Westernize' universalism, to 'de-nationalize' or 'de-ethnicize' thought and action in a decentred world. It is above all to succeed in conceiving a common world, in which the programme of equality must be reinvented, with a cosmopolitan narrative on the first page.

NOTES

Preface to the English Edition

1 Michael Billig, *Banal Nationalism*, London: Sage, 1995.

Introduction

1 Information from Migreurop and Frontierenews.it, 14 July 2012.
2 Mike Davis, *City of Quartz: Excavating the Future in Los Angeles*, London: Verso, 1990.
3 Carl Schmitt, *The Nomos of the Earth in the International Laws of the Jus Publicum Europeaum*, New York: Telos, 2003; Wendy Brown, *Walled States, Waning Sovereignty*, Cambridge: Zone Books, 2014, p. 43. See more widely Brown's commentary on the spatial dimension of political order and law (*Walled States*, pp. 43–7).
4 See L. R. Chavez, *The Latino Threat: Constructing Immigrants, Citizens and the Nation*, Stanford: Stanford University Press, 2008; also Martin Lamotte, 'États-Unis/Mexique: les milices veillent . . .', *Hermès*, 63, 2012, pp. 101–8.
5 I describe in chapter 3 the contemporary figure of the *métèque* who corresponds to these paradoxical border situations, where illegality and utility combine to produce legal, urban and physical precariousness, strengthening his or her link with the other figures of the 'pariah' and the 'wanderer'. [Agier uses this French term, stripped of the derogatory connotation it has often acquired, in its original sense, as a translation of the ancient Greek *metoikos*; see p. 59. – Translator.]
6 A study conducted jointly with Sara Prestianni, a photographer and at this time the coordinator of the Migreurop network, the results of which are reported in Michel Agier and Sara Prestianni, *'Je me suis réfugié là!' Bords de routes en exil*, Paris: Éditions Donner Lieu, 2011.

Chapter 1 The Elementary Forms of the Border

1 Régis Debray, *Éloge de la frontière*, Paris: Gallimard, 2011, p. 12.
2 Debray, *Éloge*, p. 77.
3 Debray, *Éloge*, p. 45.
4 Michel Foucher, *L'Obsession des frontières*, Paris: Perrin, 2007, p. 18.
5 Besides his career as a professor and researcher in geography, Michel Foucher has also had a high-flying career as a geostrategic consultant and diplomat.
6 Wendy Brown, *Walled States, Waning Sovereignty*, Cambridge: Zone Books, 2014.
7 Marc Augé, *Le Temps en ruines*, Paris: Galilée, 2003, p. 15.
8 Fredrik Barth, 'Introduction', in *Ethnic Groups and Boundaries: The Social Organization of Culture Difference*, Boston: Little Brown, 1969, pp. 9–37.
9 Arjun Appadurai, *Modernity at Large: Cultural Dimensions of Globalization*, Minneapolis: University of Minnesota Press, 1996.
10 The *orixás* are divinities in the Afro-Brazilian *candomblé* cult, most of whom were 'transported' in the nineteenth century from the Gulf of Guinea to Bahia. Other rituals (processions in particular) and other divinities came from earlier phases in the slave trade, in this case from central Africa.
11 An intermediary divinity between humans and spirits, the protector of thresholds, crossroads and paths. The function of Exu (or Legba) is found in West Africa (on the littoral of the Gulf of Guinea), where this tutelary and propitiatory function is applied to the entire house and to those that it shelters (inhabitants and visitors from outside), without a particular religious activity taking place.
12 See Michel Agier, 'Between affliction and politics: a case study of Bahian *candomblé*', in Hendrik Kraay (ed.), *Afro-Brazilian Culture and Politics: Bahia, 1790s–1990s*, New York: Sharpe, 1998, pp. 134–57, where the study of Vila Flaviana is presented in detail. Recent work that renews the approach to this question, both locally and globally, includes Kadya Tall, *Le Candomblé de Bahia: Miroir baroque des mélancolies postcoloniales*, Paris: Cerf, 2011; and Kaly Argyriadis and Stefania Capone (eds.), *La Religion des orisha: Un champ social transnational en pleine recomposition*, Paris: Hermann, 2012.
13 Maurice Godelier, *Au fondement des sociétés humaines: Ce que nous apprend l'anthropologie* (2007), Paris: Flammarion, 2010.
14 Godelier, *Au fondement des sociétés humaines*, p. 215.
15 Maurice Godelier, *Communauté, société, culture*, Paris: Éditions du CNRS, 2009, p. 27.
16 See Arnold Van Gennep, *The Rites of Passage* (1909), London: Routledge, 1960, and the development of his analyses of rites of passage by Victor Turner (*The Ritual Process: Structure and Anti-Structure*, New Brunswick: Aldine Transaction, 1995), particularly apropos of ritual liminality, a subject which we will return to later. Michel Leiris's study of the rites of possession of the *zar* in Ethiopia (*La Possession et ses aspects théâtraux chez les Éthiopiens de Gondar*, Paris: Plon, *Cahiers de L'homme*, no. 1, 1958) has shown the importance of the contexts, actors and social and aesthetic effects of ritual. The analysis of the 'ritual dispositive' and its either restrained (for example therapeutic) or enhanced (contextual and identitarian) effects has

been developed by Marc Augé, *An Anthropology for Contemporary Worlds*, Stanford: Stanford University Press, 1999.

17 On the connection between Lupercalia and the foundation of Rome, I have drawn on the research of Brice Grouet, *La Rue à Rome, miroir de la ville: Entre l'émotion et la norme*, Paris: Presses de l'Université Paris Sorbonne, 2006.

18 Which would explain its pre-carnivalesque character (see the section 'Interval time: carnivals and deceleration').

19 Alexis de Tocqueville, 'Fortnight in the wilderness' (1831), in George Wilson Pierson, *Tocqueville in America*, Baltimore: Johns Hopkins University Press, 1996, p. 239.

20 See Michel Serres, *The Troubadour of Knowledge*, Ann Arbor: Michigan University Press, 1997. I shall return later to this hybrid figure of the *tiers-instruit* as one of the universal components of the foreigner.

21 See http://occupybufferzone.wordpress.com

22 See Jacqueline de Bourgoing's synthetic presentation, *Le Calendrier: Maître du temps?*, Paris: Gallimard, 2000; also Ali Magoudi, *Quand l'homme civilise le temps: Essai sur la sujétion temporelle*, Paris: La Découverte, 1992 (new edition 2001); Daniel Fabre, *Carnaval ou la fête à l'envers*, Paris: Gallimard, 1992; Jacques Heers, *Fêtes de fous et carnavals*, Paris: Fayard, 1983.

23 De Bourgoing, *Le Calendrier*, p. 23.

24 De Bourgoing, *Le Calendrier*, p. 29.

25 This is the gesture indicated in the Bantu language by the word *semba*, the literal sense of which is 'blow with the navel' [*coup de nombril*]. Brought to Brazil by the slaves who danced it, the word was either translated into Portuguese as *umbigada* (the old name for a round), or kept as such to give rise to 'samba', the name for the Brazilian carnival rhythm.

26 Mikhail Bakhtin, *Rabelais and His World*, Bloomington: Indiana University Press, 1984.

27 Christine Ramat, 'Les langues de carnaval dans les écritures des Caraïbes: le bel envers de la littérature', in Biringanine Ndagano (ed.), *Penser le carnaval: Variations, discours et représentations*, Paris: Karthala, 2010, pp. 195–210 at p. 196.

28 Florabelle Spielman, 'Le carnaval de Trinidad: jeux de masques et masca-rades', in Christine Falgayrette-Levreau (ed.), *Mascarades et carnavals* (with advice from Michel Agier), Paris: Dapper, 2011, pp. 227–55.

29 See Christian Cécile, 'Mas et rites de Guadeloupe: un carnaval contestataire', in Falgayrette-Levreau, *Mascarades et carnavals*, pp. 157–77.

30 Marcel Détienne, *Comment être autochtone? Du pur Athénien au Français raciné*, Paris: Seuil, 2003, p. 146.

Chapter 2 The World as 'Problem'

1 http://www.migreurop.org/article2302.html. See Migreurop, *Atlas des migrants en Europe: Géographie critique des politiques migratoires*, Paris: Armand Collin, 2012.

2 Tara Brian and Frank Laczko (eds.), *Fatal Journeys: Tracking Lives Lost during Migration*, Geneva: International Organization for Migration (IOM), 2014.

3 Atiq Rahimi, 'The Ninth Night', in *Le Retour imaginaire*, Paris: POL, 2005.

4 Immanuel Kant, 'Perpetual peace: a philosophical sketch' (1795), in *Political Writings*, ed. H. D. Reiss, Cambridge: Cambridge University Press, 1970, pp. 93–130.

5 Several contemporary philosophers have taken up this theme and developed it at length. After René Scherer (*Zeus hospitalier: Éloge de l'hospitalité*, Paris: La Table ronde, 1993) and Jacques Derrida (*On Cosmopolitanism*, Abingdon: Routledge, 2001), see in particular the works of Étienne Tassin, *Un Monde commun: Pour une cosmopolitique des conflits*, Paris: Seuil, 2003; Étienne Balibar, 'Cosmopolitisme et internationalisme: deux modèles, deux héritages', in Francisco Naishtat (ed.), *Philosophie politique et horizon cosmopolitique*, Paris: UNESCO, 2006, pp. 37–64; Guillaume Leblanc, *Dedans, dehors: La condition d'étranger*, Paris: Seuil, 2010; and Kwame Appiah, *Cosmopolitanism: Ethics in a World of Strangers*, New York: Norton, 2007.

6 Antonia Birnbaum, 'Ville, cité, site: déplacement de l'hospitalité', *Dé(s)générations*, 13, 2011, pp. 44–64 at p. 48.

7 Saskia Sassen, *A Sociology of Globalization*, New York: Norton, 2007.

8 Jean-François Bayart has developed a global-level social stratification schema that shows the emergence of a global elite of experts (*Global Subjects: A Political Critique of Globalization*, Cambridge: Polity, 2008); and Georges Com (*Le Nouveau gouvernement du monde: Idéologies, structures et contre-pouvoirs*, Paris: La Découverte, 2010) analyses the new bureaucratic elite who manage the world.

9 See Claire Rodier, *Xénophobie business: A quoi servent les contrôles migratoires?*, Paris: La Découverte, 2012 and Ruben Andersson, *Illegality, Inc.: Clandestine Migration and the Business of Bordering Europe*, Oakland: University of California Press, 2014.

10 Arjun Appadurai, *Modernity at Large: Cultural Dimensions of Globalization*, Minneapolis: University of Minnesota Press, 1996.

11 Appadurai, *Modernity at Large*, p. 274.

12 Marc Augé, *Le Temps en ruines*, Paris: Galilée, p. 15.

13 These issues are examined further in chapter 4.

14 See Catherine Wihtol de Wenden, *La Question migratoire au XXIe siècle: Migrants, réfugiés et relations internationales*, Paris: Presses de Sciences Po, 2013. The demographic data used here come from this source, which itself draws on the 2012 annual report of the OECD, *Perspectives des migrations internationales*, Paris: OECD, 2012 (http://dx.doi.org/10.1787/migr_outlook-2012-fr).

15 Jean and John Comaroff, *Zombies et frontières à l'ère neoliberal: Le cas de l'Afrique du Sud post-apartheid*, Paris: Les Prairies Ordinaires, p. 78.

16 Aurelia Segatti and Loren Landau (eds.), *Contemporary Migration to South Africa: A Regional Development Issue*, Africa Development Forum, Washington, DC: AFD/World Bank, 2011. See also the study by Dominique Vidal, *Migrants du Mozambique dans le Johannesburg de l'après-apartheid: Travail, frontières, altérité*, Paris and Johannesburg: Karthala-IFAS, 2014.

17 Clara Lecadet, '"Tinzawaten c'est le grand danger pour nous les immigrés!"', *Hermès* (dossier 'Murs et frontières'), 63, 2012, pp. 95–100. On the contemporary global phenomenon of expulsions, see Nicholas De Genova and Nathalie Peutz (eds.), *The Deportation Regime: Sovereignty, Space, and the Freedom of Movement*, Durham, NC: Duke University Press, 2010.

18 The term used by Michel Foucault in *Blanchot*, New York: Zone Books, 1987.

19 I have discussed these issues both empirically and theoretically in *Managing the Undesirables*, Cambridge: Polity, 2011. The network of camps and encampments across the world is presented in a collective essay in global ethnography, *Un monde de camps* (edited by Michel Agier with the assistance of Clara Lecadet, Paris: La Découverte, 2014).

20 Michel Foucher, *L'Obsession des frontières*, Paris: Perrin, 2007.

21 Wendy Brown, *Walled States, Waning Sovereignty*, Cambridge: Zone Books, 2014.

22 Brown, *Walled States*, p. 30; and Eyal Weizman, *Hollow Land: Israel's Architecture of Occupation*, London: Verso, 2007, p. 179.

23 Eyal Weizman, *Hollow Land*, and *The Least of all Possible Evils: Humanitarian Violence from Arendt to Gaza*, London: Verso, 2011.

24 Gadi Algazi, 'La Cisjordanie, nouveau "Far Est" du capitalisme israélien', *Le Monde diplomatique*, August 2006.

25 See Emmanuel Blanchard and Anne-Sophie Wender (eds.), *Guerre aux migrants*, Paris: Migreurop/Syllepse, 2007.

26 See the studies of Didier Bigo as well as various dossiers on this question from the review *Cultures et Conflits*. Also Stephen Graham, 'Ubiquitous borders', in *Cities under Siege: The New Military Urbanism*, London: Verso, 2010, pp. 89–152.

27 See Teresa Caldeira, *City of Walls: Crime, Segregation, and Citizenship in São Paulo*, Berkeley: University of California Press, 2000.

28 Brown, *Walled States*, p. 117.

29 See Zygmunt Bauman, *Liquid Modernity*, Cambridge: Polity, 2000, particularly the first chapter, 'Emancipation', pp. 16–52.

30 Brown, *Walled States*, p. 129.

31 Brown, *Walled States*, p. 165.

Chapter 3 Border Dwellers and Borderlands

1 [See note 5 to Introduction. – Translator.]

2 On these 'border landscapes' or 'borderscapes', see Thomas M. Wilson and Hastings Donnan, *A Companion to Border Studies*, Hoboken: Wiley-Blackwell, 2012, as well as the dossier 'Composer (avec) la frontière: passages, parcours migratoires et échanges sociaux' (compiled by Nicolas Puig and Véronique Bontemps) for the *Revue Européenne des Migrations Internationales*, 30:2, 2014.

3 On relative degrees of foreignness from the point of view of anthropological study, see chapter 4.

4 Collectif Précipité, *Manuel pour les habitants des villes*, vol. 1, *Nous sommes dans la frontière 2003* (book and CD), 2011.

5 We should also bear in mind, so as to measure the scale of this condition, that the number of so-called 'illegal' immigrants is far larger, since according to the UN Development Programme (UNDP), two-thirds of the world's population is unable to move freely (see Catherine Wihtol de Wenden, *La Question migratoire au XXIe siècle: Migrants, réfugiés et relations internationales*, Paris: Presses de Sciences Po, 2013).

6 See Pauline Carnet, *Passer et quitter la frontière? Les migrants africains*

'clandestins' à la frontière sud espagnole, doctoral thesis, University of Toulouse Mirail/University of Seville, 2011.

7 Anaïk Pian, Aux nouvelles frontières de l'Europe: L'aventure incertaine des Sénégalais au Maroc, Paris: La Dispute, 2009, p. 155.

8 Julien Brachet, Migrations transsahariennes: Vers un désert cosmopolite et morcelé (Niger), Bellecombe-en-Bauges: Le Croquant, 2009. See also Jocelyne Streiff-Feynart and Aurelia Segatti (eds.), The Challenge of the Threshold: Border Closures and Migration Movements in Africa, Lanham: Lexington Books, 2011.

9 Collectif Précipité, Manuel pour les habitants des villes.

10 Pian, Aux nouvelles frontières de l'Europe, p. 171.

11 Pian, Aux nouvelles frontières de l'Europe, p. 208.

12 See Michel Agier and Sara Prestianni, 'Je me suis réfugié là!' Bords de routes en exil, Paris: Éditions Donner Lieu, 2011.

13 This story and that of other refugee itineraries are presented and analysed at greater length in Michel Agier, Managing the Undesirables, Cambridge: Polity, 2011, pp. 87–115.

14 The United States, Australia and northern Europe are the main destinations for these UNHCR resettlements.

15 On the political and urban history of the Chatila camp, some 500 metres from the Gaza Hospital squat in the Sabra district, see Hala Abou-Zaki, 'Chatila (Liban): histoire et devenir d'un camp de réfugiés palestiniens', in Michel Agier (ed. with the assistance of Clara Lecadet), Un monde de camps, Paris: La Découverte, pp. 35–46.

16 Alfred Schütz, 'The stranger: an essay in social psychology', American Journal of Sociology, 49:6, 1944, pp. 499–507 at p. 506.

17 Schütz, 'The stranger', p. 507.

18 Schütz, 'The stranger', p. 506.

19 Abdelmayek Sayad's La Double Absence, Paris: Seuil, 1999, describes these two absences (of a home country and a receiving country) combined in a single person.

20 See on this point the research and discussion in the collective work edited by Alain Morice and Swanie Potot, De l'ouvrier immigré au travailleur sans papiers: Les étrangers dans la modernisation du salariat, Paris: Karthala, 2010.

21 Étienne Balibar, 'Cosmopolitisme et internationalisme: deux modèles, deux héritages', in Francisco Naishtat (ed.), Philosophie politique et horizon cosmopolitique, Paris: UNESCO, 2006, pp. 37–64 at p. 47.

22 Sandro Mezzadra and Brett Nelson, Border as a Method and the Multiplication of Labor, Durham, NC: Duke University Press, 2013.

23 For a critique of 'methodological nationalism' in the social sciences, see Ulrich Beck, 'The cosmopolitan condition: why methodological nationalism fails', Theory, Culture & Society, 24:7–8, 2007, pp. 286–90, and The Cosmopolitan Vision, Cambridge: Polity, 2006.

24 Zygmunt Bauman, Globalization: The Human Consequences, Cambridge: Polity, 1998. See also Jean-François Bayart, Le Gouvernement du monde, Paris: Fayard, 2004.

25 In the conclusion we shall return to this discussion and to what anthropology can say about it.

26 See Beck, Cosmopolitan Vision.

27 This is the starting-point of Ulrich Beck's discussion of cosmopolitism.

28 Frédéric Keck's study of the geographical spread and experience of bird flu (*Un monde grippé*, Paris: Flammarion, 2010) is strikingly different from this approach to the varied consciousness of risk, also showing one of the possible paths for global ethnography.

29 These are cases studied respectively in Africa, Colombia, France and Brazil, as presented in chapter 5.

30 Nina Glick Schiller, Linda Basch and Cristina Szanton Blanc, 'From immigration to transmigrant: theorizing transnational migration', *Anthropological Quarterly*, 68:1, 1995, pp. 48–63.

31 Nina Glick Schiller and Andrew Irving (eds.), *Whose Cosmopolitanism? Critical Perspectives, Relationalities and Discontents*, Oxford: Berghahn Books, 2014. See also Alain Tarrius, 'Des transmigrants en France: un cosmopolitisme migratoire original', *Multitudes*, 49, 2002, pp. 42–52, and *Étrangers de passage: Poor to poor, peer to peer*, La Tour d'Aigues: Éditions de l'Aube, 2015; Peter Nyers, 'Abject cosmopolitisms: the politics of protection in the anti-deportation movement', *Third World Quarterly*, 24:6, 2003, pp. 1069–93; and Gustavo Lins Ribeiro, *Outras globalizaçoes: Cosmopoliticas pos-imperialistas*, Rio de Janeiro: Eduerj, 2014.

32 Hein de Haas, *Migration Theory: Quo Vadis?*, IMI Working Papers Series, International Migration Institute, University of Oxford, 2014, no. 100, p. 23. A reflexive and critical assessment of the place of migration studies in the new anthropological approach to globalization and fieldwork is made by Alessandro Monsutti, 'The contribution of migration studies and transnationalism to the anthropological debate: a critical perspective', in Cédric Audebert and Mohamed Kamel Doraï (eds.), *Migration in a Globalized World: New Research Issues and Prospects*, Amsterdam: Amsterdam University Press, 2010, pp. 107–25.

33 De Haas, *Migration Theory*, p. 24. See also Sylvie Bredeloup, *Migrations d'aventures: Terrains africains*, Paris: Comité des Travaux Historiques et Scientifiques, 2014.

34 Balibar, 'Cosmopolitisme et internationalisme', p. 41.

35 I use the term 'multilocality' in preference to 'trans-' or 'supralocality' in order to keep the concrete reference to places and multiple anchorings rather than to uprooting.

36 Seloua Luste Boulbina, 'La décolonisation des savoirs et ses théories voyageuses', *Rue Descartes*, 78:2, 2013, pp. 19–33. See Edward Said, *Reflections on Exile, and Other Literary and Cultural Essays*, London: Granta Books, 2001. Also Barbara Cassin, 'Entre', in Jean Birnbaum (ed.), *Repousser les frontières?*, Paris: Gallimard/Folio, 2014.

37 This also applies to urban borders: see Michel Agier, *Anthropologie de la ville*, Paris: PUF, 2015.

Chapter 4 Questions of Method

1 These more particularly concern the transformation of local anchorings (see Marc Augé, *Non-lieux*, Paris: Seuil, 1992), transformations of alterity (Marc Augé, *Le Sens des autres*, Paris: Fayard, 1994) and the formation of new social and cultural 'worlds' (Marc Augé, *Pour une anthropologie des mondes contemporains*, Paris: Aubier, 1994).

2 See in particular Johannes Fabian, *Time and the Other: How Anthropology Makes its Object*, New York: Columbia University Press, 1983.

3 See in particular Clifford Geertz, *The Interpretation of Cultures*, New York: Basic Books, 1973, and 'La description dense: vers une théorie interprétative de la culture' (translated and introduced by André Mary), *Enquête*, 6, 1998, pp. 57–105; James Clifford, *The Predicaments of Culture: Twentieth Century Ethnography, Literature and Art*, Cambridge, MA: Harvard University Press, 1988; James Clifford and George Marcus, *Writing Culture: The Poetics and Politics of Ethnography*, Berkeley: University of California Press, 1986.

4 George Marcus, 'Ethnography in/of the world system: the emergence of multi-sited ethnography', *Annual Review of Anthropology*, 24, 1995, pp. 95–117; Akhil Gupta and James Ferguson (eds.), *Culture, Power, Place: Explorations in Critical Anthropology*, Durham, NC: Duke University Press, 1997.

5 Tobias Rees, 'Introduction: today, what is anthropology?', in Paul Rabinow and George Marcus (eds.), *Designs for an Anthropology of the Contemporary* (with James Faubion and Tobias Rees), Durham, NC: Duke University Press, 2008, pp. 1–12 at p. 4.

6 Rabinow and Marcus, *Designs for an Anthropology of the Contemporary*, p. 30.

7 Rabinow and Marcus, *Designs for an Anthropology of the Contemporary*, pp. 22–3.

8 See for example Jean Copans, *Critique et politique de l'anthropologie*, Paris: Maspero, 1974. John Comaroff, 'The end of anthropology, again: on the future of an in/discipline', *American Anthropologist*, 122:4, 2010, pp. 524–38, has recently summarized the discussion on the state of anthropology at a time when its end is once again proclaimed. In a perspective similar to that which I develop here, he shows that this new crisis reformulates in polemical mode a topical question, that of the need to go beyond the disciplinary limits of anthropology.

9 See Achille Mbembe, *Sortir de la grande nuit: Essai sur l'Afrique décolonisée*, Paris: La Découverte, 2013.

10 'Anthropology is alive in its post-1980s engagements, but these are very different from in its old haunts, in its still stereotypic receptions, and in an institutional life that is still a beneficiary of what some have called its Golden Age' (George Marcus, in Rabinow and Marcus, *Designs for an Anthropology of the Contemporary*, p. 32).

11 See Augé, *An Anthropology for Contemporary Worlds*, p. 60. Moreover, the opening of new terrains often leads to a revision of ways of research and description – for example, to describe and understand life in prison, relations on the Internet, politics in refugee camps or power relations in laboratories, etc. See the dossier 'Frontières de l'anthropologie' compiled by Benoît de l'Estoile and Michel Naepels for *Critique*, 680–1, 2004.

12 See for example Laurent Berger, *Les Nouvelles ethnologies: Enjeux et perspectives*, Paris: Nathan, 2004 (new edition Paris: Armand Colin, 2005); Mondher Kilani, *Anthropologie: Du local au global*, Paris: Armand Colin, 2010; and Jean Copans, *L'Ethnologie*, Paris: Le Cavalier Bleu, 2009.

13 These two ethnic groups inevitably bring to mind Bronislaw Malinowski and Marcel Griaule respectively.

14 Jean Bazin, 'À chacun son Bambara', in *Des clous dans la Joconde: L'anthropologie autrement*, Toulouse: Anarchasis, 2008, p. 105.

15 Two collective works deal with this subject: Jean-Loup Amselle and Elikia M'bokolo (eds.), *Au cœur de l'ethnie*, Paris: La Découverte, 1985, and Jean-Pierre Chrétien and Gérard Pruner (eds.), *Les Ethnies ont une histoire*, Paris: Karthala, 1989, given that there are many case studies for the period 1980–2000 that can inspire critical reflection.

16 Jean-Loup Amselle, 'Ethnie et espaces: pour une anthropologie topologique', in Amselle and M'bokolo, *Au cœur de l'ethnie*, pp. 11–48.

17 The volume edited by Fredrik Barth, *Ethnic Groups and Boundaries: The Social Organization of Culture Difference*, Boston: Little Brown, 1969, still serves as the main point of reference for this approach. See also Philippe Poutignat and Jocelyne Streiff-Fenart, *Théories de l'ethnicité*, Paris: PUF, 1995, for a general presentation of the question of ethnicity.

18 See for example Rogers Brubaker, *Ethnicity Without Groups*, Cambridge, MA: Harvard University Press, 2006, and Livio Sansone, *Blackness Without Ethnicity: Constructing Race in Brazil*, New York: Palgrave Macmillan, 2003.

19 Rogers Brubaker and Frederick Cooper, 'Beyond "identity"', *Theory and Society*, 29, 2000, pp. 1–47.

20 See Eduardo Viveiros de Castro, *Métaphysiques cannibales*, Paris: PUF, 2008.

21 See Philippe Descola, *Beyond Nature and Culture*, Chicago: University of Chicago Press, 2014, and Bruno Latour, *An Inquiry into Modes of Existence: An Anthropology of the Moderns*, Cambridge, MA: Harvard University Press, 2013. Critical analyses of the so-called 'ontological turn' have recently been published by Henrik E. Vigh and David B. Sausdal ('From essence back to existence: anthropology beyond the ontological turn', *Anthropological Theory*, 14:1, 2014, pp. 49–73). The latter show the difficulty of conceiving and studying a supposed 'radical alterity', asking for example whether, in ontological logic, a 'Western . . . Euro-American ontology' is not another aspect of this essentialism.

22 See Michel Agier, 'Le dire-vrai de l'anthropologue: réflexions sur l'enquête ethnographique du point de vue de la rencontre, des subjectivités et du savoir', Ethnographiques.org, no. 30, *Mondes ethnographiques* (http://ethnographiques.org/2015/Agier).

23 Viveiros de Castro, *Métaphysiques cannibales*, p. 19.

24 Still more, in this procedure of reification, the concept of 'persona' can be indefinitely extended to other species than the human, an intellectual operation based on the idea of a (multi-)naturalism embracing humans and non-humans, object and subject, etc. (Viveiros de Castro, *Métaphysiques cannibales*, p. 23).

25 In the final chapter of this book I resume this discussion on the possibility of thinking the subject in philosophy (after Balibar, Foucault or Rancière) and anthropology.

26 See the section 'Decentring reconceived', p. 95.

27 Oscar Calavia Saez, 'Do perspectivismo amerindio ao indio real', *Campos*, 13: 2, 2012, pp. 7–23 at p. 15.

28 This is the point at which the Amerindian ontology of Viveiros de Castro meets the totalizing constructions defended by Philippe Descola or Bruno Latour, the latter taking the ontological point of view to the point of seeing thought embodied in the totality of the Earth conceived as matter, being and divinity under the name of Gaia (*Face à Gaia: Huit conférences sur le*

nouveau régime climatique, Paris: Les Empêcheurs de Penser en Rond/La Découverte, 2015).

29 Viveiros de Castro, *Métaphysiques cannibales*, p. 121.

30 For Henrik Vigh and David Sausdal ('From essence back to existence', p. 54), this procedure dismisses the *anthropos*, questioning the principle of shared humanity as the foundation of anthropology, and thus enabling the authors of these ontologies to introduce themselves, without any detour or precaution, into the world of both non-humans and post-humans.

31 The reader will have to be satisfied, by way of context, with a brief mention of 'the conservative revolution that, over the last few decades, has shown itself particularly effective in transforming the world, in ecological as well as political terms, into something perfectly stifling' (Viveiros de Castro, *Métaphysique cannibales*, p. 12).

32 A 'ventriloquial' function of ethnology that is criticized by Alcida Ramos, who quite legitimately opposes to it the political question of the Indians' claim to speak, their access to higher education, and beyond this, the possibility of an 'auto-ethnography' (Alcida Rita Ramos, 'The politics of perspectivism', *Annual Review of Anthropology*, 41, 2012, pp. 481–94). Nonetheless, this last point, 'auto-ethnography' or 'ethnology of self', particularly sensitive in the Brazilian academic world today, is a question that crucially requires the redefinition of decentring as epistemology and on all terrains, as I argue here.

33 For myself, I firmly oppose to this anthropological essentialism the description and analysis of a construction, both biographical and political, of a *subject of speech* and a Yanomami discourse in and vis-à-vis the regional, national and global world, as carried out in a book that is exceptional in many respects, jointly written by the anthropologist Bruce Albert and the Yanomami leader Davi Kopenawa: *La Chute du ciel: Paroles d'un chaman yanomami*, Paris: Plon, 2010. I also refer on this point and others tackled here to the political critique of Terence Turner ('The crisis of late structuralism. Perspectivism and animism: rethinking nature, culture, spirit, and bodiliness', *Tipiti*, 7:1, 2009, pp. 1–42).

34 For a discussion of the place of globalization in anthropology, see Marc Abélès, *Anthropologie de la globalisation*, Paris: Payot, 2008, and Jackie Assayag, *La Mondialisation des sciences sociales*, Paris: Téraèdre, 2010. Apropos of the thesis of a 'grounding globalization' and localized studies of facts, networks and global social movements, see Michael Burawoy (ed.), *Global Ethnography: Forces, Connections, and Imaginations in a Postmodern World*, Berkeley: University of California Press, 2000.

35 As evidenced by the accounts of Michel Leiris (*L'Afrique fantôme*, 1934, in *Miroir de l'Afrique*, Paris: Gallimard, 1996, pp. 61–869) and Georges Balandier (*L'Afrique ambiguë*, Paris: Plon, 1957; new edition 2008).

36 See Adrian Adams's 'Introduction' to a modern translation of Mungo Park, *Voyage dans l'intérieur de l'Afrique* (*Travels in the Interior of Africa*, 1799), Paris: Maspero, 1980; and my own commentary in *La Sagesse de l'ethnologue*, Paris: L'Œil neuf, 2004.

37 Maurice Godelier, *Au fondement des sociétés humaines*, Paris: Flammarion, 2007, p. 72.

38 [The Musée du Quai Branly was opened in 2006 as the French's government's official museum and research centre for indigenous art. – Translator.]

39 This is the sense in which Homi Bhabha refers to 'the docile body of difference' (*Les Lieux de la culture: Une théorie postcoloniale*, Paris: Payot, 2007, p. 73), meaning at the same time the critique of political uses of the aesthetics of the 'other' and the plasticity of cultural objects, which change meanings and are transformed as they circulate (see also Jean-Paul Warner, *La Mondialisation de la culture*, Paris: La Découverte, 2008).

40 Dipesh Chakrabarty, *Provincializing Europe: Postcolonial Thought and Historical Difference*, Princeton: Princeton University Press, 2008.

41 I deliberately say 'multipolarity' so as to emphasize the political aspect of this reality of research. This is in the same direction, for example as the discussion of Jackie Assayag (*La Mondialisation des sciences sociales*, pp. 219–25) on the necessary and polemical connections between the universal and democracy, and that of Gustavo Lins Ribeiro ('Anthropologies du monde: cosmopolitique pour un nouveau scénario mondial en anthropologie', *Journal des Anthropologues*, 110–11, 2007, pp. 27–51) on the multipolarity of knowledges. See also the dossier compiled by Élisabeth Cunin and Valeria Hernandez ('De l'anthropologie de l'autre à la reconnaissance d'une autre anthropologie', *Journal des Anthropologues*, 110–11, 2007).

42 This perspective of a world anthropology founded on systematic decentring and a supersession of cultural relativism links up on a different path with the cosmopolitical project of a 'world thought' developed by Achille Mbembe starting from Africa (*Sortir de la grande nuit*).

43 Jean-Jacques Rousseau, *Discourse on the Origin and Foundations of Inequality among Men* (1755), in *The Discourses and Other Early Political Writings*, ed. and trans. Victor Gourevitch, Cambridge: Cambridge University Press, 1997, pp. 111–231.

44 Claude Lévi-Strauss, 'Jean-Jacques Rousseau, fondateur des sciences de l'homme', in *Anthropologie structurale deux*, Paris: Plon, 1973, pp. 45–56.

45 Rousseau, *Discourse*, p. 131.

46 Rousseau, *Discourse*, p. 132.

47 Rousseau, *Discourse*, p. 164ff.

48 I use here the very enlightening terms of Blaise Bachofen and Bruno Bernardi, 'Introduction', in Jean-Jacques Rousseau, *Discours sur l'origine et les fondements de l'inégalité parmi les hommes* (1755), Paris: Flammarion, 2008, p. 28.

49 Claude Lévi-Strauss, *A World on the Wane*, London: Hutchinson, 1961, p. 389.

50 Lévi-Strauss, *World on the Wane*, p. 39. There is a remarkable interpretative lineage between Rousseau's ethnological view here and the representation of an anthropology confined in cultural decentring and the exotic society, a representation of anthropology that is still found in contemporary political philosophy. From a certain point of view, the culturalist reading still serves philosophy for thinking the other 'without state' or 'against state' as counterpoint or counter-ideal. It thus forms for certain philosophers an ethnopolitical paradigm 'good for thinking', the association with the names of Rousseau, Lévi-Strauss and Clastres, to which we can now add the most recent works of James Scott, idealizing proto-anarchist mountain societies that have recently disappeared (James Scott, *The Art of Not Being Governed: An Anarchist History of Upland Southeast Asia*, New Haven: Yale University Press, 2010).

51 Bachofen and Bernardi, 'Introduction', p. 23.
52 Louis Althusser, *Cours sur Rousseau*, recorded (1972) with a preface by Yves Vargas, Paris: Le Temps des Cerises, 2012.
53 See Vargas, 'Préface', in Althusser, *Cours sur Rousseau*, pp. 9–43.
54 Jacques Rancière, *La Mésentente: Politique et philosophie*, Paris: Galilée, 1995.
55 Fabian, *Time and the Other*, p. 21.
56 There are no longer fundamental ruptures of temporality and context between the Indian reserves of the 'pacified' Amazonian forest and the favelas of Rio de Janeiro in the process of 'pacification', with a strong military and police presence and placed under 'tutelage', notes João Pacheco de Oliveira in an article of which we can say that, besides the remarkable light that it sheds on Brazilian policy towards the margins, it has the great virtue of breaking in practice with the 'great divide' within social thought on the Brazilian nation ('Pacificação e tutela militar na gestão de populações e territorios', *Mana*, 20:1, 2014, pp. 125–61).
57 Georges Balandier, *Sociologie actuelle de l'Afrique noire: Dynamique des changements sociaux en Afrique centrale*, Paris: PUF, 1955 (5th edition 1992), and *Sociologie des Brazzavilles noires*, Paris: Fondation Nationale des Sciences Politiques, 1955 (2nd edition 1985); Gérard Althabe, *Oppression et libération dans l'imaginaire*, Paris: Maspero, 1969 (new edition Paris: La Découverte, 2002); Max Gluckman, 'Analysis of a social situation in modern Zululand', *Bantu Studies*, 14, 1940, pp. 1–30; Clyde Mitchell, *The Kalela Dance: Aspects of Social Relationships among Urban Africans in Northern Rhodesia*, Manchester: Manchester University Press, 1956, and 'The situational perspective', in *Cities, Society, and Social Perception: A Central African Perspective*, Oxford: Clarendon Press, 1987, pp. 1–33.
58 Gérard Althabe ('Ethnologie du contemporain et enquête de terrain', *Terrain: Carnets du Patrimoine ethnologique*, 14, 1990, pp. 126–31) has emphasized the importance of reciprocal engagement between researcher and subjects in defining the situation as a context of communication. Moreover, theoretical developments in the situational approach can be found in articles and books by Clyde Mitchell ('Situational perspective'); Alisdair Rogers and Steven Vertovec (eds.), *The Urban Context: Ethnicity, Social Networks and Situational Analysis*, Oxford and Washington: Berg, 1995; also Terry Evens and Don Handelman (eds.), *The Manchester School: Practice and Ethnographic Praxis in Anthropology*, New York: Berghahn Books, 2006. Finally, and this is certainly not by chance, the situational approach did not find a place in the 'philological turn' of North American anthropology in the 1970s and 1980s mentioned earlier.
59 Jean Bazin, 'Interpréter ou décrire: notes critiques sur la connaissance anthropologique', in Jacques Revel and Nathan Wachtel (eds.), *Une école pour les sciences sociales*, Paris: Cerf/EHESS, 1996, pp. 401–20 (reprinted in Bazin, *Des clous dans la Joconde*, p. 409).
60 Victor Turner, *The Ritual Process: Structure and Anti-Structure*, Chicago: Aldine, 1969.
61 Georges Balandier, *Le Désordre: Éloge du mouvement*, Paris: Fayard, 1988.
62 Slavoj Žižek, *La Subjectivité à venir: Essais critiques*, Paris: Flammarion, 2006, p. 13.

Chapter 5 Civilization, Culture, Race

1 See Samuel Huntington, *The Clash of Civilizations and the Remaking of the World Order*, New York: Simon & Schuster, 1996. A reasoned response to Huntington's arguments is given by Tzvetan Todorov in *La Peur des barbares: Au-delà du choc des civilisations*, Paris: Robert Laffont, 2008.
2 Huntington, *Clash of Civilizations*, p. 128.
3 Étienne Balibar, 'Europe, pays des frontières', in *Europe, constitution, frontière*, Bègles: Éditions du Passant, 2005, p. 108.
4 See Myriam Cottias, *La Question noire: Histoire d'une construction coloniale*, Paris: Bayard, 2007. We shall return to the racial question today further on in this chapter.
5 Georges Balandier, *Afrique ambiguë*, Paris: Plon, 1957 (new edition 2008, p. 67).
6 Georges Balandier, *Sociologie actuelle de l'Afrique noire*, Paris: PUF, 1955 (new edition 1992).
7 Claude Meillassoux, *Femmes, greniers et capitaux*, Paris: Maspero, 1977 (new edition Paris: La Découverte, 1982).
8 Marc Augé, *Pouvoirs de vie, pouvoirs de mort: Introduction à une anthropologie de la répression*, Paris: Flammarion, 1977.
9 Gérard Althabe, *Oppression et libération dans l'imaginaire: Les communautés villageoises de la côte orientale de Madagascar*, Paris: Maspero, 1969 (new edition Paris: La Découverte, 2002); and, by the same author, on the postcolonial form of power, see *Les Fleurs du Congo: Une utopie du lumumbisme* (Paris: Maspero, 1974, new edition Paris: L'Harmattan, 1997).
10 Balandier, *Afrique ambiguë*, p. 37.
11 Balandier, *Afrique ambiguë*, p. 20.
12 Michel Leiris, *L'Afrique fantôme* (1934), in *Miroir de l'Afrique*, Paris: Gallimard, 1996, pp. 61–869.
13 Michel Leiris, *Cinq études d'ethnologie*, Paris: Denoël, 1969 (new edition Paris: Gallimard, 1997, p. 10).
14 Norbert Elias, *Écrits sur l'art africain*, Paris: Kimé, 2002.
15 Elias, *Écrits sur l'art africain*, p. 26 (author's emphasis).
16 Elias, *Écrits sur l'art africain*, p. 12.
17 Balandier, *Afrique ambiguë*, p. 59.
18 Paul Gilroy, *The Black Atlantic: Modernity and Double Consciousness*, London: Verso, 1993.
19 See Anne Doquet, *Les Masques dogon: Ethnologie savante et ethnologie autochtone*, Paris: Karthala, 1999. In order for this development through tourism to be possible, there obviously has to be a reverse path taken by tourists 'converted to Africanity', which leads to displacing the object of research towards ethno-tourists and the relationships established between each category (see the dossier 'Tourismes: la quête de soi par la pratique des autres', *Cahiers d'Études Africaines*, 193–4, 2009).
20 See for example Bernard Nantet, *Dictionnaire d'histoire et civilisations africaines*, Paris: Larousse, 1999.
21 Élikia M'Bokolo, *Afrique noire: Histoire et civilisations*, Paris: Hatier, 1992 (2nd edition 2004).
22 M'Bokolo, *Afrique noire*, p. 249.

23 Deeper analyses of the artefacts of this material culture, connected with the royal function that embodies and 'subjectivizes' them, have been developed by Jean-Pierre Warner, *Régner au Cameroun: Le roi-pot*, Paris: CERI and Karthala, 2009.

24 Achille Mbembe, *Sortir de la grande nuit: Essai sur l'Afrique décolonisée*, Paris: La Découverte, 2013.

25 Mbembe, *Sortir de la grande nuit*, p. 209.

26 The studies in this region were conducted between 1997 and 1999. They were centred in the forest and rivers around the Tumaco panhandle, on the far south of the Pacific coast, as well as in Cali, in the *distrito* of Agua Blanca. The research was conducted in collaboration with a research team from International Relief and Development (IRD) and the Universidad del Valle at Cali (coordinated by Fernando Urrea and Michel Agier). A great deal of research has been developed over the last twenty years in this region, little studied previously, in particular on the question of Afro-Colombian identities in rural and urban milieus. See in particular Peter Wade, *Blackness and Race Mixture: The Dynamics of Racial Identity in Colombia*, Baltimore: Johns Hopkins University Press, 1993; Anne-Marie Losonczy, *Les Saints et la forêt: Rituel, société et figures de l'échange entre Noirs et Indiens Emberà (Chocó, Colombie)*, Paris: L'Harmattan, 1997; Odile Hoffmann, *Communautés noires dans le Pacifique colombien: Innovations et dynamiques ethniques*, Paris: Karthala, 2004; Carlos Efren Agueldo, *Politique et populations noires en Colombie: Enjeux du multiculturalisme*, Paris: L'Harmattan, 2004; Olivier Barbary and Fernando Urrea (eds.), *Gente negra en Colombia: Dinámicas sociopolíticas en Cali y el Pacífico*, Medellín: Editorial Lealón, 2004; and on the town of Tumaco, Michel Agier, Manuela Alvarez, Odile Hoffmann and Eduardo Restrepo, *Tumaco: Haciendo ciudad. Historia, identidad y cultura*, Bogotá: ICANH, IRD and Univalle, 1999.

27 Mera is said to have been born in 1872 at Florida, near Cali, and to have died not far from there at Palmira in 1926, after practising as a priest in several localities on the Pacific coast. A detailed ethnographic study of this subject is given in Michel Agier, 'From local legends into globalized identities: the Devil, the priest and the musician in Tumaco', *Journal of Latin American Anthropology*, 7:2, 2002, pp. 140–67.

28 Jean-Baptiste Renard, *Rumeurs et légendes urbaines*, Paris: PUF, 1999.

29 See Alain Charier, *Le Mouvement noir au Venezuela: Revendication identitaire et modernité*, Paris: L'Harmattan, 2000.

30 This question was tackled collectively in the context of research conducted in the Pacific region of Colombia, as mentioned earlier. We can even say, given the sum total of work concerned, that this region and this period (the Colombian Pacific in the 1990s) were particularly propitious for the emergence of a problematic of identity (de)construction, in which the institutional dimension (national or international) played a preponderant role. See for example the articles in the dossier 'Black identity and social movements in Latin America: the Colombian Pacific Region', compiled and introduced by Peter Wade for the *Journal of Latin American Anthropology* (7:2, 2002), which are quite convergent on this point. A comparable problematic, in a different context, has been developed in Brazil since the early 2000s.

31 It was in this context that Brazil, followed by Colombia, adopted constitutions

and laws with a multicultural character, in 1988 and 1991 respectively (I shall return to this later in connection with Brazil).

32 Sydney Mintz and Richard Price, *The Birth of African-American Culture: An Anthropological Perspective*, Boston: Beacon Press, 1992 (first edition 1976), p. 18.

33 See Serge Gruzinski, *La Pensée métisse*, Paris: Fayard, 1999.

34 See Cottias, *La Question noire*. A deeper analysis of the formation of racial thinking and its institutions in late nineteenth-century Brazil has been conducted by Lilia Schwarcz, *O espetáculo das raças: Cientistas, instituições e questão racial no Brasil (1870–1930)*, São Paulo: Companhia das Letras, 1993. For the racialist arguments that formed the backdrop to this period, see Arthur de Gobineau, *The Inequality of Human Races* (1853–5), New York: H. Fertig, 1999.

35 See Michel Foucault, *Society Must Be Defended*, London: Allen Lane, 2003; and Thomas Holt, 'Pouvoir, savoir et race: à propos du cours de Michel Foucault "Il faut défendre la société"', in *Lectures de Michel Foucault: À propos de 'Il faut défendre la société'* (texts collected by Jean-Claude Zancarini), Lyon: ENS éditions, 2000, pp. 81–96.

36 The descriptive concept of 'black condition' used by Pap Ndiaye acknowledged the 'fact of being black' without attributing to this an identity definition with a racial or cultural character. The black condition here is the 'description in duration of this minority social experience' which consists in persons 'being generally considered as black' (Pap Ndiaye, *La Condition noire: Essai sur une minorité française*, Paris: Calmann-Lévy, 2008, p. 24). While I share this pragmatic and situational view of what the notion of a black *condition* refers to, it remains the case that the transition from black condition (a negative social experience in relation to skin colour) to 'minority perspective', and still more so to 'minority politics', both of which are introduced by this author, is by no means self-evident and very likely pertains once again to different national genealogies of 'race war'.

37 Ndiaye, *La Condition noire*, p. 41.

38 Ndiaye, *La Condition noire*, p. 63.

39 An earlier version of this section of the present chapter was published in English in the journal of the Latin American Studies Association, *LASA Forum*, in the context of a debate on the theme 'Racial inequalities and public policies: debates in Latin America and beyond', *LASA Forum*, 39:1, 2008. The question raised here was: 'Is the use of race or colour legitimate in public policies?' I am grateful to Antonio Sergio Guimarães for this invitation to comparison. Here I have updated and developed this text so as to deepen the comparative analysis, particularly with the Brazilian case.

40 See Alain Mabanckou, *L'Europe depuis l'Afrique*, Paris: Naïve, 2009.

41 One example of this is in the account of the famous strike of workers on the Dakar–Niger railway in 1947 given by Ousmane Sembene, *Les Bouts de bois de Dieu* (1960), Paris: Pocket, 2002.

42 See in particular Jean-Pierre Dozon, *Frères et sujets: La France et l'Afrique en perspective*, Paris: Flammarion, 2003, in which the author seeks to understand on the basis of this historical moment the formation of reciprocal desires for France and Africa.

43 See successively Achille Mbembe, *On the Postcolony*, Berkeley: University of California Press, 2010, and *Sortir de la grande nuit*.

44 See Michel Agier, Rémy Bazenguissa Ganga and Achille Mbembe, 'Mobilités africaines, racisme français', *Vacarme*, 43, 2008, pp. 83–5.
45 See Georges Raeders, *Le Comte de Gobineau au Brésil*, Paris: Nouvelles Éditions Latines, 1934.
46 Roberto Da Matta, 'A fábula das três raças, ou o problema do racismo à brasileira', in *Relativizando: Uma introdução à antropologia social*, Rio de Janeiro: Rocco, 1987, pp. 58–85.
47 See Thomas E. Skidmore, *Preto no branco: Raça e nacionalidade no pensamento brasileiro*, Rio de Janeiro: Paz e Terra, 1976; Schwarcz, *O espetáculo das raças*.
48 Gilberto Freyre, *Masters and Slaves*, New York: Alfred A. Knopf, 1946.
49 On the formation of the word and myth of racial democracy in Brazil, see Antonio Sergio Guimarães, 'Démocratie raciale', *Cahiers du Brésil Contemporain*, 49–50, 2002, pp. 11–37.
50 UN World Conference against Racism, Racial Discrimination, Xenophobia and Relates Intolerance, held in Durban, South Africa, August 2001.
51 See in particular Véronique Boyer, 'Une forme d'africanisation au Brésil: les *quilombolas* entre recherche anthropologique et expertise politico-légale', *Cahiers d'Études Africaines*, 198, 199 and 200, 2010, pp. 707–30; and José Mauricio Arruti, 'Quilombos', in Osmundo Pinho and Livio Sansone (eds.), *Raça: Novas perspectivas antropológicas* (2nd edition), Salvador: Unicamp/EDUFBA, 2008, pp. 315–50.
52 Saïd Bouamama and Sophie Wahnich, 'Une citoyenneté sans identité nationale', *Vacarme*, 46, 2009, pp. 80–2.
53 A remarkable development of analyses on the violence of the identity assignment of race and the future of the 'Negro subject' at the global level can be found in the more recent work by Achille Mbembe, *Critique de la raison nègre*, Paris: La Découverte, 2013, which I refer to here. See also my commentary, 'Au cœur de la race', *La Vie des Idées*, 30 April 2014, http://www.laviedesidees.fr/Au-coeur-de-la-race.html.
54 See, for France, Gérard Noirel, *Le Creuset français: Histoire de l'immigration (XIXe–XXe siècle)*, Paris: Seuil, 1992, and *Le Massacre des Italiens: Aigues-Mortes, 17 août 1893*, Paris: Fayard, 2010.
55 See Jean-François Véran, 'Métis malgré tout: une résistance amazonienne aux politiques ethniques', *Problèmes d'Amérique Latine*, 92, 2015, pp. 27–45.

Chapter 6 Logics and Politics of the Subject

1 In the course of a conference in 1971, this question was addressed in the combined form of a synoptically retrospective summary and a critical and innovating spirit, corresponding to the watershed period that this was: Germaine Dieterlein (ed.), *La Notion de personne en Afrique noire*, Paris: Éditions du CNRS, 1973 (new edition Paris: L'Harmattan, 2000). This summary is an essential point of reference for reflection on this notion.
2 Marcel Mauss, 'A category of the human mind: the notion of person; the notion of self' (1938), in *The Category of the Person: Anthropology, Philosophy, History*, ed. Michael Carrithers, Steven Collins and Steven Lukes, Cambridge: Cambridge University Press, 1985, pp. 1–25.

3 Louis Dumont, *Essays on Individualism: Modern Ideology in Anthropological Perspective*, Chicago: University of Chicago Press, 1992.

4 On these two points, see Marc Augé, *Le Sens des autres,* Paris: Fayard, 1994; and Emmanuel Terray, 'Le rôle de l'Autre dans la constitution de l'être humain', in *Combats avec Méduse*, Paris: Galilée, 2011, pp. 15–23.

5 See for example on the 1950s and 1960s: Georges Balandier, *Sociologie des Brazzavilles noires*, Paris: Fondation Nationale des Sciences Politiques, 1955 (2nd edition 1985); and Jean-Marie Gibbal, *Citadins et villageois dans la ville africaine: L'exemple d'Abidjan*, Paris Grenoble: Maspero and Presses Universitaires de Grenoble, 1974. The same questions are found in the themes of the 'village in the city' or of 'urban ethnicities' as developed in urban anthropology and sociology (see the summary by Ulf Hannerz, *Explorer la ville: Éléments d'anthropologie urbaine*, Paris: Minuit, 1983).

6 Robert Castel, *Les Métamorphoses de la question sociale: Une chronique du salariat*, Paris: Fayard, 1995.

7 The title of his autobiography: Gabriel García Márquez, *Living to Tell the Tale* (Spanish original: *Vivir para contarla*), New York: Vintage, 2004.

8 In the expressions recently used by Robert Castel, 'Individu par excès, individu par défaut', in Philippe Corcuff, Christian Le Bart and François de Singly (eds.), *L'Individu aujourd'hui: Débats sociologiques et contrepoints philosophiques*, Rennes: PUR, 2010, pp. 293–305.

9 For a comparison of these two positions, see for example Charles Taylor, *Multiculturalism and the Politics of Recognition*, Princeton: Princeton University Press, 1992; and Jean-Loup Amselle, *L'Ethnicisation de la France*, Paris: Nouvelles Éditions Lignes, 2011.

10 On this point, and more generally on representations of the contemporary individual, I refer to the critical collective work edited by Corcuff, Le Bart and de Singly, *L'Individu aujourd'hui*.

11 In the concluding words of Marc Augé's essay *Non-Places: Introduction to an Anthropology of Supermodernity*, London: Verso, 1995, p. 120, on a theme that the author has subsequently returned to on several occasions: 'So there will soon be a need – perhaps there is already a need – for something that may seem a contradiction in terms: an ethnology of solitude.'

12 Étienne Balibar, *Citoyen sujet et autres essais d'anthropologie philosophique*, Paris: PUF, 2011, p. 5.

13 See Michel Foucault, 'The subject and power', *Critical Inquiry*, 8:4, 1982, pp. 777–95, and *Society Must Be Defended*, London: Allen Lane, 2003.

14 Mathieu Potte-Bonneville, 'Individualisation et subjectivation: remarques à partir de Michel Foucault', in Corcuff, Le Bart and de Singly (eds.), *L'Individu aujourd'hui*, p. 121.

15 For examples of the intimate learning of a mechanism of subjectivation, see Ann Laura Stoler, *Carnal Knowledge and Imperial Power: Race and the Intimate in Colonial Rule*, Berkeley: University of California Press, 2002; and Gabrielle Houbre, *La Discipline de l'amour: L'éducation sentimentale des filles et des garçons à l'âge du romantisme*, Paris: Plon, 1997.

16 Balibar, *Citoyen sujet*, p. 83.

17 Frédéric Gros, 'Sujet moral et soi éthique chez Foucault', *Archives de Philosophie*, 65:2, 2002, pp. 229–37 at p. 233.

18 Gros, 'Sujet moral', p. 233.

19 Collectif Maurice Florence, *Archives de l'infamie*, Paris: Les Prairies Ordinaires, 2009.

20 See for example Veena Das, *Life and Word: Violence and the Descent into the Ordinary*, Berkeley: University of California Press, 2006; Mariella Pandolfi and Vincent Crapanzano, 'Présentation: les passions: au cœur du politique?', *Anthropologie et Sociétés*, 32:3, 2008, pp. 7–13; Richard Rechtman, 'Psychanalyse et anthropologie aujourd'hui: une question de genre', interview with Laetitia Atlani-Duault, *Journal des Anthropologues*, 116–17, 2009, pp. 121–9; or again François Laplantine, *Le Sujet: Essai d'anthropologie politique*, Paris: Téraèdre, 2008.

21 I take up here the term used by Jacques Rancière (*La Mésentente: Politique et philosophie*, Paris: Galilée, 1995; *Disagreement: Politics and Philosophy*, Minneapolis: University of Minnesota Press, 2004) to describe politics.

22 See Michel Agier, *Managing the Undesirables*, Cambridge: Polity, 2011. I shall return later to the second 'scandalous' expression mentioned here, that of the refugee politically confronting international organizations.

23 Mathieu Potte-Bonneville, 'Au sujet du terrain: subjectivation et ethnologie', *Rue Descartes*, 75, 2012, pp. 102–13 at p. 107.

24 Slavoj Žižek, *La Subjectivité à venir: Essais critiques*, Paris: Flammarion, 2006, p. 13.

25 For a detailed presentation of this black movement in the carnival, see Michel Agier, *Anthropologie du carnaval: La ville, la fête et l'Afrique à Bahia*, Marseille: Éditions Parenthèses and IRD, 2000. In part, but only in part, this ritual of the opening of paths is inspired by the *padê* of the Afro-Brazilian cult that I discussed in chapter 1.

26 Victor Turner, *The Ritual Process: Structure and Anti-Structure*, New Brunswick: Aldine Transaction, 1995.

27 At Salvador de Bahia in Brazil, as we saw, the announcement that 'the street is for the people' ('*A rua é do povo*') marks the temporal border of the opening of carnival.

28 See Philippe Artières, *Le Livre des vies coupables: Autobiographies de criminels (1896–1909)*, Paris: Albin Michel, 2000.

29 See also Michel de Certeau (*La Prise de parole*, Paris: Seuil, 1994) and his pioneering reflections on speaking out; as well as the dossier edited by Marcel Detienne, 'Qui veut prendre la parole?', *Le Genre Humain*, 40–1, 2003.

30 J. Hageninmana, J. Nkengurukiyimana, J. Mulindabigwi and M. Goretti Gahimbare, *L'Itinéraire le plus long et le plus pénible: Les réfugiés hutus à la recherche de l'asile* [Maheba, 2000].

31 They were also among the founders and leaders of an association of Hutu refugees for the development of agricultural activity in this UNHCR site in a rural zone, with the explicit aim of settling here rather than returning to Rwanda. Eight years later, in 2010, they were still there, whereas the majority of other refugees, for the most part Angolan, had been repatriated in the years between.

32 See Agier, *Managing the Undesirables*.

33 Michel Lussault, *De la lutte des classes à la lutte des places*, Paris: Grasset, 2008. The author uses this neologism to denote the organized distribution of places in space.

34 On 'becoming-citizen' as one figure or potentiality of the subject, see Balibar, *Citoyen sujet*, p. 5.

35 On the contrast between humanitarian and political 'stages', see Rancière, *La Mésentente*, p. 167ff.
36 Peter Brook noticed this in the street theatre of the South African townships: Peter Brook, *Le Théâtre des townships*, Arles: Acte Sud, 1999. See Michel Agier, *Anthropologie de la ville*, Paris: PUF, 2015, pp. 188–97.
37 We find here, and not without significance, the dynamic indicated by the term 'regaining of initiative', which Balandier used to describe the movement of decolonization (Georges Balandier, *Sociologie actuelle de l'Afrique noire: Dynamique des changements sociaux en Afrique centrale*, Paris: 1955, 5th edition 1992).

Conclusion

1 Immanuel Kant, 'Perpetual peace: a philosophical sketch' (1795), in *Political Writings*, ed. H. S. Reiss, Cambridge: Cambridge University Press, 1970, pp. 93–130.
2 See on this point Emmanuel Terray's brilliant historical essay that compares nomadism and sedentarism in the military, sociological and political fields (*Combats avec Méduse*, Paris: Galilée, 2011, pp. 15–23).
3 Étienne Tassin, *Un monde commun: Pour une cosmo-politique des conflits*, Paris: Le Seuil, 2003, p. 18.
4 Hannah Arendt, *The Promise of Politics*, New York: Schocken, 2005.
5 Kwame Appiah, *Cosmopolitanism: Ethics in a World of Strangers*, New York: Norton, 2006.

INDEX